SWEET SUMMERS

THE CLASSIC CRICKET WRITING OF
JM KILBURN

Edited by
Duncan Hamilton

GREAT NORTHERN

Great Northern Books
PO Box 213, Ilkley, LS29 9WS
www.greatnorthernbooks.co.uk

ISBN: 978 1 905080 46 5

Design and layout: David Burrill

Printed in Great Britain

CIP Data
A catalogue for this book is available from the British Library

For Mary Kilburn

CONTENTS

INTRODUCTION

I DETECT three things whenever I read Jim Kilburn's words. Firstly, the sheer pleasure he took from watching the game. Secondly, the warmth of feeling he generated in writing about it. Thirdly, the unmistakable fact that he loved and respected cricket so much.

I could never imagine Jim wanting to hurt or damage its reputation in any way and he frowned upon anyone who did. For me, Jim was indisputably a cricket man to the very core; someone who relished his work and took a professional pride in it. In fact, I'm certain Jim took as much enjoyment from each day he spent in the sun as I do every time I pick up a microphone in the commentary box.

He was knowledgeable, developed his own style of writing and – most importantly of all – formed opinions which he was willing to put into print.

You might think that last statement is fairly obvious. If you're paid to report, don't you possess independence of thought and the wit to express it? Well, not necessarily – and I better explain why.

When I was growing up in Fitzwilliam, television didn't dominate cricket the way it does today. Even radio coverage of it was spasmodic. If I wanted to know what was happening at Headingley, I turned to the Bible of Yorkshire cricket – the

Yorkshire Post and Jim's reports, which was read like scripture throughout the county.

By the time I came into the Yorkshire side, he was already an important and imposing character, the doyen of the press box with his friend – and mine – the wonderful Bill Bowes. The two of them nearly always seemed to be together, and the talk was usually about cricket.

Jim was someone I'd call 'old school', a description which I use wholly as a compliment to him. He didn't chase asinine quotes to 'create' a story that really didn't exist for the sake of a controversial headline. He didn't indulge in petty tittle-tattle. And he didn't betray confidences.

What he did was express an honest and crisp opinion on what he saw and felt during a day's play. It was the bedrock of his principled approach to writing.

If I played badly, he said so. If I played well, he said so too.

Nowadays, I believe there are too many writers attached to cricket who know bugger all about it and have no opinions – sensible, valid or otherwise – about what's happened on the field. As the nature of the media has changed, and regretfully become more focussed on sensationalism rather than hard fact, a lot of journalists find it convenient to string together a series of other people's opinions rather than form any of their own. It's a terrible pity and is also detrimental to the reader as well as to cricket.

At the beginning of my Test career, when I'd struggled and needed some advice, I went to Bill Bowes. And, of course, I found him with Jim. I chatted to Bill, who helped me as much as he could. Jim never reported a word of it. He didn't even hint at the technical and very private conversation I'd had with Bill – despite the fact he'd heard every bit of it.

Jim was someone I could trust implicitly. Later on in my career, as the desire for tabloid scandal profoundly altered the relationship between journalists and players, I was always wary about talking to reporters who I didn't know. You could find something you'd said – usually innocuously or half in jest – either grossly inflated or ripped out of context and then spread across the back pages in huge dark type.

Jim was different.

Geoffrey Boycott

Preface:

'I am here to write about the cricket'

JAMES MAURICE KILBURN, always known as 'Jim', was one of cricket's major romantic poets; the Coleridge to Neville Cardus' Wordsworth. Kilburn believed that 'beauty we see in cricket because cricket is beauty', and for more than 40 summers – 'sweet' summers, as he described them – his cultivated essays captured the essence of it. For Kilburn, the blunt statistics of the game were used merely as evidence of quality. But, as he made clear, 'figures cannot convey the splendour of an evening's innings' and so his words did the job instead.

He gave imaginative life to everything he saw, and his perceptive vignettes of players were always gilt framed by the landscape into which each one was set: the ground, the weather, perhaps a distant church tower, the mood and feel of the occasion. What fascinated Kilburn, and which illuminated his writing, were the technical aspects of cricket and the disparate skills and characters involved in its pure hard combat. He wrote about them analytically and with a supple intelligence: the way a bowler's knotty fingers gripped the ball, the skill in a wristy flick that sent a loose delivery scorching past point and the tactical chess between captains. With intense observation, he was able to fasten on to a splinter of detail and fashion it into a phrase that gave high definition to a man or a specific moment: Walter Hammond's walk to the wicket: 'He came like a king and he looked like a king in his coming'; Brian Statham's removal of his sweater, which was achieved 'by stretching one hand over his shoulder to the small of the back indicating an uncommon suppleness of joints'; Fred Trueman's argumentative streak: 'Trueman always had breath to spare for an expression of opinion'; Jack Hobbs 'burning the grass with boundaries'; Don Bradman as a 'textbook of batting come to life with never a misprint or erratum'.

Bradman repaid the compliment. He described Kilburn as a 'great writer' and told him: 'Your cricket writing made a massive contribution to a memorable era'. The Don had good taste. Kilburn created portraits as vivid as lightning of, among others, Keith Miller, Bill Bowes, George Hirst and Herbert Sutcliffe. But he regarded cricket's aristocracy as 'figures of gold' and – in another sign of his rich romanticism – freely confessed that he became nervous watching them. 'I felt more anxious,' he wrote 'for Hobbs and Wooley at the beginning of their innings than they presumably felt for themselves'.

While he was a Yorkshireman writing for the *Yorkshire Post*, frequently rejecting job offers from national newspapers based in London, Kilburn's outlook was never narrowly northern. The Welsh language has *cynefin* to denote a fierce attachment to a square of land. There is no direct English translation, but the definition of that word adheres itself obviously to Yorkshire, where passionate pride in the county and devout protectionism towards it is inherent. Under the circumstances, it would have been terribly easy for Kilburn to have focused parochially; particularly as Yorkshire was the axis on which the County Championship turned: winners seven times between 1931 and 1939 and a further nine times between 1946 and 1968. Kilburn always took the broader view. The 'helpful wicket' of the *Yorkshire Post* enabled him to write about whatever, and whoever, gripped his interest. He had no desire or ambition to leave it.

As a consequence, Kilburn quickly established himself as a respected and influential correspondent, during one of those Golden Ages of cricket writing, alongside Cardus, RC Robertson-Glasgow, EW Swanton and Australia's Ray Robinson. Kilburn more than matched his contemporaries. Like Cardus and Robertson-Glasgow, he had the sensitivity of touch to craft a line that caught the light. Like Swanton and Robinson, his articles were formidably authoritative and opinionated. He didn't go in for fence-sitting. 'What I thought praiseworthy, I praised. What I thought inadequate, I condemned,' he said. Along with cricket, which he studied obsessively, his head was full of literature; his books and articles are garnished with quotations from writers and poets such as Shakespeare, Stevenson, Kipling and Brooke.

SERENDIPITY began Kilburn's cricket writing career. Born in Sheffield in 1909, he went to university there, taking a degree in economics, and briefly became a teacher at a Harrogate prep school before spending a year in Finland, where he sent travel articles to the *Yorkshire Post*. On his return, the editor, Arthur Mann, immediately agreed to meet him. Oddly for a newspaper which took cricket seriously, the *Yorkshire Post* no longer had its own correspondent attached to Yorkshire. The post had been vacant for three years following the retirement of AW Pullin, who wrote under the pseudonym *Old Ebor*. Mann liked Kilburn's writing, and he liked Kilburn. As a young boy, Kilburn had been tutored by Hirst in the Scarborough nets and eventually became a solid enough all-round cricketer for Bradford in the Bradford League, where he bowled off-breaks at a nippy pace (he was 6ft 5 inches tall) and batted decently. He won both Bradford League and Priestley Cup medals in the late 1920s. The editor of the *Yorkshire Post* knew all about Kilburn from the Bradford League reports in his own newspaper.

Kilburn was welcomed into Mann's office, which resembled a library in a gentleman's club: a high ceiling, a vast leather topped desk, glass fronted mahogany bookshelves, a coal fireplace and Spy and Ape prints of Victorian statesmen hanging on the wall. Mann listened as Kilburn spoke convincingly about cricket and writing, and he then promptly put him on probation for three months. He was given £3 per week and described as 'A Special Representative'. His first assignment was daunting: the Roses match at Sheffield. Kilburn sat on the back row of the Bramall Lane press box and 'spoke only when I was spoken to'. His writing spoke eloquently for him. So eloquently, in fact, that Cardus wrote to the newspaper and said of Kilburn: 'To my mind yours is the best cricket reporting today'. It was the equivalent of a papal blessing.

Kilburn was hired permanently, became 'Our Cricket

Correspondent', his salary raised to £6 and augmented by expenses: 7s 6d for home games, one guinea a day when staying in a hotel and 25s a day for London or seaside matches. He was 25 years old. Within months he got a regular by-line, which was a rare thing. The newspaper's front page carried nothing but classified advertising, and staff writers and contributors remained anonymous or, just as Pullin had been, were identified through a sobriquet. In many editions, Kilburn had the only by-line in a 16 page *Yorkshire Post*.

It has to be said that Kilburn was not a journalist, but a writer. He knew nothing of newspapers or news values. He vehemently disapproved of chasing quotes or tit-bits of gossip, and never indulged in either. The reporting of dressing room tittle-tattle was demeaning and unnecessary, he argued; the *Yorkshire Post* was paying for *his* view. If asked to cover something he regarded as detached from, or superfluous to, what was happening inside the boundary rope, he would reply firmly: 'I am here to write about the cricket'. Norman Yardley wrote: 'If all cricket correspondents could be persuaded to adopt Mr Kilburn's style and principles, cricket would be the better served'. Geoffrey Boycott said Kilburn 'maintained standards of tact and integrity' throughout his career.

His principles made Kilburn a confidant of players such as Hutton and Bradman, who came to trust him implicitly. In retirement, he and Bradman exchanged long and detailed correspondence. Bradman's air mails came in blue Biro; Kilburn preferred the fountain pen with which for years he wrote his pieces for the *Yorkshire Post* (the newspaper's copy paper eventually became so shockingly cheap and thin that legibility reluctantly obliged him to use a ball point). His obituary in *The Cricketer* detailed his working methods. 'Jim

Kilburn sat on the front row, a tall, impassive, magisterial figure puffing at his pipe . . . He wrote his daily pieces in his own hand and, however eventful the last hour's play might be, he had finished when the last ball was bowled. He then held the paper aloft, a messenger emerged from the back of the box and bore it away. Less organised and less gifted workers watched in envy'. Ian Wooldridge went further. He said that Kilburn thought the typewriter was 'the devil's own invention' and added that his 'neatness of handwriting and speed' made his reports 'one of the nightly miracles of the English cricket press box'. Wooldridge continued: 'While many of his rivals are still contorted by the creative agony of arresting opening paragraphs, some with a large Scotch in one hand, their second cigarette in the other and a dozen screwed up pieces of paper at their feet, Kilburn is clipping together six folios of cream-laid notepaper, replacing the cap of his fountain pen and bidding his colleagues a *sotto voce* 'Goodnight'. No 'i' is undotted, no 't' uncrossed'.

Those accounts emphasise two things: Firstly, Kilburn was important enough to the *Yorkshire Post* to have his own messenger, the way a Lord routinely has a butler. Secondly, he was a man of conviction and discipline. He neither talked over the day's play nor actively sought the opinions of others. He was sure of what he had to say, and uncompromising in the way he said it. In the office, Mann, and subsequent editors, decreed that the copy must appear in the newspaper untouched and that Kilburn alone should determine the content of his reports. It is inconceivable that anyone would get the same latitude today. Newspapers now mostly rely on quotes, however anodyne or trivial, rather than judgment.

Even if he had not been such a prose stylist, Kilburn's writing is worthy of attention and re-examination. Not only because he was a knowledgeable interpreter of cricket – well balanced, tough-minded and scrupulously honest in his verdicts – but also for the valuable historical and social perspective that reading him provides. Most of all he demonstrably cared about cricket. His heart was in it – and belonged to it. The title of his autobiography *Thanks to Cricket* was chosen as a genuine expression of how much he owed to the game and what it had given him. It was his 'devotion'.

Kilburn cast light on to eras long gone – and that appear only tangentially connected to the present – but which are deserving of more than just sentimental reflection. The easiest thing to say after reading him is: *How times change*. In 1934, when Kilburn began writing for the *Yorkshire Post*, Bradman effortlessly stroked 304 in the Headingley Test, Yorkshire's daily attendance for County Championship matches nudged 8,000 and amateurs mostly enjoyed superior dressing room or hotel accommodation to professionals. There were no motorways, no TV coverage and radio was still in its crackling infancy. In 1946, the journey to Australia for the first post-war Ashes series took a tedious three and a half weeks by boat; Kilburn was squashed into a cabin with Swanton, who wrote: 'Jim Kilburn and I shared a cabin so small that we literally could not stand up in it together – a trial of friendship which I'm glad to say survived'.

When Kilburn retired in 1976, the Packer revolution of World Series Cricket – coloured clothing, floodlights, the white ball and the original bulky helmets – was less than a year away. By then Kilburn's longevity had enabled him to witness the genius of Bradman, the extraordinary gifts of Hutton, the arrival and dominance of Garry Sobers, the departure of the amateur, an end to uncovered pitches, a waning of interest in the Championship, the establishment of three one-day competitions and the widespread commercialisation of cricket. While Kilburn fretted about the route cricket was taking, his response was not a blanket rejection of progress. He gave helpful and sage advice about where it might lead. He believed cricket was in danger of losing its spirit and purity, and what he had to say about it made him a high-minded and slightly idealistic critic, but also a prescient one. His worry about the proliferation of one-day cricket and its impact on the County Championship and Test matches might equally apply today to the spread of Twenty20. His point about generating good publicity for the game echoes in the debate about TV rights for Tests: free to air or satellite, anyone? His concern at declining moral standards in cricket, and his thoughts on the meaning of sportsmanship, still resonate far beyond the boundary ropes of his sport. And, as anyone in the Broad Acres will tell you, Kilburn hits the bullseye again when he touches on the high level of expectation among Yorkshire members and the pressure it puts on the players. Yorkshire has never played for fun. Perhaps things *haven't* changed as much as we think.

The romantic streak in Kilburn is thankfully never far from the surface. It comes out in his claim that: 'No day passes upon a cricket field without some joy is brought to someone'. The joy it brought him is explained in his account of the start of a new season. 'We go again where we have so often been before to find new paint upon the same pavilion railings, to see new figures tread the old steps well worn by the feet of the mighty ones of yesterday'.

It is also visible in his essays on cricket grounds. He adored

Worcester and venerated Lord's. Of walking through The Grace Gates, he said: 'I always feel I am stepping into history.' The quintessential Kilburn was nonetheless found at Scarborough during its Festival. 'Cricket on holiday,' he called it. It was 'one last battle' for the season before 'bats and pads are packed mournfully away for the winter' and where 'yesterday's players come to sit in the summer's last sunshine and talk over achievements long since written in history'. When one Scarborough Festival was over, he longed for the next. Wherever stumps were pitched, Kilburn's abiding principle was that cricket needed to be played 'with pleasure to give pleasure'; otherwise it was pointless.

As an eight year-old, one of his heroes became and always remained Sir Lancelot, the 'knight of knights'. He wanted his cricketers – and the cricket he saw – to be similarly brave and chivalrous. The aesthetics of cricket were paramount to him. He appreciated classical style and artistry, and fair play and sportsmanship. He abhorred sharp practice and the mitigating gloss that any perpetrator tried to give it. As he saw it, anyone who stepped on to a cricket field tacitly gave an oath of loyalty to cricket, and this meant upholding the honour, traditions and codes of the game, which he regarded as sacrosanct and inviolable. He gave a loathing stare in the direction of anyone who thought otherwise. When Yorkshire won the Championship of 1967 through 'dubious manoeuvring' – a euphemism for time-wasting – Kilburn excoriated them. He called the means a 'disgrace' and went on: 'They lost prestige, but if their excesses and the consequences help bring a general change of outlook in the way county cricket is approached and played good will derive from evil'. His credo was simple: 'The bell tolls for all of us every time we cheat a little, every time we encourage or overlook a misdemeanour, every time we silence the still small voice that asks: 'Was that unsportsmanlike?'

In Keith Miller's final Test innings at Lord's, after Fred Trueman had claimed his wicket, Kilburn wrote: 'Miller looked down the pitch at the triumphant Trueman and waved a gesture of appreciation for the fine out-swinger that had conquered him . . . I count the moment among my treasures of cricketing experience'. Impeccable behaviour and gracious conduct was essential in Kilburn's mannered world; ill-discipline and bad etiquette frowned upon. The split second acknowledgement between Trueman and Miller, victor and vanquished, embodied for Kilburn what cricket was truly about – virtue.

He revered players who possessed it, and celebrated the greatest of them so vividly that black ink and plain paper become moving images: Verity fizzing each ball; Trueman's daggered glares; Miller as tough as galvanised steel; Bradman's regal grace. Kilburn's closeness to cricket and to the men who played it gave him an insight into the scalding stress that Hutton's 364 brought with it, Verity's rigorous self-examination of his art ('To dismiss a modest batting side on a turning pitch was to him no more than the routine of a bank cashier completing a simple balance') and the joie de vivre of Percy Holmes. If Holmes was the first to arrive at the reception desk of a hotel before an away match, he would tell the clerk: 'Register us as Percy Holmes and his circus'.

Studio photographs make Kilburn look austerely formal and patrician. But there is a dry, mischievous humour in some of the pieces, such as his verdict on Maurice Leyland's bowling to a rampant Bradman. 'No one expected him to get a wicket,' wrote

Kilburn 'he was neither good enough nor bad enough for that'; the parallel he drew between Emmott Robinson and the characters of Dickens; and his account of what he saw one baking afternoon in Adelaide: 'At the kerbside five or six strikingly attractive young ladies were standing beneath a sign that read: *Queue for Kilburn*. An envious companion assured me that the girls were merely waiting for a local bus'.

LESS than a year after he covered his final Test match for the *Yorkshire Post* in 1976, Kilburn began to lose his sight. Age-related macular degeneration left him with just peripheral vision. He could neither read nor watch cricket. But he listened to commentary on radio, and continued to talk about the game and take an interest in it. He died in Harrogate, aged 84, on 28 August 1993. Fittingly, Yorkshire were playing at Headingley that day. As well as his writing for the *Yorkshire Post*, he left behind 10 books and was a significant contributor to two more. He wrote regularly for both *The Cricketer* and *Wisden*.

Of everything he wrote about cricket, one sentence encapsulates Kilburn's unshakeable love for it and his belief in its capacity to stir emotions. 'Cricket is of us,' he wrote 'as the very breath in our lungs, (and) makes poets of the incoherent and artists of the artisans'. Even without cricket J M Kilburn would have been a poet and artist. With it, he soared. He enriched it with his pen as indisputably as Bradman enriched it with his bat.

Duncan Hamilton
Bramley, Yorkshire, 2007

Chapter One:
THE SPIRIT OF THE GAME

May Days

THE opening of each cricket season is a voyage of most joyous adventure, for it brings promise of the thrilling unknown, together with the prospect of sailing again certain charted and well-loved seas. We go again where we have so often been before to find new paint upon the same pavilion railings, to see new figures tread the old steps well-worn by the feet of the mighty ones of yesterday. We go to see new faces, hear new names, yet still the game remains the same, the fresh and the mellow mingling and sweet.

The early days are always exciting, for form is uncertain and wickets a maze of bewildering contradiction; though May days of adventure are, paradoxically, not for youth but for sober experience. Every year the same story is told; the young cricketer comes eagerly forth, bat in hand, pads and boots gleaming white, and passes, a moment later, on his chastened way back to the pavilion, victim of mistiming or prey to cunning spin. His elder colleague comes more quietly to the field. There is less downright challenge in his step and lovingly he feels the soft turf once more beneath his feet, drinks in the pale sunshine and breathes the spring air in quiet appreciation. This man knows that his innings are now numbered, feels that his remaining seasons are precious, and calls upon the impetuous failures of yesterday to help him along his present way. The old ones, the wise ones, make runs in May days, for they have known other Mays and feel within themselves that they cannot, as cricketers, know many more.

As May turns into June, and the hard wickets of July and August follow, all batsmen worthy of the name will make runs, for high summer is the batsmen's delight and all Nature gives him assistance. That is why youth perseveres; that is why today's failures are borne as patiently as may be – 'I did not score today, but later in the season there will come a time . . .

Not infrequently we have to suffer for our early cricket enthusiasm; spring days are not always fair and spring airs not always balmy as the poets would have us believe. 'Rain stopped play' is a common cry when the English season begins. Sometimes mackintoshes alone are not enough to keep warmth and comfort in spectators; great-coats and scarves, reminiscent of football days, can often be seen mingling with white flannels and even the greatest enthusiasts have been known to watch the play from within the sphere of influence of the Long Room fire.

Perhaps the season of 1935 must be awarded the highest honour or infamy as the bringer of the coldest May that ever froze a suffering fieldsman. Then not a single Oldest Member, wrapped in his overcoat and fixed immovably in the warmest corner, was heard to grumble in scorn, 'Cold, sir? Pah! Why, in 1868 when we played the Bohemians there was seven inches of snow in the outfield, and when I clean bowled FWV Coates-Bedlington with the loveliest off-break you ever saw, sir, I was robbed – robbed, I say, sir – of my just reward, because the bails were frozen to the stumps and refused to drop. That was cold, sir. You moderns are soft and pampered'. The cricketers of 1935 will have a tale of hardihood to tell to their grandchildren, and the tale, no doubt, will lose nothing in the telling.

Through all those bitter winds with snowflakes scurrying from leaden skies cricket seemed unreal, an unkindly mockery of a kindly game. Batsmen came to the wicket muffled in scarves and hampered by as many sweaters as friends and fortune could bestow. Bowlers started their work by peeling off two outer layers and then proceeded to the job still be-sweatered. No man could say a word against them: in the ordinary way to bowl in a sweater looks as wrong as to play in brown boots, but this was out of the ordinary way in cricket, and players were justified in going to any lengths to preserve some semblance of comfort and some possibility of blood circulation.

But for most bad springs there is a good one in store, and poor cricketing days will find somewhere a compensating balance. Good or bad, spring days bring light hearts, for with cricket of any sort before us again, life begins anew, dark winter fades to dark oblivion, and the merest speck of blue in the sky is enough to send us eagerly down the road on our way to the ground.

In Search of Cricket

Going to the Match

ROBERT LOUIS STEVENSON'S assessment of hopeful travel is not always applicable to cricket but going to the match is one of my pleasures. In the days of earliest recollection it was a tram-ride up the long hill to Undercliffe out of the bowl of Bradford's city centre. From tram-stop to ground entrance was only a few hundred yards and there was always ample time in hand, but the excitement of anticipation prohibited walking. I had to run; I might have been missing sight of players in pre-match practice.

Tram-cars could scarcely rate as transport of delight in themselves, but they transported me to much cricketing delight in their service during the 1920s and 1930s. 'Specials' ran to Headingley and Park Avenue and Bramall Lane, and on a lucky day you might share a seat, or standing room, with a player you were going to watch at play. Herbert Sutcliffe first met Percy Holmes on a tram-car in Leeds – going to Headingley, of course.

Tram journeys stay in my mind as part of a day's cricket at Edgbaston and at the old Aylestone Road ground in Leicester. When two or three of us travelled together we gambled on the ticket-numbers. I have forgotten the rules of our game, which merely determined who paid the fares. Brighton had the most inviting tram-ride of all, along the sea-front from the Old Ship Hotel to the appropriate stop in Hove. You were going to cricket, you had a sense of holiday and you gave yourself a bonus of ozone on the open top-deck. The most alarming tram-rides to cricket of my experience were in Sydney, where the open-sided 'toastracks' required agility and resolution to embark and a cultivated indifference towards the perils facing a conductor swinging his way along the running-board.

Going to cricket at Lord's and at Scarborough have given me special delights. The approach to Lord's is attractive only in romantic conception because the wall along St John's Wood Road is forbidding and the Main Gate has an institutional appearance, but entry through the Grace Gates never fails to stir my imagination. I always feel as though I am stepping into history. So it is, of course, and Lord's on a Test match morning offers the fascination of living history to the observant early-comer. In the forecourt opening from the Grace Gates, in the passageway behind the pavilion, on the grassy mound at the back of the Warner Stand, there are reunion reminders of yesterday's battles. Casting aside the years and assuming the peak of form you can usually compile a Test team from the conversational groups encountered in a fifty-yard stroll. I know of nowhere else on earth where so much of cricket's flavour is so readily concentrated.

Scarborough at Festival time breathes cricket. Its economy is based on the thousands who choose early September for the family seaside holiday because cricket is being presented at the North Marine Road ground. Hotels adjust themselves to the cricket programme. Shops relate their wares to cricket. The talk at convivial gatherings, public or private, concerns the play of the day or the morrow. Cricketers are seen on the field and heard, or heard of, in the evenings. Recent adjustments in the Festival programme and in social holiday habits have cost Scarborough some of its September cricket character. The civic emphasis is not as strong as it used to be. Flags and bunting no longer decorate the main streets and cricket is no longer the dominating theme of shop window displays. A cricket song or joke is not now inevitable in the variety shows and the Spa is not a recognised place of cricket assembly in the evenings. Scarborough is still essentially a cricket centre during the Festival, but less manifestly so because the motor-car brings and takes away a daily visitation.

The abolition of the amateur cost the Scarborough Festival some of its character. It meant the abandonment of a long-standing fixture, though that might have been necessary anyway, and it meant a literal diminution of colour in the occasion. Festivals were less sober-hued than championship engagements. Monochrome of sterner business could be discarded for the brighter trappings of I Zingari, Free Foresters, Crusader and Authentic in cap and blazer. The generation of WHT Douglas could be seen entering the ground already in flannels, sometimes carrying a precautionary umbrella. University colours or an England cap and blazer were not considered ostentatious or out of place, provided they were worn with due qualification and dignity.

Going to the match at Scarborough develops personal ritual as varied as temperaments and time-facility. For some there is sandwich-collecting from a favourite bakery. For others there is the earliest possible arrival to ensure a wanted vantage point, the waiting hours to be passed with book or crossword puzzle. Patsy Hendren liked to drive to the ground in an open horse-drawn carriage. My leisurely approach on foot seeks to include a small diversion giving a glimpse of the sea. Down the years from childhood to qualification for old age I have never gone to Scarborough Festival cricket without the tremor of anticipation that heralds adventure.

Overthrows

Sight of the Great

MY lifetime touches cricket's Golden Age, but my time in cricket has left me just outside the boundaries of that glamorous era. Grace and Ranji, Trumper and Noble, Blythe and Bosanquet I know in detail, but only at second-hand by their pictures and performances and by descriptive writing and the folklore of their contemporaries. Their cricketing characters are as real to me as any enchantment, but I have not encountered the actual presence of their greatness. Within my generation, however, I have known comparable greatness and am duly grateful for the sight and sound and feel of it. Into my span came the mature Hobbs and Woolley and Macartney; the full careers of Bradman, Hammond, Hutton, Compton, of Tate, Bedser, O'Reilly and Verity; of McDonald and Larwood and Trueman and Lindwall; the blossoming of May and of Sobers. Personal observation has given me Hobbs and Sutcliffe in opening partnership, Tyson and Statham bowling together, Chapman, Lock and Lloyd fielding.

Supreme greatness transcends precise definition and analysis. It is an impression. To dissect is to destroy. It needs figures but it cannot be circumscribed by figures; it needs manner but the manner is infinitely variable. It raises an emotional response beyond the bounds of logical argument. It evokes inspiration without envy.

To accord this greatness and therefore to share it vicariously is the highest form of pleasure cricket can give and for me the pleasure is enhanced rather than diminished by a mingling of trust and apprehension. I felt more anxious for Hobbs and Woolley at the beginning of their innings, than they presumably felt for themselves. Early dismissal could not lessen them in my esteem but until they were established at the crease I was selfishly fearful lest some accident of cricket should deprive me of the thrill of their splendour, of a basking in their authority.

In county cricket I had to apportion desires and loyalties. When Yorkshire played Surrey I could hope for Surrey all out 125, providing Hobbs or Peter May made 100 of them; Kent or Gloucestershire could be routed for my rejoicing if Woolley and Hammond were left unharmed. This reaction was more than a childish fancy. It remained with me all through my cricket watching, through my years as a professional observer when I was theoretically in lofty detachment. Much the same sentiment apparently affected others. Arthur Mailey has confessed that when he once defeated and dismissed Trumper his satisfaction involved an emotion akin to having 'shot a dove'.

The trepidation experienced when the great began to bat or bowl was vastly outweighed by the sense of wonder and fulfilment when their artistry was presented. On the principle that 'we needs must love the highest when we see it' the great cricketers have contributed to the quality of living. The authority, the mastery, the 'class' that stamps supremacy in any art form initiates a response we can no more avoid than we can explain. Appreciation of the exceptional comes to us as a conclusion reached without conscious steps in logic. Those of us without technical expertise know without knowing why; those with ability and experience of their own recognise without having to analyse in detail. 'There is nothing I can show him,' said George Hirst of the fledgling Hutton; 'You cannot fault his method,' said Warner of the same Hutton a few years later. The sight of Bradman drew spontaneous tribute from the wisest cricketer of all and Wilfred Rhodes was not accustomed to wearing his heart on his sleeve.

A contemporary of mine in school and Barnsley CC teams was Harry Bedford, who reached the Yorkshire first eleven in 1928. As a club cricketer Bedford was a useful all-rounder, but Yorkshire's principal interest was in his leg-break bowling and they gave him his chance on an end-of-season tour comprising three or four championship matches in the South. One game was at the Oval where Hobbs made a century. Bedford, who was a delightfully modest and friendly cricketer, told me afterwards that he had been fascinated. 'I forgot everything else when Hobbs was batting,' he said. 'It was simply wonderful'.

This is the beneficent influence of greatness displayed. It expands experience and it elevates us beyond any disagreeable elements in comparison and competition. The quality of true greatness, like that of mercy, is not strained:

It is twice blessed;
It blesseth him that gives and him that takes.

Intentions

FROM its origins and by its design cricket was intended to be a pleasant pastime. The conventional conception of the game pictures good-natured play in a pastoral setting. It has been described as 'the meadow game with the beautiful name' and it has given to the world a message of morality in the phrase: 'It isn't cricket'. The precepts of cricket stand high in the ranking of its pleasures. They remain in the trappings with which it is surrounded and in the sophistication it has developed. Cricket is still supposed to be played, still thought of in generality, as it was originally conceived – in friendly enmity. The pleasantness of cricket has always been its supreme appeal.

Ideals and practices have frequently diverged. There have been ill-tempered cricketers, cheating cricketers, anti-social cricketers. In some periods of its history cricket has known corruption, defiance of law and political encroachment. It has known personal dispute and public discord, but it has not abandoned regret and a sense of shame over manifest shortcomings. Majority opinion wants cricket to be a pleasant game for the gratification of people in pleasant mood.

Players and administrators of first-class cricket have known exceptional difficulties in recent years. They have been required to preserve the essence of their game under pressure from iconoclastic practices. Cricket, like other forms of sport, has been challenged by thinking and behaviour that 'isn't cricket'. In some aspects sport has conceded that foul play may be regarded as fair play. An Association footballer loses no prestige among his fellows and the team supporters by deliberately cheating; he is, indeed, applauded for the 'professional foul' because 'there was nothing else he could do' to save a goal. An athlete is encouraged to believe that the use of medical stimulant is justified by resulting performance. Tantrums on a tennis-court are recognized as tactical ploy or acknowledged with sympathetic applause. A national coach in

Rugby Union football has advocated 'better cheating' as the response to successful cheating in the line-out.

Lines at the edges of cricket morality have wavered. Official rebukes to individuals at home and to teams touring have had to be issued and penalties imposed. The fervour of national and local patriotism has occasionally induced crowd-stupidity and the common courtesies have been sacrificed for cash in interviews and ghosted writing.

First-class cricket could, no doubt, be presented and justified as a commercial undertaking, with its values correspondingly adjusted. Its pleasures need not be measured in terms of good-natured striving in opposition, of scorn for the mean advantage, of appreciation without abandon, of contest without controversy. They would have to be different pleasures, appealing to a different breed of player and follower. They would not be the pleasures recalled and defined by George Hirst when he leaned across the rails of the pavilion balcony at Scarborough on his retirement day and said: 'What can you have better than a green field with the wickets set up and to go out and do your best for your side?'

Cricket is perhaps the most complicated of all games in subtleties of technique and tactics, of actions and reactions, of variety in self-expression. It meets the challenge of physical endeavour, mental alertness and reflective satisfaction, but it has a simple heart. It provides every reward in recreation, but the full rewards are available only from pleasant cricket – cricket without rancour, cricket without selfishness, cricket with purpose essentially in itself. Cricket can be played in this way from the school field and the village green to the Test match arena. It can be played in this way by the casual participant and the dedicated careerist, amateur or professional. It can be played in this way as a pastime or as an occupation. It can be seen and enjoyed in this way by those without playing talent or experience.

High-level cricket might give way to a public presentation involving bats and balls and stumps, with significance in politics, in commerce and in sociology. It might become a means to an end beyond and more exacting than itself and in such destiny there is no right or wrong but thinking makes it so. All I claim for my own belief and for those who have formulated and reflected that belief is the certainty that cricket without a pleasant character would be cricket transformed and diminished.

Overthrows

Business and Pleasure

IN days far distant when a rough-carved branch, the stump of a tree, and a simple sphere were the implements of the game, cricket was purely recreative and no other factor than pure enjoyment entered into its objects.

Today cricket has developed far beyond the imagination of its early players and has become an affair of intense importance to half the civilized world. The fortunes of a few flannelled men upon a green field are responsible for the state of mind of thousands of people in different quarters of the earth. The game has become a business, a means of livelihood to hundreds, and the principal item of news in the daily journals of the British Empire. No longer is bat and ball the pastime of the idle hour, unpremeditated and immediately forgotten. There is a very real danger that the essence of simple enjoyment will be driven from our cricket, whether played upon international arena or in the field of Farmer Johnson. There is more than a suspicion that our games and their results are becoming invested with too much seriousness and that in a complicated age enjoyment is becoming dependent upon sensationalism.

How many cricketers, players, and spectators, of today are satisfied with quiet hours beneath the sun, happy in the careless freedom of contented minds, unwearied because this wicket or that does not fall or this batsman or that does not achieve a century? How many of our players are not slaves to the occasion, carrying always upon them the weight of a wearying responsibility and seeking ever 'the bubble reputation'? How many men go day by day from the pavilion rejoicing only in the feel of bat or ball in the hand, without ever a thought of the morning's publication of the averages, 'the world forgetting by the world forgot' in the purely intrinsic pleasures of cricket? It is, I should imagine, impossible ever to retrieve the lost simplicity of games; money, personal success, partisanship, and future prospects are now too inevitably bound up with cricket to be disentangled and set aside. Cricket need be no worse for their intrusion, always provided that these factors never become predominant.

There is still great joy to be had from the playing of cricket of all grades, but before that joy can be fully experienced the simplicity of pleasure must be wholly appreciated. From the joy of the player comes the joy of the spectators and there would be no complaint of dull and worthless cricket were every player to radiate his own enthusiasm for participation.

Too many of our cricketers bring solemnity and gloom in their very walk down the pavilion steps.

Too often does a batsman feel aggrieved if it is suggested to him that a boundary is a happy creation and a century not so much a matter of duty as an expression of well-being. Too many bowlers display obvious misery upon being asked to bowl for more than half an hour at a time, and to the last ounce of effort. Too many fieldsmen regard the non-batting hours as a necessary penance to be undergone with the minimum of exertion.

We do not ask genius from all our cricketers; we do not (or we should not) demand historic deeds upon every summer's day. We would rather have an hour's honest enjoyment than a week's pained effort. We want our batsmen to be thankfully conscious of their own ability and ever ready to display their talents for their own and our delight. We want our bowlers to use all their energies in bowling for bowling's own sake, independent of scoreboard readings or the day of the week.

A truly first-class cricketer is not one who condescends to appear before us and perform because he is expected to do so. The greatest technician is an empty shell and a bore beyond compare without the willing spirit, and the most desperate 'rabbit' radiates pleasure and inspiration if his endeavour be earnest and whole-hearted. The cricketer himself finds his greatest happiness in simplicity of aim; there are those who cannot go upon the field without worrying hour upon hour over the tactics of the captain and suggesting this move or that as more suitable to the requirements of the situation. There are those who cannot sit as spectators for half an hour without dwelling upon the incompetence of the present as compared with the past, and airing views and knowledge to a totally uninterested neighbourhood.

The happiest cricketer is he who, on the field and off, accepts without complaint the gifts of the moment, neither dwelling lingeringly upon yesterday nor dreaming idly of tomorrow. No day passes upon a cricket field without some joy is brought to someone and no day passes without some pleasure lost for want of seeking. The greatest cricketer, to himself and his companions, does his immediate task to the best of his ability and with cheerful willingness; obvious endeavour is the most lovable characteristic of any player of any game, and more of it in modern cricket would go far towards the solution of all the problems that beset us. Whether cricket be well or badly played, let it at least be always enjoyed, for we know in our heart of hearts that the 'trier' is: 'The happy warrior . . . he/ That every man in arms would wish to be'.

In Search of Cricket

An August Day

CRICKET'S leaves are falling fast, for the autumn of the season is upon us and the fresh green of timid springtime strokes against the turning ball has changed to the bold bright colours of the confidence that has infinite faith in the wicket and knows the burnt turf as a broad polished highway to the boundaries. In these days a batsman paints his innings in vivid browns and reds and golds and has a final riotous fling before the cold winds sweep him away for the winter and leave his fields chill and desolate, whilst the guardian groundsman repairs the ravages of summer in the brief hours of daylight at his disposal.

Cricket in late August and early September is in tomboyish mood, for the sobering influence of farewell is not yet at hand and every day brings hot sunshine and holiday mood. Now is the batsman in his element, the major problems of the campaign settled, worries and responsibilities behind him, and new records close at hand. There is leisure here to look and love. The beauty of the game is brightly shining, and its lovely spell is woven tightly round us. Precious game that brings us each morning, as the sun rides high and gathers strength for a blazing breathless afternoon, to the familiar gates and cheerful 'Good-day to you, Sir', greeting; that bids us pause to gaze upon the players drifting from the cool pavilion shadows, and marvel at the freshness and the sameness of it all; that holds us all day long in watching wonder and unspoken sympathy as brave dreams become realities before our eyes.

Cricket was born in England and is England's own whomsoever may sail the seas to take Ashes and rubber away from us; cricket is of us, as the very breath in our lungs, makes poets of the incoherent and artists of the artisans. Not one of us that takes a bat or bowls a ball or watches a game but gives and receives a precious heritage. Cricket takes us from ourselves because we give ourselves to it, and its appeal is permanent and infinite because it is a part of all of us. Its pictures are unending because each one is seen with a different eye and in a different mood. Cricket's chief attraction is its universality, for poor indeed and unhappy is he who has not at some time in some small way known its joys. Every boy who has defended a lamp-post wicket is in blood brotherhood with Bradman, and knows Hobbs or Sutcliffe as himself raised to and beyond the power of n; every man who has by reflex action or conscious effort flicked a boundary past point knows a thrill of intense physical delight when he sees Woolley bat.

Our sweetest cricketers, whom day by day we applaud and admire, have the happy qualities of human idols, for we, too, have tasted of their wine and shared of their moments, yet never dare aspire to their station. The cricket of Canterbury or Old Trafford or Lord's is but the cricket of the railway goods yard differently circumstanced and accoutred with more care. A low, swooping slip catch is as beautiful in Brixton as in Bournemouth, just as a swallow makes curving delights of flight round dust-bins and rhododendron bushes alike. Beauty we see in cricket because cricket is beauty, and no alteration of environment can remove an inborn quality. We praise great cricketers because somewhere within us we can feel their ambitions, understand their ideals, and picture their desires. We know through our own experiences the difficulties, the trials and troubles that beset them, and we can sympathise in failure and share in joyful success.

There is the warmth of comradeship in every ball bowled or every stroke played in cricket. That is why thousands upon thousands will sit patiently beneath the scorching sun until the cool shades of evening and find in each hour something to remember. It is worse than idle to complain of the ignorance of a cricket crowd; ignorance of detail there may be because of the distance of the prospect, but there is never ignorance of the purpose of the game which is, first and last, the creation of living beauty in a particular medium.

Cricket is ethically independent of the scoreboard, and I have known a crowd enthralled where no scoreboard existed, and had it been present would have told a dull tale. When we read that Hammond has made 170 in an innings of two hours' duration we do not picture it in figures, but in sweeping curves of flannels, brown arms and white bat and the ball making swift patterns across the grass. When we are told that Larwood has bowled down seven wickets we do not think of flying stumps so much as of pounding feet and a whirling arm circling and circling in magical curve. As cricketers we are all artists, and as artists we are more nearly god-like in our mortality. All this is done for us by a game, a dear, lovely game that will be ours until green fields and sweet sunshine have passed from the earth.

In Search of Cricket

Chapter Two:
CRICKET HEROES

Treasured Recollections of Len Hutton

IN the 21 years of his first-class cricket career Leonard Hutton has carried factual achievement beyond the acceptable limits of romance. In 1934 he played for Yorkshire as an unsophisticated youth of obvious talent and rare devotion to the game. He was happy to be playing cricket anywhere, somewhat astonished to find himself in the Yorkshire team and no doubt cherishing an ambition to represent England in some hazy future.

Now his retirement has been enforced and he looks back upon summer days that brought a world record Test match score, the captaincy of England and a reputation as the leading batsman of his time. He has missed nothing that cricket could offer him, and if at the age of 17 he had been able to see himself at 37 he would have rejected that picture as an incredibility.

Yet the logic of his development is within appreciation now

that his complete career can be reviewed. Success as a county cricketer could have been withheld only by the denial of opportunity. Translation to Test match status was no more than a matter of waiting, and the waiting was neither wearisome nor lengthy. Test match experience added to incessant study of play, and players brought a seniority and wisdom that indicated leadership when leadership was needed, and when the political atmosphere of cricket was favourable to a change in traditional outlook.

The chapters of the Hutton story follow an orthodox pattern though they contain material of the most striking novelty. Hutton became a Yorkshire figure in his first season for the county, playing an innings of 196 against Worcestershire. He became a national figure when he first played for England in 1937, scoring 100 against New Zealand. He made 100 in his first innings for England against Australia and he came to world-wide fame in the fifth Test match of the same series when he batted for 13 hours and 20 minutes to score 364 runs. After that he was no longer 'L Hutton, the Yorkshire and England batsman,' but simply 'Len Hutton' universally recognised. The immediate satisfactions of his achievement were to be enjoyed only briefly. South Africa saw his batting in its most joyful assurance during the MCC tour of 1938-39 and England delighted in the same untroubled mastery when he averaged 96 in the Tests of 1939 against the West Indies. His next Test match innings was delayed for seven years.

No overseas service was demanded of Hutton during the Second World War, but military activities threatened to end his cricket career and certainly exerted profound influence upon it. An accident cost him a broken arm, and the complications of recovery cost him the pain and anxiety of grafting operations with a permanent disability at the end of it all.

Hutton was 23 years old when Hitler's war broke out; he was in his 30th year when first-class cricket was resumed and never to be entirely free from consciousness of his shortened arm. Change in his outlook towards his own cricket and to cricket in general was inevitable. The change involved an increase of caution. He could not avoid the realisation that important years and some freedom of action had been stolen from him. Circumstances had increased his public and private responsibility and it was not in his nature to turn aside from challenge. He made adjustments.

He adjusted his batsmanship to the requirements of different cricketing conditions, playing the hook shot less frequently because he found it unreliable with a crippled arm, and playing with less freedom in general because he believed that his primary business was to lead the scoring. For the sake of his reputation and for the sake of Yorkshire and England he could not afford brief innings, however touched with glory. 'Why not try to hit these Australian bowlers?' he was once asked when England were in a perilous position. 'That's all very well for you' was his studied retort. 'People expect you to get out. They expect me to stay in'. People did expect Hutton to stay in and they came to expect so much of him that anything less than a century represented failure. His dismissal for 0 demanded headlines on the sports pages and momentary loss of form meant an inquisition into his past, present and future concerns.

He was left under no misapprehension over his significance in the world of cricket. He preserved his modesty, he kept his own counsel and he never ceased to think. The longer he thought the more strongly he became convinced that successful cricket was a business requiring as much study and concentration and devising as any other successful business. Without becoming arrogant he lost tolerance towards cricketers not prepared to follow his own single-minded devotion. Without pressing his own claim he became an obvious candidate for the captaincy of England.

In 1952 he was appointed, and he has not yet been superseded. He led England in five rubbers and never lost one of them. He won the Ashes in England and retained them in Australia. All captains are subject to public criticism, but Hutton knew himself peculiarly vulnerable. He knew that because he was an innovator, as professional leader, his every action would be minutely scrutinised and not without prejudice; he knew that captaincy would add to the isolation his playing stature had already created; he knew that he could expect little forgiveness in failure. He wanted to captain England, of course, because he counted the invitation the very crown of his career and he wanted to win it in his own right – as the leading player and the leading student of the game. The prize was worth the struggle, not so much to gain it as to hold it by proof that it had been rightly offered. He led his country in 23 Test matches, and but for illness would have led in several more. Neither captaincy nor batsmanship came easily to Leonard Hutton. He would have valued those attainments the less if they had. His main satisfactions in cricket have been derived from the study of its problems, the endless scheming and preparation to overcome the challenge of opponents, wickets and weather. He tired only of easy cricket. An hour of struggle against bowlers of the highest calibre or against the turning ball on an awkward pitch gave him more pleasure than boundaries for the taking. 'It's nice batting when you've made a hundred,' he would say, but he meant that it was enjoyable to be on holiday with the problems of work successfully cleared away.

Cricket has given him much. Experience, travel, fame and financial comfort. He has given much to cricket. The inspiration to seek perfection of technique and to combine with it the virtues of patience, endurance and forethought. He has added greatness of achievement to an innate gift of greatness and scaled peaks considered before his time to be unassailable. He will be remembered forever as the batsman whose method could not be faulted and the captain who concentrated to win. In the middle his magnificence was inescapable. Thousands upon thousands of fervent admirers gave him their confidence and approbation; sighed their relief as they saw him take off his cap and brush back his hair at the end of an over of watchful defence; thundered their applause as the loveliest off-drive of modern times left the fieldsmen in the covers immobile; raised their ovation on the completion of another century or another innings of precious memory. We who were privileged to see have recollections to treasure, and when cricket talk runs free and comparisons are raising doubts and deliberations the quiet of the indisputable will fall when Hutton's name is mentioned. 'Hutton,' we shall say, 'Ah – Hutton'.

August 1955

ONE day in the summer of 1934 a seventeen-year-old boy was observed enjoying a private joke. 'What are you laughing at?' he was asked. 'Me, playing for Yorkshire,' replied Leonard Hutton. Yet it always seemed natural enough that Leonard

Hutton should play for Yorkshire, and for England. He was born into a family well known in Pudsey club cricket, and his interests and ambitions were bound up in cricket from the time he could handle a bat and ball. His remarkable talent soon made itself evident and, strongly recommended by Herbert Sutcliffe among others, he came to the notice of the Yorkshire authorities (as, indeed, did Sutcliffe himself) about the time he was changing from short trousers to long ones. At the age of sixteen he was making runs for the county second team; at seventeen he was appearing in first-class cricket.

Yorkshire used him discreetly in his introductory season, for at that stage of his career there was more concern for his physique than for his technical ability, and 28 innings were all he was asked to play; in them he made 863 runs, with a score of 196 against Worcestershire to prove that his concentration and stamina were worth cultivating. In 1935 Hutton had poor health and it was not until late in the season that he made his only first-class century of the year, but in 1936 he won a regular place in the Yorkshire side and scored over 1,000 runs. He was, in that year, by no means a dominating batsman, for defence remained his primary consideration, and it was in his faultless technique that he gave most satisfaction to observant spectators. Of his essential quality, however, there was never any doubt, and in 1937 he came to man's estate with a season of complete triumph. He was third in the first-class averages with an aggregate of 2,888; he hit ten centuries; he played for England in the three Test matches against New Zealand, scoring a century at Old Trafford; and he was an obvious choice for one of *Wisden's* Five Cricketers of the Year. His highest score was 271 not out against Derbyshire at Sheffield, and in the match following he spent his 21st birthday making

153 in a first-wicket stand of 315 with Sutcliffe against Leicestershire at Hull. Hutton's career was firmly established.

By the end of another year all the world knew his name. The 1938 Australians, led by Bradman, won the fourth Test at Leeds and were sure of retaining the Ashes when they went to The Oval for the timeless fifth Test, but they were still anxious to guard an unbeaten record and, of course, the honours of the rubber remained to be decided. On Saturday, August 20th, England won the toss and Hutton went in first. He stayed in all the Saturday, all the Monday, and until half-past two on the Tuesday afternoon, by which time he had made the world's record Test match score of 364. It was not only the biggest but it was also much the longest of all Test match innings, for it lasted 13 hours and 20 minutes and was built up of 35 fours, 15 threes, 18 twos and 143 singles. There was a possible stumping chance at 40, otherwise scarcely a sign of error until a slightly mis-timed off-drive provided a low catch at cover.

Throughout the whole time the wicket remained perfect, the occasional light showers doing more good than harm, and the Australian attack was limited in the absence of their fast bowler, but whatever the comfort of the circumstances the innings was a colossal feat of concentration and endurance. All temptation to relax, to play a speculative shot, to take some risk in forcing the pace was resolutely put aside from first to last. Whether or not Hutton enjoyed himself he alone can say; there was no sign of it in his demeanour or in his manner of batting. The aftermath must certainly have brought him very mixed feelings. There were universal congratulations and there were considerable financial rewards, but there was no more privacy for Leonard Hutton. His photograph stared back at him every time he opened a newspaper or looked at an advertisement hoarding. He was a public figure wherever he went and he could never play another game of cricket without some sense of self-consciousness and responsibility. His failures became matters of national significance and his life was no longer his own. He learned as painfully as any monarch how uneasy lies the head that wears a crown.

The effects of that innings of 364 could never be erased from Hutton's subsequent cricket. In the winter of 1938-39 he offered some splendid batting to South Africa and he was in the best of form through the home season of 1939, but during the war an accident cost him a broken left forearm and he endured months of pain and anxiety because of unsatisfactory healing. Leonard Hutton, the young man with the cricket world at his feet, often wondered whether Leonard Hutton would ever have chance to play cricket again. The arm recovered, the war ended, and Hutton did play cricket again, apparently as well as ever. He was still, without a moment's query in selection, England's opening batsman, still the Test match record holder, expected to emulate himself. But Test matches for Hutton now became a very serious business. He was a known antagonist, a champion on whom hostility must be concentrated not only for the prize of his own wicket but for the value in shock upon his side. In the Australian tour of 1946-47, Hutton would have been a success had he been anyone but Hutton. His figures were good, but not good enough – for a batsman who held a record or 364. He was judged by a standard of 364, and he fell short of it. The Australian fast bowlers troubled him and it is possible that his responsibilities lay more heavily upon him than he cared to admit. The tour of the man of 364 was the tour of a man of smaller centuries – and consequent disappointment. Hutton did not fail in Australia, any more than Bradman failed in 1932-33. He, like Bradman, was merely reduced from his own reputation.

In the home season of 1947 Hutton's health and Hutton's Test match achievements were never permitted to be anything but a major topic of cricket conversation, and in 1948 when the Australians came again there was widespread speculation over Hutton in relation to fast bowling. The sensation of the season was his omission from the third Test. He came back for the fourth Test and he played an innings, fast bowlers or no fast bowlers. At The Oval he was the only batsman to look a batsman in the dreadful England total of 52. Perhaps his 30 on that occasion was as fine a piece of batsmanship as his 364 ten years before, but having scored 364 Hutton tends to be regarded as a permanent scorer of 364.

It would be sad injustice to cricket and to Hutton were figures to obscure the art of his batsmanship. He is indeed a beautiful player. His every movement at the wicket has a tidiness, an economy, a 'rightness', that stamp him unmistakably among the truly great. On difficult wickets against the turning ball he is surely close to perfection, confident in judgement, swift in footwork, faultlessly balanced. When run-getting is comparatively easy his off-drive and his forcing shot off the back foot are only credible because they are seen, and seen time and time again. There is no stroke he does not play, and play in strictest accordance with the canons of the text book. He is a complete illustration of batting, the polished product of much experiment, much study and much practice. He could no longer be caught laughing to himself at the thought of Hutton playing for Yorkshire and England, but he is infinitely deserving of the satisfaction that should come to an artist reflecting upon the delight his artistry has given to thousands and thousands of people all the world over.

Leonard Hutton (Yorkshire) was born in 1916 in Pudsey. He made 19 Test centuries and scored 6,971 runs for England from 1937 to 1955. He scored 129 hundreds – 11 of them double centuries. He was knighted in 1956. He died, aged 74, in 1990.

Statham and Trueman: The Flood Tide and the Tempest

HAPPY the country with no history may be debatable as a political aphorism but happy the cricketing country with high-class fast bowling is self-evident truth. Fast bowling superiority has governed the results of Test match rubbers for generation after generation, though, of course, in the absence of fast bowling or fast bowling conditions other factors have decided the issue from time to time.

In the years between 1951 and 1961 JB Statham and FS Trueman have made between them 104 appearances for England. In that period England have lost only two Test rubbers, one in Australia and one against Australia in England, and have been defeated only 17 times in 89 matches. The successes were not all directly attributable to the achievements of Statham and Trueman playing together or to one or the other, but the significant influence of fast bowling in general and of Statham and Trueman in particular scarcely brooks argument. This influence of fast bowling is inadequately measured in the analyses of fast bowlers. The figures themselves have been startling on occasion but the essential value of fast bowling lies in the creation of authority. Analyses count in numbers; fast bowling accountancy involves moral effect and the relative value of batsmen dismissed. Fast bowling represents the alarming element in cricket, the thunderstorm inducing awe and disturbance whatever the material results of its passage. Fast bowlers usually take as many wickets for others as for themselves. Statham and Trueman, playing so much together, have followed parallel careers with little more than their speed and success in common. Each has touched the topmost heights of his profession aided in considerable measure by the contemporary incidence of the other; either would have been welcomed in England teams of any age. They have been co-operative and competitive, complementary and contrasting. Brian Statham came quietly upon the Test match stage. At the age of 20 he was flown across the world as reinforcement to the decimated ranks of MCC on tour in Australia. He played against New Zealand in the supplementary programme and against South Africa in the home series of 1951. His early performances reflected his character; they were undramatic. Statham's rise to eminence was gradual and assured, based on a talent steadily developed, on perseverance and stamina. His outlook on bowling has always been admirably professional. Whatever the circumstances, he has been reliable, industrious and competent. Statham has sometimes bowled unsuccessfully for England but never badly by the basic canons of bowling.

Indeed, it has been said of him that he often bowls too well in the sense that the experienced batsman has greater opportunity of anticipation than against a more erratic and therefore more unpredictable attack. His length and direction verge upon the mechanical in their extraordinary accuracy. The element of surprise in his bowling is reduced by the very excellence of his technique. His great personal triumphs for England have been based on long endeavour rather than surging inspiration. The magnificent return of seven for 39 against South Africa at Lord's in 1955 involved 29 overs unchanged. In his 1960 mastery of South Africa at Lord's he bowled 20 overs in the first innings to take six for 63 and 21 overs in the second innings for 34 runs and five wickets. Fast bowlers in general neither receive nor expect any high degree of sympathy towards their cricketing labours. They do not need it. They rarely have to toil in unfavourable circumstances – on soft wickets, uphill, against the wind; their threat is obvious and they glory in their power, usually excused even consideration of the retaliatory bumper. Statham is an outstanding exception. His virtues are a basis for his misfortunes. No fast bowler has been more regularly condemned to achieve his conquests twice or three times over. The number of times he has defeated the stroke to see the ball miss the stumps or the edge of the bat is incalculable and incredible. Without the philosophic resignation that is his natural blessing and cultivated re-action he would have commited suicide, or turned batsman, long ago. Statham is the most phlegmatic of all fast bowlers. The mind's picture is of an unimpressively slight and youthful figure approaching business with a casual air. There is no elaborate routine of muscle-flexing and to all appearances Statham is not unduly concerned with the details of field-setting. One feature alone of preparation is remarkable; Statham pulls off his sweater by stretching one hand over his shoulder to the small of the back indicating an uncommon suppleness of joints. The run-up is smooth but not fearsome. The action is high with a marked cross-over of the feet before the delivery stride. The balance is delicate and when it is disturbed Statham sometimes stretches his length in an alarming fall. To most bowlers such accident would mean severe injury or, at best, an upset of rhythm and confidence. Statham has begun a Test match with a horrifying tumble, picked himself up and entered a long spell of swift and accurate bowling. He is notably undemonstrative in either achievement or disappointment. Opposing batsmen, defeated and dismissed, give their parting glance of subjection to find the conqueror standing relaxed at the end of his follow-through or stooping to pluck a blade of grass. Triumph was never more modestly acknowledged. Batsmen defeated but miraculously preserved may be made aware of good fortune by their own conscience but rarely by Statham's attitude. If his hand be raised it is not so much in protest to the gods as to receive the ball returning from the sympathetic wicket-keeper. There is no extravagance in Statham. The fires within him maintain an equable range and he would readily attribute the majority of his 213 Test match wickets to persistence and accuracy rather than to any flares of inspiration. His challenge is to the technical skill of batsmanship as distinct from the temperament of batsmen. He seeks to impose misjudgment of pace, miscalculation of swing, not fear for life and limb. He takes wickets more as a benevolent despot than as a tyrannical pirate. His nickname is The Greyhound. Freddie Trueman, called Fiery, equal partner in one of the most significant bowling combinations of all cricket, might have been deliberately designed as the antithesis to Statham. Statham obliterates opposing batting like the inexorable flood tide; Trueman shatters by tempest. Not for him an entry by stealth. At Headingley he brought to his first Test match the sensation of four Indian wickets whirled away with the score still at 0. In the third match of that 1952 series he found the ideal circumstances for the encouragement of a young fast bowler making his way in a glamorous world; a lively pitch, a strong following wind, superb fielding support and demoralised batting. In nine overs at Old Trafford Trueman took eight wickets for 31 runs. Success has not been Trueman's invariable portion in Test match cricket but sensation has surrounded him. He has been torpid and terrifying; dramatic in appearances and dramatic in omissions. All his cricketing career has been coloured by controversy, some of it inevitable, some spurious, none evaded. Trueman is a forthright and explosive character. By nature and by training he has become the popular personification of fast bowling. In his long run and long delivery stride with pronounced arching of the back his antagonism is plain for all to see. At his best pace speed alone has represented a formidable challenge and he has never felt any obligation to resist the testing of a batsman's physical courage. Aggressiveness has sparkled from his attitude and frustration has drawn his heartfelt comment, vocal and gesticulatory. It could fairly be argued that Trueman's type of attack has been as valuable to England as the talent in his bowling. High talent indeed is required to take 194 wickets in 45 Test appearances, but Trueman's influence has probably exceeded the mathematical register of his performances. His presence has stimulated optimism in his own team and anxiety in his opponents. His omission from

Test teams at home and from touring sides abroad has not necessarily involved England failure and his inclusion has sometimes originated England embarrassment, but he has always given his side the encouragement of belief that they would not be left naked to their enemies. By the features of his bowling and the principles of his assault he has raised his most thrilling hours to the great experiences of cricket. If Trueman's only bowling had been a Saturday afternoon spell for England against Australia at Lord's in 1956 his cricketing immortality would be assured. England, 114 behind on first innings, needed urgent and impressive recovery. Trueman, roused to the full magnificence of his fast bowling fury, almost contrived it in one of the most commanding and memorable attacks ever launched from the Nursery end. In the inspiration of the occasion he made an epic of an episode. Through over after over of awesome speed and vigour he flung himself against the Australian batting in endeavour raised to desperation, yet still controlled. The spellbound silence of anticipation dramatised his run up; in gasps of incredulity the ball flashed past bat and stumps into the hands of a distant wicket-keeper; in a chatter of amazement and hope he walked back to his mark. This was no moment for the theatrical gesture or self-conscious by-play. A whole world of endeavour was concentrated on a cricket pitch. The game transcended its own technicalities. Trueman took wickets, though as it happened he did not deliver this match into England's hands. He battled in a losing cause but this was his apotheosis as an England bowler; for this he will be remembered by all who watched as a bowler of rare skill, high endeavour and temper of the finest forging. By the look of the scorebook it may seem that Statham and Trueman have been in competition more than in partnership. Their best returns have been when they were playing in a team without the other; only in the West Indies in the second Test of 1960 have they shared all the wickets of a completed innings. The figures show less than the achievements. Statham and Trueman being contemporary have made each other more formidable, have made the England attack greater than either alone could have rendered it. Between them they have built a renown for such pressure upon the batsmen of the world that England at home and England abroad have never gone weakly or hopelessly into the field when their services were available. Their fires are dying now but the flames they kindled during the years of their mastery leave a glow across the cricketing sky to warm the heart in gratitude. Statham, the Greyhound, and Fiery Fred have deserved well of their country.

Wisden 1962

Fred Trueman (Yorkshire, Derbyshire) was the first bowler to take 300 Test wickets. His final total was 307 from 67 matches at 21.57. He took 2,304 first-class wickets at 18.29. He was born at Stainton in 1931 and died in his beloved Yorkshire in 2006, aged 75.

Brian Statham (Lancashire) was born in Gorton in 1930 and died in Stockport in 2000 only a few days short of his 70th birthday. He played in 70 Tests, taking 252 wickets (24.84). For Lancashire he took 2,260 wickets at 16.37.

Tom Graveney: Days of Wine and Roses

TOM GRAVENEY has always looked a cricketer of the West Country, though he was born in Northumberland. His schooldays were passed in Bristol, and when they were over he chose voluntary Army service before conscription to reach commissioned rank. By the time he returned to Bristol in 1947 his elder brother, Ken, had become a Gloucestershire player, and Tom was introduced to the county club as 'a kid brother I can't bowl out'. Cricket was not a compulsion for Graveney. He had talent that encouraged him towards a career in professional golf, and he had opportunity to train in accountancy. He accepted cricket and satisfied anticipations as a batsman of uncommon grace and authority. By 1951 he was playing for England.

On appearance alone Graveney's place in England teams could never have been questioned. His batting, founded on the classical forward strokes, contained an elegance that distinguished him even in the highest company, and when derivations were sought for his style, Hammond was invariably the quoted model. In fact Graveney could have drawn inspiration only from Hammond's name. The two players were not contemporary and resemblance in the eye of beholders was beauty seen and beauty remembered.

Graveney's early international career was unspectacular without being unsuccessful, but ironically his successes sowed doubts of his adequacy; he did enough to create assumptions that he should be doing more. By the most exacting standards he was found wanting in critical moments, lacking concentration at the crunch. He was discarded for the vital matches in the 1954-55 tour of Australia, and modest performances in the Test rubbers immediately following brought depreciation, with regret but not injustice.

Whenever Graveney was out of the England side England cricket was not necessarily weakened but it seemed slightly unrepresentative, as a June garden without roses or a banquet without wine. Roses blossomed and wine was relished in innings of 258 and 164 against West Indies in 1957, but another tour of Australia was disappointing and Graveney left the Test match scene for three years. They were years of disturbance in his county cricket. He left Gloucestershire to join Worcestershire, but immediate registration for his new county was not permitted and he had to endure the summer of 1961 without appearing in the Championship. Success for Worcestershire and against Pakistan earned a third tour of Australia, but the outcome was disappointing and again a cricketer of international quality passed into the international wilderness.

Graveney emerged from his experiences a harder, grimmer player. Worcestershire's Championship contention stiffened his sense of batting responsibility; advancing age in itself eliminated some of the batting frivolities. In 1966 England lost the first Test to West Indies, and they turned back to Graveney as ten years earlier they had turned back to Washbrook and to Compton. The parallels were remarkable. Washbrook scored 98 in his innings of recall, Compton scored 94, and Graveney scored 96. Washbrook and Compton met the needs of a specific hour; Graveney stayed to build a new international reputation. He played Test innings of substance and dignity and charm at home and in West Indies, and he remained an unquestioned selection until he fell into contractual dispute during the Old Trafford Test of 1969.

Graveney may have disappointed some cricketers by playing in Graveney's way, but he has adorned cricket. In an age preoccupied with accountancy he has given the game warmth and colour and inspiration beyond the tally of the scorebook. He has been of the orchard rather than the forest, blossom susceptible to frost but breathtaking in the sunshine. Figures give him too little credit and too much. They rate him among the most prolific of scorers with a hundred centuries achieved, and ignore the failures to command where command was expected in a critical hour. They obscure serenity and fragility alike. Figures cannot convey the splendour of an evening's innings or the anti-climax of first-over dismissal next morning.

Graveney's batting has always been open-handed and open-hearted, though not always open-eyed. He has tended to read Test match and festival in the same context, his cricket a medium for uncomplicated contest of talent with his own gifts offering an opportunity but not an obligation to succeed. Graveney has presented his ability without enforcing its acceptance. He has felt no guilt in edging a slip catch, because error is a human frailty and he has never sought to eliminate the humanity from cricket.

The difference between his earlier and later batting, indicated by more marked stability, represents not so much a change of heart or change of method as a restriction of adventurous activity through the insistence of advancing years. Graveney has not attempted to circumscribe himself;

the swing of his bat has been reduced by the natural process of age, and he still counts cricket in all its forms a game to be enjoyed. Taking enjoyment as it came he has given enjoyment that will warm winters of memory.

The Cricketer, May 1970

Tom Graveney (Gloucestershire, Queensland, Worcestershire) was born in Northumberland in 1927. He hit 11 Test hundreds in 79 matches, scoring 4,882 runs (highest score 258) at an average of 44.38. His first-class record was 47,793 runs at 44.91. He was President of the MCC in 2004.

Walter Hammond: The Royal Walk

AT 20 for two Walter Hammond came out to bat. In an Impressionist painting he would have trodden a red carpet down the pavilion steps and across the outfield on his way to the crease. In no possible way could Royal progress have been more regal than in Hammond's walk to the wicket. It was made at normal pace, without the hurry of anxiety or the deliberation of tactical device. It focused the attention of every man, woman and child in Lord's by the strength of its assurance and the beauty of its physical attributes.

Hammond's walk was the most handsome in all cricket, smooth in the evenness of stride, precise in balance. It was a flow of movement linking stillness to stillness. It was, as much as any feature of athletics, the poetry of motion. Hammond came to the wicket through many different approaches. At

Bristol he had awkward steps to negotiate from a first-floor dressing-room; at Headingley he had to press his way through spectators; at Gloucester among other places he would prise himself from a deck-chair. By repute he was not a compulsive watcher of cricket and there is record of his having to be nudged from sleep to take his innings and of his making apology for desertion of a card-school.

Wherever and however he appeared he was graceful and magnetic, but at Lord's in 1938 he epitomised himself. He adorned the picture by being so perfectly in keeping with it.

In his walk from pavilion to pitch he stirred the heart and dimmed the eye with pride for cricket in a magic moment. He came like a king and he looked like a king in his coming.

I am conscious of my tendency to invest the commonplace with a romanticism of my own making; I am inclined to colour with a 'Light that never was on sea or land' and I am not above suspicion of exaggerating virtues and over-looking flaws in consideration of cricket heroes and heroics. 'Heavens above,' I can hear the realist protest, 'what a song and dance to make about a batsman simply walking to the wicket'. There is no defence against such complaint. Hammond was, in physical terms, doing no more and doing it no better than on hundreds of occasions. He always walked with grace and confidence and dignity, but this time there was an added quality as clear, to me, as though he had been wearing a purple cloak. It was the assurance of being the right person in the right place at the right time.

I was not alone in thinking so. Over the years innumerable people who were at Lord's that day have remarked on the impressiveness of Hammond's entry in the atmosphere of excitement created by the fall of wickets to McCormick's lively bowling.

Some of that impressiveness is no doubt a product of hindsight, a reflection of glory that followed. Had Hammond been leg-before for 0 we should probably remember his walk out more readily than his walk in, but Hammond was not lbw for 0 and his entry did presage and perhaps contribute to one of the great innings of cricket. On 30,000 watchers, sitting or standing, comfortable or crushed, the effect of Hammond at the crease was soothing. Facts insist that the alarms of the morning were not over, for England lost their third wicket at 31, suggesting that McCormick could still extract lift and swing from the new ball. Hammond quelled the alarms by saying to Australia's bowlers and using deeds for words: 'Enough; this is a batting occasion.' By lunch-time the character of the day had been established. Hammond had scored 70 and Paynter had stayed with him, virtually unremarked in the shadow of the Hammond splendour. There had been no assault born of passion on the bowling, no hitting in desperation, no grim defiance of a fearsome enemy. The whole glory of Hammond's batting was its easefulness. The force employed was made the more astonishing by its disguise under rhythm. Nobody troubled to chase the ball to boundary as Hammond directed it through the covers or between the bowler and mid-off, but Hammond's driving contained no element of brutality. Its power was in its artistry.

Hammond went on to make 240. The Test – in June 1938 – was drawn.

WALTER HAMMOND in his hey-day offered all the glory and the colour of medieval chivalry. He graced a cricket field by stepping on it. He brought to combat the dignity, the skill, the authority of rightful rank. The trappings and the panoply surrounded him. He was never seen without being remembered. In his time a Test match could not seem a Test match in his absence.

Hammond's cricket reached the topmost peaks of the game. More than anyone else of his generation he reflected gleams of a golden age and carried us all beyond the care of local loyalties to an experience of the spirit. He thrilled us, held the imagination, raised us beyond ourselves in his presence, and the darkening to his final curtain cannot obscure the unquestionable greatness of the whole play. It was a satisfaction to watch Hammond do no more than walk from one position in the field to another, from first slip to first slip. His was the very poetry of motion, flowing, smooth and vital. Sometimes he made no runs and did not bowl, and still earned his keep by catches. Three times he held six catches in an innings and once he held ten in a match. He was everything the slip fieldsman is supposed to be in theory: he was balanced, he never 'grabbed' at the ball and though he used both hands whenever possible he had full confidence in either right or left alone. His timing often made his achievement incredible in retrospect, yet the most natural activity imaginable during the execution. Hammond's bowling was as easeful as his fielding and his batting. There was a delicacy of touch and hidden vigour in it. An economical 'sideways' action gave him control and subtle variation of pace and helped him to swing the new ball. Had the gods denied him batting talent he could have found fame as a bowler.

There was no denial of batting talent; in technique, temperament, power and grace Hammond was superb. It was said that his on-side play had its limitations, that he possessed no hook shot; McDonald at Old Trafford was not conscious of the deficiency one historic morning in May. When Hammond did not hook, it was because Hammond did not choose to hook. On the off side, where Hammond mostly did choose to play, he was acknowledged as without peer. Fast bowlers of his time thought him the best player of slow bowling in the whole world; slow bowlers pointed out that fast bowlers also paid for his wicket. His magnificence was undeniable and his display of it was lavish. He played incomparable innings for England over a period of nearly 20 years and the multitudes of Lord's and Sydney rose in homage to him, but it is not beyond argument that he gave the highest expression of himself at Bristol or Gloucester or, best of all, at Cheltenham. He could wear the robes of state with assurance and nobody ever saw him cheapen a cricketing occasion, but he was perhaps at his most comfortable and impressive when circumstances gave him a deck-chair to sit in until it was his turn to bat and he could stroll out to make a century for his own entertainment. In the end the game lost savour for him because he was too public a figure. His own genius and the responsibilities placed upon it spoiled his cricket - so he gave it up. There is no need to make comparisons between Hammond and his contemporaries, or indeed between Hammond and any cricketers of any time. He stands among the few who can be excused the noun in apposition. It is sufficient to say WR Hammond, omitting as superfluous 'the Gloucestershire and England cricketer'.

Cricket Decade

*Walter Hammond (Gloucestershire) made 50,551 first-class
runs from 1920 to 1951. He scored 7,249 runs in Tests,
including 22 hundreds. He also took 83 Test wickets at fast-
medium. Born in Buckland, Dover in 1903, Hammond died in
Natal in 1965. He was 62 years old.*

G H Hirst:
Golden Figure of the Golden Age

GEORGE HERBERT HIRST was born a Yorkshireman, bred
a Yorkshireman and came to represent the ideals of a
Yorkshireman. He illustrated expectations and then exceeded
them. He carried character to the ultimate plane. He made
generally accepted pictures of a Yorkshireman; short and
stocky; round-faced and with a suggestion of bandiness in the
legs. He wore a cap and smoked a pipe and spoke slowly with
a regional accent. There was an air of physical strength and
mental contentment about him, even in the frailness of old age.
He was entirely without affectation. Because he was so
essentially himself there would have been a rightness in
George Hirst as representative of any of his county's typical
characters. He would have been esteemed in the engineer's
overalls or at the farmer's 'ordinary' on market days; he would
have fitted into the pattern of the wool trade exchanges or
filled a fisherman's jersey and sea-boots. It so happened that
his talent and his inclination was for cricket and for talent and
inclination there is always cricketing opportunity in Yorkshire.
George Hirst became one of the greatest of all cricketers and

never wanted any other way of life.

He was not born a cricketer in the sense of family associations and occupation, but he came to cricket and to football through the natural consequences of boyhood in a village on the outskirts of a town absorbed in sporting interests. Most of the boys of Kirkheaton played cricket and football and talked and heard talk of the cricketers and footballers of Huddersfield and district. George Hirst could scarcely have avoided cricket and football in Kirkheaton of the 1880s and he became a better cricketer than his companions because he was blessed with a co-ordination, a physical strength, a resolution beyond theirs. He had no advantages of training or environment, but he had the supreme advantage of being what he was. At the age of eighteen his Kirkheaton achievements had carried him into the Yorkshire team. He was a fast left-arm bowler, an enthusiastic hitter and an uncomplaining fieldsman. He proved an unexciting 'discovery' and it was not until three years later, in 1892, that he became a regular member of the county side. He then achieved 177 runs in 16 innings and took 27 wickets for an average of 19.51. Modest beginnings led to long and almost incredible triumph. When Hirst retired he had scored 36,203 runs and taken 2,727 wickets; he had played 24 times for England (in a period when Test matches were comparatively uncommon); he had, in 1906, become the only player ever to reach 2,000 runs and 200 wickets in one first-class season. He had written his cricket in figures of gold.

He had done more. He had moved from village adolescence to the maturity of world-wide renown and won universal respect and admiration for himself, his county and his country. In cricket he was the beloved Yorkshireman. Respect was accorded him for technical ability as a batsman, bowler and fieldsman; admiration for his achievements; affection for his personality. George Hirst would undoubtedly have found a high degree of success without the acquisition of what is known in the current idiom as his 'gimmicks'. His bowling was based on the virtues of good length and direction. His batting showed the soundest of principles. George Hirst never altered his opinion that 'the old method is the best – length first; finger spin, flighting the ball, swerving and the other devices afterwards, but with length never subservient to anything'. That was George Hirst in an interview, of course, but it is a fair, if stilted, expression of his convictions. Of batting he said: 'Quick footwork is three parts of batting and it helps the arms to make the stroke and follow-through. If a man stands easy and comfortable at the wicket it does not matter whether he is one or two-eyed.' In those classic dissections by Beldam and Fry of the players of the Golden Age Hirst was selected to illustrate great batting, great bowling and great fielding. As a batsman he is shown with an upright, unstrained stance, feet slightly apart, hands together and high on the handle, face full towards the bowler. The whole attitude exudes determination and assurance. Hirst at the wicket looked as though he feared no bowler, and his look did not belie him.

The determination and assurance persist through the demonstration of off-drive, hook, on-drive, pull and defensive back-stroke. Textbook canons were never more strictly followed. In the off-drive the front foot is far across towards the pitch of the ball, the follow-through full and high and the body leaning to the direction of despatch. In the backstroke the head is over the ball, the lower hand dropped to the bottom of the handle, bat and leading forearm are in one straight line. Had he played entirely by the textbook George Hirst could have been an admirable model for right-handed batsmen. In practice he wrote his own appendix and advanced beyond imitation except at gravest peril to the less-gifted. George Hirst added the George Hirst pull to batting. In his best form he would seize upon the short half-volley pitched on or even outside the off-stump, stretch to it with the left foot and sweep across the line of flight with a full swing of the bat. The result was devastating, particularly upon off-break bowlers finding some help in the pitch. They called upon high heaven to witness the unreason of it all and by the time they appreciated that GH Hirst was born wise and skilful rather than lucky another match had been won or saved for Yorkshire. CB Fry, that shrewd assessor, saw into the heart of things when he wrote of George Hirst: 'On slow, wet wickets and on difficult sticky wickets he is one of the most dangerous batsmen, as he is very sure of his pull-driving and his hooking. In point of fact, although his strokes sometimes look daring to the verge of rashness, he watches the ball very closely and is very quick with his bat. Indeed, it is his quickness more than anything else that enables him to take what usually are regarded as liberties with the bowling.'

Quickness of movement and care in watching the ball formed the technical foundation of Hirst's batting; adventurousness gave its quality. Without a call to adventure George Hirst's cricket rarely touched its best. He rejoiced in challenge. The more difficult the situation, the greater his effort. The more hopeless the cause, the more probable his success. He made 56 centuries for Yorkshire and very few of them were superfluous to the needs of this moment. His smaller innings of rescue were beyond counting. No match was to be considered lost with George Hirst still batting or to bat.

With this capacity for rising to the occasion George Hirst earned the affection of all Yorkshiremen and the admiration of all cricketers. Yorkshiremen understood the fighting spirit. They love a fighter and they gave their greatest love to the greatest of all cricketing fighters. The sight of George Hirst passing through the pavilion gateway raised the hearts as it raised the voices. The strength, the calmness, the warmth of him surged into the crowds. He never courted popularity, never played to the gallery, yet he was always a friend among friends. He commanded response because he gave to the limit of his gifts.

In bowling George Hirst began with the assets of youth and an exceptionally strong constitution. He was left-handed, he bowled fast and he possessed abounding vitality. As soon as he acquired control of length and direction he became a good bowler and successful. When he had developed his special facility he became a great bowler and at times unplayable in the highest of company. No doubt the essence of his famous swerve lay in his natural action in which the arm was not notably high and came across a considerable body turn supported by a powerful lift from the small of the back. The curve of flight would tend to follow the arc of propulsion. The photographs in Beldam and Fry show the approved placing of the feet and a smooth follow-through.

The photographs do not show the bewildered helplessness of batsmen who contemplated an off-side stroke and found the ball passing behind their legs. There was no orthodox answer to what one victim described as 'a good throw from cover-point'. Nobody taught George Hirst his swerver. He found it by accident, observed it with care, developed it by thoughtful experiment, and mastered it by patient application. He was not a 'straight' bowler one minute, or one season, and a swerve bowler the next. He was never entirely dependent on swerve for bowling success. George Hirst's swerve was unique only in his development of it. He noticed that in certain conditions the ball tended to behave in a certain way and he saw in this behaviour a weapon of attack additional to good length, speed, liveliness and the natural break of the left-arm bowler. Swerve was not a substitute for the other bowling arts but an extension of them. A moist atmosphere, a 'green top' pitch, a gentle breeze from third-man, gave Hirst his ideal conditions and with the ball held seam-up and bowled to a full length there followed such performances as nine for 41 against Worcestershire, when Worcestershire were dismissed before lunch on the first day, yet nearly 1,000 runs were scored in the remainder of the match. Morning and evening and the new ball brought the sudden wreckage of many an innings when George Hirst was enjoying what he called one of his 'funny' days.

When conditions were against his swerve Hirst was far from helpless. A turning wicket did not eliminate him from the attack, because he changed his grip to seam-across and whipped the ball away from the bat for the benefit of fieldsmen crowding the slips instead of the leg trap. He had a remarkable capacity for keeping his foothold on muddy turf and could thus remain a fast or fast-medium bowler in unhelpful circumstances, for through the greater part of his career it was not the custom to cover the ends of the pitch during rain. Hirst and Rhodes bowled together throughout more than one innings. They demolished an Australian Test innings after rain at Edgbaston in 1902 whereupon the chastened travelled to Headingley to be put out for a total of 23 by Hirst and Jackson. The history books are full of feats verging upon the incredible. It is as well they are. The marvels of George Hirst would never have been revealed by George Hirst. He would talk cricket, and happily, all day long, but it would be your cricket or the cricket of a third party, not the cricket of George Hirst. He was not falsely modest or shy; he was genuinely interested in the hopes, fears, prospects and accomplishments of other people. He could not avoid knowing his own worth, but he never made comparisons and he regarded his reputation as an asset to be used for giving pleasure to others. His kindliness was unwavering.

To me it was perfectly exemplified by his methods of inquiry. He never failed to ask the performances of young cricketers and in my experience he never said 'How many did you get?' but always 'Did you get any?' The unsuccessful batsman finds it much less embarrassing to reply 'No' than 'None'. In all probability the distinction never consciously occurred to George Hirst. His sympathy was as natural as his courtesy. In all his coaching he suggested rather than insisted, never asserting the superiority of his own method, but indicating an experiment as between equals. He would watch, to all appearances approvingly. Then he would question knowledgeably. Then he would indicate the means to an improvement. 'How are you holding the ball for your off-breaks?' – 'Try it this way'. 'Do you find they are going rather wide?' – 'Try placing your front foot there'. His generosity in approval warmed the heart. If there was anything good to say George Hirst was sure to say it; if nothing could be found George Hirst was silent. Hundreds of young cricketers made his acquaintance during his years as coach to the Yorkshire County Club and to Eton College. Not one of them was sent empty away for lack of George Hirst's interest and endeavour. If he thought it necessary for the sake of encouragement he would gladly give the appearance of diminishing his own stature by allowing himself to be bowled during net practice or suggesting that he was at wit's end to dismiss a batsman young enough to be his grandson. To know him was to be his friend; and to be his friend was to be his admirer, but all the admiration, all the acclamation that followed him across the world and home again never so much as threatened to turn his head. He, as much as any man, could walk with kings without losing the common touch. His universal popularity was proclaimed in his benefit match, played at Headingley in 1904. The August Bank Holiday weekend was blessed with fine weather and the total attendance at the match was 78,792. By the monetary values of those days, when Yorkshire professionals were paid £5 for a home match and £6 for an away match (paying their own expenses) the benefit proceeds of £3,703* represent a public tribute unequalled before or since. On the field George Hirst was a tremendous opponent, batting, bowling and fielding with all his heart, but there was no arrogance in his power, no blindness in his loyalty, no tyrannous use of his giant's strength. When he was making his record Yorkshire individual score of 341 against Leicestershire he found opportunity to congratulate a young Leicestershire substitute upon brilliant fielding in the covers.

When, at the age fifty-eight, he was persuaded to make a final appearance in the Scarborough Festival he was beaten and bowled by Bowes after a few minutes at the crease. He directed his course to the pavilion so that he passed the bowler.

*£3,703 is the equivalent of almost £300,000 in 2008.

'Well bowled, Bill,' he said. 'That would have been too good for me at any time.' He was Yorkshire's coach when a slight, shy fourteen-year-old boy attended the practices at Headingley to receive the accolade, 'There's nothing more I can show him'. The boy was Leonard Hutton. George Hirst never turned away from cricket and cricketers as the interest of his life. Long after his retirement to his Huddersfield home he would meet and talk over past and present with Wilfred Rhodes. On his 80th birthday he visited the Scarborough Festival and as he walked round the ground to the President's tent honour would be paid him, starting as a gentle ripple of applause as he was first recognised and rising to an acclamation that drew attention from the play and finally stopped it. His sympathies extended beyond his contemporaries and he always contrived to see the best in the cricket of days following his own. He appreciated the inevitable changes of technique and strategy and avoided invidious comparisons. He went out of his way to offer congratulations and good wishes of unmistakable sincerity. In many treasure-chests there is a letter of careful calligraphy signed GH Hirst, written to mark a milestone in a career or lend encouragement to the approach of an occasion. He was always glad of an opportunity to meet players of later renown and discuss with them, always on equal terms of authority, current conditions and outlook. He was the last person to suggest that the best of cricket was contained in the era of George Hirst. His vitality and his stamina were wonderfully preserved and into the fifties he followed a season of energetic coaching and vigorous club cricket with a willing turn as umpire in Festival matches. Umpiring, he said, gave him a close view of the good players of the time. He accepted the advancing years with the grace of a contented mind, comfortable with his pipe and cricketing company. Though the little hair remaining had long turned white and the sturdy legs stepped shorter and more stiffly, alertness stayed in the kindly eyes and a quality of brightness in the husky voice. As the increasing frailness of great age became evident he could still say cheerfully to inquirers of another generation, 'Oh, I'm like Bill Bowes, here; I bowled two overs too many too often'. One May morning, another cricket season just begun and Yorkshire playing far away in Gloucestershire, he came to his quiet end. All over the country, all over the cricketing world, the pavilion flags fluttered their last salute. The long obituaries could only repeat the wondrous stories already well-known, truths that had become legends, of timely centuries, decisive bowling spells and brave fielding at mid-off, but George Herbert Hirst left more than could ever be told in the score-book. He left affection in the memory of all who knew him, or met, or watched him. His faults and virtues, failures and successes, the strength of his endeavour made a character within the understanding of everyone.

This was the happy warrior, this was he
That every man in sport would wish to be!

Cricket Heroes 1959

George Hirst (Yorkshire) was born in Kirkheaton in 1871 and died in Huddersfield on May 10, 1954, aged 82. He batted right handed and bowled (medium fast) with his left. He scored 790 runs in 24 Tests and took 59 wickets. In first-class matches for Yorkshire, he scored 36,356 runs and claimed 2,742 wickets.

Brian Close:
The Art of Physical Courage

BITTER-SWEET has been the characteristic flavour of Brian Close's cricket career. He has stretched his fingertips to clouds of glory and stumbled in a morass of disappointment and controversy. He has enjoyed the highest distinctions and suffered salt in deep wounds. In twenty years he has known few seasons of quiet content. He was born at Rawdon near Leeds into a cricketing family and his youthful sporting talent was so pronounced that he was plunged into county and Test cricket at the age of 18. Hindsight indicates that too much was undoubtedly asked of him too soon, but true kindness would have involved some cruelty had he been denied the opportunity to score 1,000 runs and take 100 wickets and to play for England against New Zealand in his first season of 1949.

Controversy was thrust on him in 1950 when he was selected to tour Australia during his period of National Service. His mere presence in the side attracted public comment and his performances concentrated it. He scored 108 not out in the opening first-class match and 0 and 1, in culpable fashion, in his only Test. Long before the end of the tour Close had become a cricketing reject. His climb to rehabilitation was long and slow and was not advanced by personal decisions that discounted well-meant advice and proved unfortunate in outcome. He hoped for a profitable career in professional football and lost a season's cricket through football injury. He drifted into a state of inconsequential performance verging on the fatalistic. In success he was impressive; in failure he appeared to cultivate indifference. Occasional undertakings for England failed to stifle misgivings, and a dramatic batting error against Australia at Old Trafford in 1961 seemed to confirm a widespread belief that temperament would always wither the blossom of his talent. Inherent talent was not questioned. Set against all the left-hand batsmen of his time Close looked comparable with the best in artistry, in power and in potential. Confining himself within the range of the orthodox he was majestic, but he allowed an impression to grow of accomplishment unharnessed and of immaturity extending far beyond cricketing adolescence. His play suggested that he had not found its purpose.

Yorkshire appointed Close their captain in 1963 because the office was vacant and because professional seniority gave him claim to succession. Within one season he had proved himself brilliantly successful. Clearly exercising authority, shrewd in tactics and leading by example at the crease and in the field, Close not only inspired Yorkshire but invigorated himself. In the five Test matches against West Indies he was a resolute batsman, an innings of 70 at Lord's touching the heroic. At the end of the season Close was a tired cricketer, mentally and physically, but he knew the satisfactions of fulfilment.

He was not required in another Test series until 1966 and then only for the last match of a rubber already decided. West Indies had won three of the first four matches and depression had settled over England cricket when Close was given the leadership of a reconstituted side. His experience was characteristically dramatic. England won the match and Close's captaincy was rated a decisive factor in the result. A new world of promise was opening to him in his 36th year.

It was shattered in 1967. As captain of Yorkshire, Close wanted the County Championship and as captain of England he wanted Test match success over India and Pakistan, not only for its own sake but in preparation for a tour of West Indies and for the visit of Australia in 1968. By mid-August Yorkshire were Championship leaders but only by such a narrow margin that two points from a drawn game at Edgbaston were balanced against opprobrium for delaying tactics in the field when Warwickshire were trying to force victory. Yorkshire's conduct was publicly condemned and on the eve of the last Test against Pakistan Close was held responsible in a formal rebuke.

He was not invited to captain MCC in West Indies and in 1968 he did not lead England against Australia. He had lost foothold, again, on the slippery pathway of esteem. Through all the vicissitudes of his career he has never lost the appreciation of cricketers for talented performance, for investigation of the game's possibilities and for unflinching physical courage. Close as a young player raised a thrill of delight in response to his powerful and confident left-hand batting, his easy right-arm action for off-spin or swing bowling and his agility in the field. He was handsome in all his athletic pursuits.

Close in mid-career drifted away to the fringes of distinction because his batting too rarely reflected the full extent of his ability and his bowling talent was not consolidated into artistry under discipline. By the evidence of his best innings no England side should have been complete without him, yet his intermittent appearances could not be counted an injustice. Appointment to captaincy turned self-assurance into channelled purpose. Close was never a more impressive cricketer, in technique and temperament, than when he assumed the responsibilities of leading Yorkshire.

The Cricketer, August 1970

Brian Close (Yorkshire, Somerset) was born in Rawdon, Leeds in 1931. He played 22 Tests and scored 887 runs. In 786 first-class matches, he scored 34,994 runs.

Herbert Sutcliffe:
Master Batsman and Man's Man

IT is a common cry that modern cricket lacks such personalities as graced it in the 'Golden Age' when every county had one man or more who attracted the crowds as much by himself as by his performances. It is unfortunately true that one innings has become very like another innings and one white figure in the field could easily be mistaken for another white figure. At most first-class matches today a scorecard is an absolute necessity, for even bowling methods have become abominably stereotyped. There are still, however, one or two figures whom none could fail to recognise. Herbert Sutcliffe is unquestionably one of them. When he stands in the field his shining black hair and immaculate flannels serve as clear identification, and when he is at the wicket his presence is unmistakable.

Sutcliffe holds so many records that he who knows not this player's reputation knows nothing of cricket. To watch one of Sutcliffe's innings is to have complete understanding of his power. He always seems to me rather to hurry to the wicket, everlastingly anxious to be batting and eager to test the quality of a bat which looks brand-new every time he opens an innings. Nine times out of ten the first ball will be outside the off-stump, and just so often will Sutcliffe step across, bring his feet together with military precision, lift that beautiful bat high out of harm's way and gaze past point as the ball thuds into the wicket-keeper's gloves. This padding-up announces as clearly as spoken words: 'My dear bowler, you are wasting your time: I am proposing to make a century today and I am certainly not going to jeopardise my chances by feeling for anything outside the off-stump.' The bowler is invariably heedless, but when Sutcliffe performs precisely the same operation at half-past five in the afternoon scepticism begins to depart. Sutcliffe's appearance is, of course, in keeping with his character. He looks cool and calm, and he behaves coolly and calmly. The bowler who beats Sutcliffe's bat and misses the stumps by a 'coat of varnish' may save himself the trouble of throwing up his arms and calling upon high heaven to witness the luck of the man. Sutcliffe will be quite unimpressed by such display. In all probability he will not even turn round to assure himself that the bails are still on. I have seen Sutcliffe beaten and morally bowled three times in six balls, yet at the end of the over he stood aside, leaned on his bat and crossed his legs in exactly the same way as when there are 200 chanceless runs to his name.

To be morally out is a conception beyond Sutcliffe's ken when applied to himself, and of all cricketers he is the most unlikely to end his innings through worry. When a man of this temperament adds to his accomplishments a wonderful technique, he is obviously approaching the ideal for the stress and strain of Test match cricket. The certainty of Sutcliffe's defence, the power of his hooking and driving, and the accuracy of his placing would probably have brought him many runs for England in any circumstances. But without the alliance of those inward qualities which make him never happier than when difficulties abound and the situation calls for almost superhuman effort he could not have astonished the world as he has done. Sutcliffe's records and runs are dear to his fellow Yorkshiremen, who recognise and respect high ability; his physical strength and his patience through the hottest of cricketing days are admired because Yorkshiremen envy and honour a man's man; his willingness to enter the struggle and his success with everything against him are the real keys to his great popularity, because Yorkshiremen and cricketers everywhere dearly love a fighter. Not only along the ways of county cricket has Sutcliffe marched triumphantly; equal success has come to him in Test matches, and his work for England, at home and abroad, has been a source of wonder and envy the world over. Many of Sutcliffe's efforts for England have been made in adverse circumstances, for he and Hobbs had invariably great responsibilities in the way of big scores against them or difficult batting conditions. How they triumphed is a matter of history, and no cricketer can read without pride of the gallant deeds of defiance inspired by the inherent greatness of these players. Sutcliffe has given a great deal to cricket. On the field he has built upon the foundations of those who went before and himself added a superstructure that is at once beautiful and inspiring. Always he has played the game as it should be played, in high courage and sporting endeavour, and given of his best at all times. Off the field, he has set himself an equally high standard, and no action of his has ever reflected other than creditably upon his profession.

In Search of Cricket

Herbert Sutcliffe (Yorkshire) was born in Summerbridge, Harrogate in 1894. He made 4,555 runs in 54 Test appearances, including 16 centuries. His first-class career brought him 50,670 runs (151 hundreds). He died in 1978, aged 83.

Percy Holmes and his Circus

PERCY HOLMES, who died on September 3 at the age of 84, was one of the most enjoyable of cricketers. He gave pleasure to those who watched and to those who played in his company. His own satisfaction in batting and fielding, and with the cricketing life of his time, was never obscured by an assumed indifference.

He came early to Yorkshire's notice through precocious success at club level, but his establishment in first-class cricket had to be postponed until after the First World War. In 1919 he won his county cap, scored 1,887 runs and began his historic association with Herbert Sutcliffe. When he left the Yorkshire team in 1933 he had made over 30,000 runs, completed 67 centuries and shared in a world-record opening partnership. For so accomplished and consistently successful a batsman his international appearances were remarkably limited. He played for England against the fearsome Australians at Trent Bridge in 1921, but not again until he toured South Africa in 1927-8 and only once more in England, as late as 1932. He was the victim of circumstances more than of any inadequacy in himself. Denied an immediate success he had no opportunity to try and try again.

There was no denying his quality. He looked a batsman of uncommon talent, sound in method and enterprising in manner. Swift footwork made the hook and the late cut his characteristic strokes and all his batting carried an air of briskness and eager anticipation. He signed himself with a little flourish of the bat at the end of his forward strokes and he was the most accommodating and trustworthy of partners in running between wickets. His approach to the crease and his preparations to receive the ball had a military precision. He marched rather than walked, back straight, head held high. His general practice was to wear only a right-hand batting glove and his flannels and pads were invariably neat and clean. For fielding, when the grass was dry, he preferred light, rubber-soled footwear and he was as tireless on the boundary edge as he was alert in the slips. He was accepted everywhere as a good companion in cricket, neither unduly downcast in failure nor ostentatiously elated in success. Yorkshire called him 'Wappy' in acknowledgment of one of his favourite hostelries near Huddersfield and when he chanced to be first to the reception desk, as the team were booking in for an away match, he created a composite nickname that Yorkshire applied to themselves for years. 'Register us,' he said, 'as Percy Holmes and his Circus.' The crown of his career as an individual batsman was an innings of 315 not out at Lord's, chanceless and containing 38 fours. In partnership his day of days was at Leyton in 1932 when he and Sutcliffe opened the Yorkshire innings with 555. Holmes, hampered by lumbago, contributed 224 not out. This was his last big innings and will be for ever his memorial. This most unselfish of cricketers was happy to share success.

The Cricketer, 1971

Percy Holmes (Yorkshire) made 30,573 first-class runs, including a highest score of 315 not out. He was born in Huddersfield in 1886 and died there in 1971. He was 84 years old.

JB Hobbs: Hail and Farewell

IT is nearly thirty years since John Berry Hobbs, who has now announced his retirement from first-class cricket, played in his first championship match for Surrey; nearly thirty years since he made his first century in first-class cricket; nearly thirty years since he first trod that Oval turf which has known so many of his triumphs. From Hobbs (JB), a young man of great promise, he has travelled a long and glorious road to become Jack Hobbs, known the world over and accepted as 'The Master' of cricket. In his springtime cricket was a flourishing flower, full-blown and sweet-o'-scent, for with him on the fields were Trumper and Noble, MacLaren and Jackson, Hirst and Rhodes and a whole host of others whose flames are immortal and memories green. Here Hobbs found fortune, for there was stimulating challenge to his genius and knights worthy of his jousting.

No batsman yet seen has evolved such mastery over all the vagaries of bowler and wicket. When the sun shone and runs came merely for the asking, he took them with a thankfulness beyond mere acceptance. He found no pleasure in painstaking effort, in watching the numbers go round; he made every innings a text-book of batting with illustrations entirely his own. A hard Oval wicket meant a good score for Hobbs – that was certain: but how the score would be made was beyond all hope of prophecy. Days were not always thus, for sometimes rain fell and spin bowlers snapped their fingers in glee. Into their hutches the rabbits went tumbling, but Hobbs, amazing the world, remained firm at his end. The pages of cricket reports echo again and again, 'Hobbs played a brilliant innings, where all others failed'. Nor was he a plant of one garden. In every cricketing county of England his magic was seen, and he charmed South Africa and Australia as he charmed the men of his own native land. When Hobbs first carried his bat for Surrey and for England, bowling strategy was not as in these times. Fast bowlers were fast, scorning swing and relying on speed, length, and break-back. Hobbs mastered these. Medium-paced off-spinners, such as Trumble and Hearne, reaped their harvest of wickets. Hobbs mastered these. Then came the googly with all its attendant alarms. Where others were beaten or hesitant, Hobbs reigned supreme, scoring still with freedom and ease, sure of himself and his power.

The years passed and the fires of Hobbs's youth flared less brightly. A new theory of bowling brought a new batting technique, and nothing in post-war cricket has revealed more grandeur than the autumn of this man's career. From the brilliance of his classical foundation grew the safety and power of his on-side play. No longer was his bat a lance, pennant flying, eagerly routing the foe. The lance became a wand, charming the enemy to impotence and bringing success through calm and assurance. Nothing could have been more beautiful than this later quietening of Hobbs; there were no regrets for the passing of that amazing speed of eye and footwork that were essential to his earlier brilliance.

'Grow old along with me, The best is yet to be,' said Hobbs, and played as Victor Trumper would have played had ever the years grown over him. Hobbs was never an inhuman, mechanical cricketer; he had a fine sense of duty to the game and its supporters. Runs as represented by marks in the score-book had for him only the value they had to his side. He has thrown away his wicket many times in an attempt to entertain the spectators; he has got himself out as though saying, 'You must be tired of me now'. His records, the bare framework to his picture, are in themselves a source of wonder. He has passed the century 197 times; over 61,000 runs has he made in the aggregate; 323 runs he shared with Wilfred Rhodes for a first-wicket partnership in Test cricket. On sixteen occasions in one season he made a score of more than 100. Is it credible that any one man will ever do more? Yet not for these things alone, or even mainly, will he be beloved in our memory. We shall think of him, trim and tidy, coming out to open the innings; we shall see the twirling of the bat before each ball, the easy, perfectly-poised stance at the wicket, those dancing feet move swiftly back or forward, and we shall dream of him 'burning the grass with boundaries', his bat flashing forth every stroke known to cricket. With Grace and Trumper and

Ranji he stands incomparable – our debt is beyond all hope of payment.

In Search of Cricket

Jack Hobbs (Surrey) made 5,410 Test runs in 61 matches (his highest score was 211), including 15 centuries. His first-class innings – between 1905 and 1934 – brought him 61,760 runs (highest score 316 not out) and 199 centuries. He was knighted in 1953 and became one of five Wisden *cricketers of the century in 2000. Born in Cambridge in 1882, he died in Hove in 1963, aged 81.*

Hedley Verity: The Thoughtful Student

VERY rarely in its history has cricket known so persistently thoughtful a student as Hedley Verity, of Yorkshire and England. CB Fry was perhaps the batsman complementary to this bowler, but not even Fry, whose study reduced batsmanship almost to scientific formulae, gave his attention more wholeheartedly to the game than does Verity. Rumour credits Verity with planning destruction for batsmen in the course of his morning shave, and cloaks him with an aura of cricket that surrounds him in eating, sleeping, and all conversation. Rumour, no doubt, exaggerates, but of Verity's deep study of cricket there can be no manner of doubt.

There was a time, or so it seemed, when this absorption threatened to become as manifest a fault as in the ordinary way it is a virtue, for there have been occasions when Verity became 'sickled o'er with the pale cast of thought', and spent so much time in laying plans to deceive his enemies that he neglected to use the weapons the gods had given him, and ignored spin upon turning wickets to engage in the less obvious delights of a battle of wits. To 'think' men out when you are without allies and in unhelpful circumstances is admirable devotion to duty, but to waste opportunities in experiment when the wicket cries aloud for nothing other than length and spin is to ride in the face of fortune. It always seemed to me that Verity took some time to recover from the effects of that unique plan of campaign pursued by Jardine's team in Australia. There it was Verity's task to hold the enemy in a state of as near as possible to stagnation whilst England's principal attacking forces were regathering strength. Verity came back to our county cricket with what I can only describe (and with much reluctance, for the phrase is far from beautiful) as a 'maiden-complex'. He seemed content with negative success and appeared satisfied to permit batsmen to stay at the crease providing they acknowledged themselves under his control. This characteristic proved, happily, but a phase, and there is now no bowler in the world more to be feared when the ball will turn. The benevolent despot has become the insistent conqueror. In this mood Verity is a great bowler indeed. Many times has he been declared the natural successor to Peel and Wilfred Rhodes, but here, I fancy, less than justice is being done to Verity and to those who went before. Verity is not quite in the true line of slow left-arm spin bowlers.

With Rhodes there went a sense of peace and inevitability that I, at least, cannot experience with Verity. Rhodes from the ringside you knew as perfection almost to the extent of monotony. Not for the spectator's sight was that delicate variation of pace and of length; for him there was only the same sweet action, the same smooth curve of flight, and the persistent drop-drop-drop upon the batsman's doorstep. You knew Rhodes would get his wicket; when the ball would turn, it did turn, and the fall was expected every minute; when the wicket was good, patience was necessary, but the result was only delayed, always forthcoming sooner or later. A man cannot take considerably more than 3,000 wickets for Yorkshire alone by waiting for turf that favours him. Unless you were batting against him you could only appreciate the true genius of Rhodes in retrospect. It all seemed so simple at the time. Verity has less delicacy. His antagonism is much more marked. He is faster through the air than was Rhodes and by virtue of his height he gets higher from the pitch. Indeed, it is not upon the truly sticky wicket that Verity is at his most deadly; he has nothing like the finger spin of Colin Blythe, and he is perhaps most potent when the ball 'stands up' rather than turns quickly. So it was at Lord's on that memorable Test match day in 1934. Verity's menace you can see and share from the spectator's seat. You can appreciate the fact that the ball leaves his hand with some imp of evil in it; Verity himself announces it as he stoops forward at the end of his follow through or throws up an expectant arm as the batsman plunges blindly to the approximate pitch.

Verity upon a day of success is the personification of hostility. A batsman fallen a victim to him might return to the pavilion assuring himself: 'Couldn't help it; it's quite impossible to play the man today'. In the bowling of Rhodes there was greater allurement, and the batsman was rarely left satisfied; then he thought, as he walked the long, lone walk, 'I am an ass; I'm quite sure I need not have got out to that ball – I wonder what I did wrong'. For thirty years the world's greatest batsmen kept wondering what they had done wrong, and I do not suppose they ever solved the problem. Verity's attack has one feature that is very rarely found in the equipment of slow bowlers: his faster ball, beautifully hidden until the last half of his arm's swing, comes down at considerably above medium pace. Here, of course, his physical attributes help him, for his height makes it unnecessary for him to toss the ball up, and perhaps more than anyone, save Colin Blythe, Verity gets results from this fast ball. Even to the suspicious it is dangerous, because of the really remarkable change of pace. How much Verity owes to his fieldsmen is quite beyond calculation. It is idle to say that had he played for any county other than Yorkshire his success would have been materially lessened, for who knows but that Verity's bowling would have developed fieldsmen elsewhere? As it is, we can say that if ever Verity goes into business and requires assistance, no partnership would be more appropriate or familiar in sound than that of 'Mitchell* and Verity'. The number of astonishing catches Mitchell has taken for Verity is legion, and the fieldsman's anticipation is now so remarkable that times beyond counting we see him darting from the gully to the bat's edge even as the ball is pitching. This is fielding to perfection, and Verity must be uncommonly grateful to have it at his disposal.

In Search of Cricket

Arthur 'Ticker' Mitchell; an excellent catcher at slip and in the gully. Wisden *described him as a 'wonderful man in a crisis'.*

If Verity had Lived . . .

HEDLEY VERITY died of wounds in an Italian military
hospital after being taken prisoner in Sicily. He would have
been 40 years old had he lived to return to cricket, ageing by
the general standards of a bowler's career but young by the
measure of the exceptional like Wilfred Rhodes and A P
Freeman. Logic indicates that Verity would certainly have
come back to cricket and to further cricketing distinction. A
five-year break would have cost him a list of outstanding
performances but not the essence of his talent. More readily
than most players he could have put cricket aside and picked it
up again because he had mastered his craft to make technique
a second nature. I believe that cricket lost far more than a
Yorkshire and England bowler with the death of Verity; I think
it lost an enormous influence for good.

Verity's bowling in post-war cricket would have been a
guiding star. By example and advocacy he might have been
able to turn post-war cricketers away from the false gods and
easy options of on-side bowling that compelled on-side batting
and then enchained it. He would have wrung startling analyses
from the poor pitches of the early 1950s and would at the same
time have scorned them in patient and irrefutable argument.

In Verity's cricketing philosophy the easy triumph was not
the most satisfying. To dismiss a modest batting side on a
turning pitch was to him no more than the routine of a bank
cashier completing a simple balance. It was a professional
obligation. Failure, or unnecessary delay, would have been

professional weakness. Verity's idea of cricketing heaven was to bowl against Australia – with Bradman, of course – not when conditions left batsmen helpless but when one factor offered the bowler opportunity. A small rough patch on the pitch, an encouraging breeze, a time element, something first of all to be discerned, then exploited, with success or failure always delicately balanced, gave Verity his greatest cricketing inspiration and joy. He wanted a challenge for his bowling mind as well as for his fingers. There were times in county cricket when he appeared to be deliberately making the game harder for himself by insisting on achievement in a predetermined manner; when he seemed to spend three overs preparing an lbw snare against a batsman who, unharassed, would probably have mishit into the covers anyway.

Purposeless cricket had no attraction for Verity, even on minor occasions, and though he was the most self-contained of players his sense of responsibility prohibited any show of selfishness. In a Yorkshire team playing against Leeds University in a pre-championship match arrangements had been made for play to continue until an agreed hour though the result had already been determined. Verity was batting when an insignificant No.11 came to the crease with half an hour left for play and that No. 11 was offered full scope for such innings as he could contrive. Verity defended with care and shared the strike with meticulous calculation in fulfilment of his own moral obligation. He felt his partner deserved an innings and he made it a responsibility to ensure that innings.

Verity's cricketing code was unimpeachable. His ironic lob, bowled and no-balled, at The Oval was not administered in anger but as pointed protest against the course of a match. The famous over at Bramall Lane in which HB Cameron, the South

African, hit three fours and three sixes was not an over of desperate confusion or self-protection. Cameron was permitted to drive, invited to drive, because Verity intended him to be caught. A few boundaries did not change the principle. Verity's principles would not have changed had he been able to appear in post-war cricket. He would have maintained a professional pride that could not have failed to be impressive and influential. He would have deprecated with quiet irony any attitude of easy self-satisfaction. Verity had been taught, in the hard school of Wilfred Rhodes and Emmott Robinson, that seven for 26 is not entirely creditable when it could and should have been seven for 22 and he would have passed on that lesson to where, for ten important years in the history of cricket, it was greatly needed. A post-war Verity would, I feel, have been influential in the councils of cricket. He was a thoughtful observer and a shrewd prophet and as an outstanding player he would have been able to illustrate his points. He could have given early warning against the encroachment of 'instant' bowling with its debilitating effect on batting; he would have exposed the fallacy of the ill-prepared pitch as a means to securing results; he would have deprecated the decline in professional standards that gave status to the half-trained and half-interested.

Whether or not he and a dozen others from the same mould could have channelled cricket differently remains a matter for academic discussion without means for conclusion. Verity was not there and the dozen others were not there for long, or with adequate resources. Few cricketers already on a pinnacle in 1939 were of an age to remain enthroned in the 1950s. Hammond and Bradman bridged the war-gap but mainly to make their farewells. Hutton, Compton, Edrich and

Washbrook stayed to extend personal triumphs but found difficulty in creating a bond of sympathy with untutored contemporaries. Bowes could and did illustrate the basic bowling virtues for a season or two, but physical legacy from a prisoners' camp prevented him from demonstrating application in his particular medium.

Bill Bowes and Hedley Verity were close friends in cricket. Their association had a natural foundation in membership of the same side as they rose to distinction and their successes were complementary rather than competitive. They were partners in bowling, not rivals. Not only could each view the triumphs of the other without envy, but both had the means and desire to open a pathway to triumph through unstinting support. On firm turf, when Bowes was expected to take the wickets, Verity could be trusted to concentrate on overall economy. When the ball was turning and Verity led the attack Bowes gave him full scope by keeping down runs from the other end. This co-operation shown over and over again in Yorkshire matches, was memorably demonstrated in the Lord's Test of 1934. Weekend rain after England had scored 440 and Australia 192 for two wickets delivered the match into bowlers' hands, but to earn full advantage England needed to enforce a follow-on. Major responsibility for taking wickets lay on Verity and he achieved his purpose, but Bowes, his bowling partner for most of the decisive morning, played an immensely significant part. Deliberately confining himself to impeccable accuracy at medium pace, Bowes gave Verity the scope he needed. Australia followed on. Verity took 15 wickets in the match, Bowes took four, but the players knew that figures were inadequate measure of performance.

A Yorkshire Tie for Verity

MONDAY, September 20, I shall always remember. By dawn the Orsova was in the Bay of Naples, and by mid-morning a small party of us were ashore on a mission of tribute. We were seeking the grave of Hedley Verity, who lies buried in the military cemetery at Caserta, where, a prisoner of war, he died of wounds received in Sicily in 1943. Caserta lies some 16 miles inland from Naples, and established a place in history in the 18th Century when the Bourbons built a royal residence there. The palace they constructed in golden coloured stone is an expression of the regal splendour of its time, the product of an age vividly contrasting wasteful luxury and purposeless poverty. Squandor and squalor rubbed shoulders, each contaminating the other. As it was built, the Bourbon palace of Caserta, with its impressive arched entrances and its gardens spreading over two miles of countryside, served the few and oppressed the many. When Italy found liberation in the Second World War the palace became Allied headquarters of the Mediterranean theatre of operations. A little way along the road climbing from Caserta to the hills is the hospital used by the Italians for their Allied prisoners of war. In the cemetery of that hospital Captain Hedley Verity, of The Green Howards, was first buried. There another Yorkshire cricketer, Frank Smailes, found the grave of his colleague in peace and war and established an appropriate memorial. Now Hedley Verity lies nearby in the cemetery built and maintained by the Imperial War Graves Commission, a garden of smooth lawns, clean paths and simple gravestones ranged in simple pattern. Trees shade the boundary walks and tended flowers grace every stone, and in the background stand the watching hills. It is a quiet place, a hallowed and an honourable home, truly a corner of a foreign field that is for ever England. Brief search along the soldierly ranks of marble headstones brought us to Hedley Verity's grave. Among the flowers already growing there Len Hutton placed a spray of white roses fastened together with a Yorkshire tie. He said nothing. Nothing needed to be said. We who knew Hedley remembered sharply. We took photographs, we left sign of our pilgrimage in the visitors' book and, as the burning sun of Italy climbed into the noontide sky, we turned away from the garden of quiet to the dust and glare of the road to Naples.

1954

Hedley Verity (Yorkshire) figured in 40 Tests, from which he harvested 144 wickets, including an 8-43 (average 24.37). He took 1,956 first-class wickets (average 14.90) in a career than ran from 1930 to the outbreak of war in 1939. He was born in 1905 at Headingley and died – aged 38 – in combat at Caserta in Italy in 1943.

Bill Bowes: One Stump Left Standing

BILL BOWES was in every sense an outstanding figure on the field, a gift for caricature, a focal point for both casual observation and the devoted attention commanded by local loyalties. The most unsophisticated spectator could discern the menace in his bowling and rejoice in scattered stumps or enforced catches behind the wicket. The surface impression created by Bowes was both true and false. He was the huge fast bowler who could make the ball lift sharply to the obvious dislike of all but the most accomplished batsmen. He was the traditional last man in who made fewer runs than he took wickets in his first-class career. He was the mid-on granted affectionate toleration.

The deeper picture told a greater truth. Bowes was much more than a bowler of size and strength and a joke in batting and fielding. He was as serious a student of cricket as any of his contemporaries and an impeccably honest appraiser of his own talents and virtues. Nature gave him the advantages to enter cricket; education carried him to the front rank of cricketers. Nothing could have been more misleading than an impression that Bowes ran up to the bowling crease and delivered the ball as fast as he could with hope for a directive. He did rejoice in his ability to make batsmen flinch, he did undertake a labourer's work in bowling, he did resign himself good-naturedly to the popular conception of his batting and fielding, but from his earliest days he was always more, much more, than a cricketer of simple physical prowess. He played his way into the MCC staff, 'grinding the batsman's fingers against the bat handle', as PF Warner reported after a net trial, but he thought his way to Lord's before seeking appointment. He thought the rest of his way to selection as opening bowler for England.

In his early years of first-class cricket his name was associated with the bowling of 'bumpers', or 'bouncers' in later terminology. He could and did pitch short, raising objection or approval according to point of view, but the

Bowes bumper was never an expression of physical exuberance or the outcome of intention to deliver the ball at maximum speed without consideration for consequences in length and direction.

Bowes cultivated the bumper as he cultivated the out-swinger, the inswinger and change of pace. When, if ever, he bowled it by accident he was the first to realise that he was bowling badly. His bumpers were designed, their purpose to discover batting reaction, response in the pitch and tactical possibilities in the current state of the game. By experiment Bowes found that the bumper bowled indiscriminately was not an economic proposition. He calculated that one bumper extracted as much physical effort as three or four normal deliveries. The element of calculation in Bowes's bowling was not always evident from the spectator's viewpoint, but it was by calculation that Bowes advanced himself from a naturally good bowler to a great one. He was encouraged, virtually compelled, to calculate under the tutorship of Wilfred Rhodes and Emmott Robinson, by the whole attitude of the Yorkshire teams in which he played and by his close association with Hedley Verity, another calculator.

By calculation – supported by intensive practice – Bowes taught himself the outswinger and such remarkable command of direction that he ran out of challengers in bowling at one stump. By calculation he adapted his bowling to circumstances that made him masterful against any batting when the ball would swing and lift and respected for his persistence when all the conditions were in the batsmen's favour. The passing years and privations as a prisoner of war took the power out of his bowling and after the war he knew better than anyone that he was reduced to technique and experience. He could bowl well but not greatly and after two seasons he retired, against Yorkshire's persuasion and before a successor had been found, but convinced of the rightness in a calculated decision. He stayed in cricket. He gave years of unstinting coaching service to Yorkshire and he qualified himself as a professional cricket-writer who came to be an acknowledged authority and a leader in the management of the Cricket Writers' Club.

In the sense of retained association and endless helpfulness Bill Bowes never retired from cricket, but he made two notable retirements from bowling. His last first-class match was for Yorkshire at Bournemouth in 1947. The weather was perfect, the pitch was placid and in Hampshire's first innings of 308 Bowes took five wickets for 52 runs in 30 overs.

He could no longer disturb the batsmen by pace but he could command their strictest attention by his own control of length and direction. In the August sunshine he summarised the basic bowling arts.

In the practice nets he explained and demonstrated those arts to the aspiring. Time and again he presented the principle of the 'cartwheel' action that he had proved to be the foundation of accuracy. Towards the end of one coaching session he took the ball from a struggling pupil and, pitching on the ideal length, picked out the off-stump behind a thoroughly beaten young batsman. He bowled again, still explaining his purpose, and only one stump was left standing. By this time the players had all stopped their own activities to watch and listen, the batsman had acquired unwanted attention and Arthur Mitchell, coaching at the batting end, called: 'You might as well finish the job.' Bowes did. He beat the batsman for a third time in succession and removed the one stump. The coaching session was over.

Bill Bowes entered cricket-writing, or at least found the opportunity to enter cricket-writing, because he was Bill Bowes the cricketer. Many others have passed through the same doorway. The majority, glowing briefly in the flattering light of the reception desk, are soon elbowed aside to disappear with the consolation of an inflated fee. A few find a foothold and create a second career. Bill Bowes chose to make a career of cricket-writing. Much of my own cricketing satisfaction over the twenty years of middle age has derived from association with him. We have watched cricket together, often with the same hopes and fears; we have talked cricket together, over innumerable hours; we have co-operated rather than competed on the toast-list at dozens of cricket dinners. Probably because we were brought up in much the same traditions we have evolved a common outlook and common opinions on many aspects of cricket, but contrary to circumstantial evidence we have never written or attempted to write in any form of partnership. Many times, but always without consultation, we have hit upon the same theme for emphasis in a day's play or reached the same conclusion in a cricketing controversy. Not once have we made an agreement of convenience before expressing our individual convictions.

Bill Bowes (Yorkshire) made 15 Test appearances, taking 68 wickets at 22.33. For Yorkshire, he played 372 times and claimed 1,639 wickets (16.76). He was born in Elland in 1908 and died, aged 79, in Otley in 1987.

Sir Francis Stanley Jackson:
Leader of the Orchestra

IN comparatively few appearances on the cricket field, FS Jackson won an undisputed position as one of the greatest players of all time. No one ever came closer to illustration of the complete cricketer, and one glance at him was enough to denote England batsman, England bowler or England fieldsman. He looked a great player, and his performances matched his promise, for to exceptional technical skill he allied a spirit incapable of accepting hopelessness in any situation. He came into first-class cricket by the dignified gateways of Harrow and Cambridge, and he brought with him the grand manner of success as of by divine right. It was not in his nature to consider the possibility of failure, and when the improbable happened there was almost embarrassment, as though a wrong note had been played by the leader of a symphony orchestra. Beauty and utility and self-confidence blended superbly in Jackson's cricket. On bad wickets or on good, in crisis or in comfort, he was as likely as anyone to make a score, and not a score of mere accumulation but in an innings of free driving and skilful forcing shots to leg. In 1900 he came back to first-class cricket after considerable absence in South Africa, and in his very first match at the Scarborough Festival he made a century with all the assurance of a season's practice behind him. His bowling was faster than medium, with the liveliness born of a smooth action, and he gave unfailing attention to good length. Natural gifts rather than any prolonged practice provided him with accuracy, and when the ball would turn, his off-break could be devastating. Opposing batsmen knew no peace of mind, for there was shrewd judgment in all Jackson's cricket and he was busy every minute of the match.

Yorkshire Profiles

Sir Francis Stanley Jackson (Yorkshire, Cambridge University) was born in 1870 in Leeds. He was a cricketer and Conservative politician (at Harrow School Winston Churchill was his fag). He made 15,901 first-class runs and took 774 wickets; and in 20 Tests, he scored 1,415 runs and claimed 24 wickets. He died, aged 76, in 1947.

W H Rhodes: The Wisest Cricketer

THE story of Wilfred Rhodes told as a schoolboy romance would stretch credulity to breaking point. No sooner had he entered first-class cricket, at the age of twenty-one, than he placed himself among the great bowlers of all time, and was a batsman in crisis only, making history for England as last man in at the Oval and at Sydney. In his thirties he was England's opening batsman, and with JB Hobbs he created a Test match record on the Melbourne ground during a tour in which he bowled so little that he did not take a single wicket. In his forties Yorkshire had need of his bowling again, so he resumed his collection of 100 wickets and more season upon season, and in his forty-ninth year his fellow-members of the England selection committee persuaded him back to international cricket for a final triumph. At fifty-two he retired, having claimed conquest over more than 4,000 batsmen and made nearly 40,000 runs. Rhodes bowling was a lovely sight. He illustrated to perfection the slow left-hander, patiently alluring when wickets were good, impossible to counter for long when the ball spun swiftly away to the slips. His three deliberate steps to the wicket, the smooth, economical curve of the arm, the immobile watchfulness as the harassed batsman tried to sum up the problem of flight made one of cricket's imperishable pictures.

Rhodes was a bowler by the light of nature, and he made himself a great bowler by building on natural facility. His batsmanship grew from the accumulated experience and persistent experiment of the wisest cricketer of them all. Eyesight and common-sense and time formed the basis of his run-getting. He got himself into the best position for seeing the ball, he countered the bowler's deceits with his own wisdom, and in due course the runs came to him. His principles were utilitarian. Whenever he could he played back, because back-play reduces risk to a minimum, and Rhodes was concerned with batting as a business proposition. Playing back was the creed of his coaching, and it is because of his efficiency based on back-play that Rhodes counts Bradman first among batsmen. No one has better grounds for expressing an opinion.

Yorkshire Profiles

Wilfred Rhodes (Yorkshire) hit 39,969 first-class runs and took 4,204 wickets. He made 58 Test appearances: 127 wickets and 2,325 runs (highest score 179). Born in Kirkheaton in 1877, he died in Dorset in 1973, aged 95.

Emmott Robinson:
The Yorkshire Character

CHARLES DICKENS should have written on Emmott Robinson, for this notable little Yorkshireman had every attribute of a Dickens character. In the field he was unmistakable; his flannels wrinkled over the top of his boots, his toes turned in, he walked with a roll, and his demeanour told the exact state of Yorkshire's fortunes. If you came late to the ground and Yorkshire were fielding you did not need the scoreboard to tell you the situation; you looked at Emmott Robinson and you knew at once whether some unfortunate had dropped a catch or whether wickets had been falling in seemly regularity. Emmott Robinson lived Yorkshire cricket twenty-four hours of every summer's day, and then thought about it all the winter. He was the most completely Yorkshire character – virtues, failings, appearance and all – ever to play for the county, and had he never taken a wicket or made a run or held a catch, he would have been an important factor in psychological warfare. In fact, of course, he made thousands of runs and took hundreds of wickets and catches. He was a new-ball bowler of considerable potency, and through the 1920s his shambling run-up, prefaced by a little kick-off as though he were starting a motor-cycle, marked daily onslaught upon the enemy's opening batsmen. With his sweater on – a wrinkled sweater – he would station himself alarmingly close to the batsman and create catches. As a batsman himself he fought uncompromisingly through all manner of crises. As

Yorkshire cricket, he was a perfect illustration.

Yorkshire Profiles

Emmott Robinson (Yorkshire) was born in Keighley in 1883 and died in Leicestershire in 1969. He was 86. He scored 9,774 first-class runs and took 902 wickets.

Maurice Leyland: Prepared for Adventure

MAURICE LEYLAND has been much the most successful of all Yorkshire's left-handed batsmen, with his character as strong as his off-drive. Indeed, his triumphs, both for Yorkshire and for England, were founded upon the self-discipline without which technical skill, like patriotism, is not enough. Nobody was ever more satisfied than Leyland with a chosen profession; he has always enjoyed cricket and the cricketer's life at home and abroad, and whenever there was a tour in prospect he would say: 'They can pick me. I'll always go'. Sanguine and unruffled by nature, he schooled himself to the very peaks of what is known as the big-match temperament. Sometimes he failed because the bowling was too good for him, but he never failed through any lack of heart or determination. In his ordinary, everyday innings he was prepared for adventure – and could be found committing sins to horrify the purists, but when occasion insisted, his bat was as straight, his method as faultless as the most exigent text-book could demand. It is nonsense to say that a sense of crisis never affected him; he was as sensible to atmosphere as the next man, but anxiety was a stimulant and not a conqueror. Perhaps equally as remarkable as his personal performance was the inspiration of his colleagues by the calmness of his attitude in time of trouble. His immense popularity had its basis in his homeliness. He appreciated the delight of spectators in fours and sixes because those were also his delights, and he never forgot his responsibility to those who watch, or lost his sense of fun. He was completely unself-conscious, yet always aware of the crowds, to whom he behaved as a friend and consequently won universal friendship. His great talent and his unfailing appreciation of the appropriate made him the man for every occasion. In county match, Test match or Festival he could be relied upon to strike the mood of the moment and to offer either light-hearted entertainment or the sternest of battle, according to the needs of the day. Maurice Leyland's place is very secure among the great players and personalities of cricket.

Yorkshire Profiles

Maurice Leyland scored 33,660 first-class runs and took 466 wickets. He played in 41 Tests and averaged 46.06 (highest score 187). He was born in Harrogate in 1900 and died there in 1967, aged 66.

Lord Hawke: Guide and Philosopher

FOR one whose cricketing quality was useful rather than outstanding, Lord Hawke built up for himself a tremendous place in the history of the game. His was perhaps the most significant voice of his time, and that time extended far beyond playing days into a generation with ideas vastly different from those of his own youth. As Yorkshire's captain for twenty-eight years and President from 1898 until his death in 1938, his work can scarcely be overestimated; he gave a character and purpose to the side, established a Yorkshire 'cap' as the qualification for an honourable and assured profession, and constructed the tradition by which a Yorkshire cricketer became a public figure of standing and renown. His care was at all times for the player, for his county and for the game as a whole. His faults were easily forgiven, for they were the faults of one who loved beyond wisdom, and he had something of the spirit ascribed to W G Grace in the saying: 'May the best side win! Certainly – and ain't we the best side?' No doubt Lord Hawke was uncommonly fond of having his own way, both on the field and in the committee room, but, after all, the way he wanted must have had much merit, for there have been few to deny him the highest of positions as 'guide, philosopher and friend'. In his pronouncements at Yorkshire annual meetings he spoke his mind, but invariably with kindly encouragement for the young cricketer and sincere affection for the old. Sometimes he laid himself open to misinterpretation, as when he said 'I pray God no professional will ever captain England,' and found he had created a world-wide storm by the expression of what was no more than a fervent hope for the preservation of amateur cricket of international standard. Lord Hawke believed in captaincy by amateurs, but not to a point of bigotry, for he was Yorkshire's President when the county leadership was offered to a professional. In his own captaincy he approached the martinet, but his was a benevolent despotism, winning from the players who served him a true affection and an abiding loyalty. He was not regarded by his team as 'one of themselves'; he was more than that – a man in authority who used the position for the good of those under him, and without self-interest. In his service to others he found his satisfaction, and his memorial is the status of cricket and cricketers in the life of a nation.

Yorkshire Profiles

Martin Bladen Hawke (Yorkshire, Cambridge University) was born in Gainsborough in 1860 and died in Edinburgh in 1938, aged 78. He scored 16,749 first-class runs, and made five Test appearances.

Alfred Mynn:
A Giant Fed on Beef and Beer

ALFRED MYNN was a cricketer who lived from 1807 to 1861 and played, in matches of which records exist, from 1829 to the year of his death. He was, by contemporary evidence and subsequent acclaim, an uncommonly accomplished cricketer and an outstanding character of his time, a fascinating subject for a biography written by Patrick Morrah.* Mr Morrah suggests that Alfred Mynn came to cricket through the chance of family removal from one Kent village to another. In Goudhurst, where Mynn was born, there was no organised cricket; Harrietsham, his home from the age of 18, was a centre of the game, then developing under private patronage in relatively isolated communities.

Mynn was translated from the casual cricket of the village green to more sophisticated and profitable spheres through the interest of John Willes, landowner and innovator of the round-arm bowling that changed the face of cricket in the early 19th century. Willes saw in Mynn the ideal raw material for the manufacture of a fast bowler with the shoulder-high action. The young and untutored Mynn possessed, in his biographer's description, 'a natural grace remarkable in so large a youth. His ambition lay in bowling and his asset was sheer pace. 'Like many another young aspirant before and since he took an enormous run and hurled the ball down with all his great, though largely wasted, strength; it was liable to go in almost any direction, but wherever it went it went there fast'.

Alfred Mynn and the Cricketers of his Time, Patrick Morrah.

Physically, Mynn was a giant. He was more than 6ft in height, he weighed 18 stones at the peak of condition, and his strength was exceptional even by the standards of an agricultural community. He had also the gentleness of a giant, 'of a happy and imperturbable temperament and accepted success and failure with a good humour that endeared him to all'. Coaching by Willes reduced the long run to six purposeful strides and innumerable hours of patient practice cultivated accuracy, though Mynn, in common with most round-arm bowlers, usually achieved more wides in a match than the underarm or overarm bowler would expect in a career. By 1832 Mynn had reached cricket rated as first-class. He played for the Gentlemen against the Players at Lord's.

Throughout his career he was nominally an amateur, though his biographer leaves no doubt that his appearances must have been sponsored and that his living was subsidised to permit concentration on cricket. He married, raised a family of daughters and engaged in extensive social activity without any visible means of support. The cricket of Mynn's time contained no international matches, no county championship, no regular fall of fixtures. The leading players undertook a dozen different loyalties in a season, often appearing as the 'given man' in local games for which they held no residential qualification. Mynn played for Western Counties, for West Surrey and for East Sussex.

His distinction, however, was based on performances at Lord's for the Gentlemen, for Kent and in single-wicket matches from which he derived his title of 'Champion of England'. He played for the Gentlemen against the Players over a period of 20 years and was in large measure responsible for the survival of the fixture, which was threatened with extinction because of the overwhelming superiority of the Players.

Mynn's bowling restored balance; he took 11 wickets in the 1841 match, nine in 1842, eight in 1843, 10 in 1844 and 1846 and, in 1848 when he was over 40 years of age he took eight wickets in the 1st Innings to win the game for his side. 'But whatever his triumphs for the Gentlemen and in other representative matches,' writes Mr Morrah, 'it is in Kent cricket that the name of Alfred Mynn shines with the greatest lustre'. The tribute illustrates literary limitations in the biography, but its sincerity and justification are beyond question. Mynn, Felix, Wenman, Hillyer and Fuller Filch formed the strength of a tremendous county team that not only established supremacy through a decade but created the Canterbury Festival and founded the County Cricket Club. His achievements on the field and his personal charm everywhere constructed a shield against public disfavour when he proved unable to fulfil his sporting and financial engagements. In his early years, he played when he was unfit to play, and in his later years he extended his career beyond the limits of physical capacity. These are common failings among the great and popular and far from heinous, but Mynn was also irresponsible in living beyond his means. Mr Morrah rejects an assertion that 'Mynn was often imprisoned for debt and bailed out by his supporters on the eve of a match,' but he does acknowledge and attempts to clarify the troubles of 1845, when Mynn's cricketing appearances were infrequent and irregular. In that year, he spent several periods in the debtors' gaol and he also filed a petition in bankruptcy.

It was Mynn's nature to live his life fully and well according to his inclinations. He was probably almost illiterate, but he was acceptable in any company where 'his friends were constantly amazed at his capacity for eating and drinking. His recipe for a cricketer's diet was beef and beer'. Single-wicket matches were common encounters of the time, partly as a natural outcome of local pride and rivalry, partly because they provided a ready subject for the prevalent gambling. Playing conditions varied but the most favoured practice was to allow each player only two or three fieldsmen; runs could be scored only in front of the wicket and the batsman could not leave the crease to play the ball for runs, 'The laws,' observes Mr Morrah, 'might have been framed for the particular benefit of Alfred Mynn'. Single-wicket cricket as he knew it passed from favour as the art of batting expanded on improving pitches, and easier travel extended the programme for county teams. The giant remains gigantic in the memories so devotedly recalled by his biographer.

September 1963

Alfred Mynn was born in 1807 in Goudhurst, Kent and died, aged 54, in Southwark in 1861. He made 4,955 first-class runs and took 1,036 wickets.

Harold Larwood:
Fast Bowler Without Peer

AMONG all the cricketers of this generation few will be remembered longer than Harold Larwood, who found his greatest fame amid as fierce a storm of controversy as cricket ever knew. Larwood and leg-theory will go inseparably into history, and there is more than a suspicion of danger that Larwood's true virtues will be overshadowed or neglected in discussions to come.

This would be unfortunate and unjust, for thus would a great cricketer lack worthy appreciation. By any standards of judgment or achievement Larwood must take a place amongst the best fast bowlers of all time. In England and Australia he has proved himself a master many times, and the company of Richardson, Lockwood, Kortright, Macdonald and their fellows is not complete in his absence.

No suspicion of Larwood's talents would come to you from a casual glance at him in the field; he has none of the physical attributes traditionally expected of the fast bowler, for he is of no more than medium height; he has no terrifying leap to precede his delivery; he has not even, so far as I know, a particularly hostile expression. When Larwood is not bowling he does not look like a fast bowler as Walter Brearley or Gregory looked like fast bowlers. In action, however, his pace and energy are never in doubt. His run is smooth and patently progressive, his arm high at the moment of delivery and his follow-through a model for the imitative. His strength lies in his back and shoulders; thus comes his speed. His length and direction are governed by the correct placing of his feet and body; thus comes his accuracy.

It is in the matter of accuracy that Larwood is without peer amongst fast bowlers. Actual speed of one man as against another must always remain a matter of argument, but of Larwood's astonishing control of length and direction there can never be two opinions. Herein is Larwood's greatest attribute, for without accompanying control mere pace has little terror for batsman with any pretensions of class on wickets that are mostly made for their liking. It is because Larwood is master of his pace and does not use it blindly in sheer exuberance of spirit that he has know such high and such prolonged successes. He rarely gives a batsman peace, for even at the times of his most ferocious attack, or when the inward fire is waning the loose ball is an unexpected event.

Fast bowlers invariably tend towards the mechanical. Theirs is an elemental physical attack, and it is upon force rather than subtlety that they rely. If they cannot batter their way through the batsmen's defences they are at a loss. They aim at no stroke at all or a mere reflexive flick that cannot be controlled. That, of course, is why they are so fascinating to watch. The responsive thrill is constantly with us whenever they are in action. Your slow left-hander has much of his art to himself, the delicacy of his moves, the deep thoughtfulness of his plots sometimes escape us, and sometimes we must wait with infinite patience before full realisation comes to us. We can appreciate the objects and the merit of fast bowling from the very sight of it. Every one of us, at one time or another, wanted to bowl fast and see stumps flying or hear the screamed 'How's that?' from a triumphant wicketkeeper.

Spin bowling we hail with wondering approbation, shaking mystified heads over its marvels; fast bowling we understand instinctively and admire the more because we can fancy ourselves in emulation. Yet the best fast bowling has more of method than of madness in it. It is not solely a matter of hurling down the ball at the best pace muscle can command to the best length practice can ensure. There is an artistry of speed no less than an artistry of spin. The chief delicacy of the fast bowler is the break-back that comes more often from the body-swing than from any manipulation of the fingers, and Larwood has this weapon in his armoury, as had Richardson and Lockwood of other days.

Every now and then you will see the batsman go bravely across the wicket to the line of flight and suddenly bend to a right angle as the break-back comes across at lightning pace to hit or miss the leg stump. That is great fast bowling. That Larwood is the master of the off-break he has shown us in recent seasons when circumstances have forced upon him an attack below his fastest.

Today he does more than bowl fast; he can go upon a soft wicket and get life and results from it with off-spinners that lack nothing in accuracy and splendour. He is doubly armed in that he is not helpless when purely fast bowling is out of the question. When Larwood's bowling turn is done his cricketing usefulness is not ended. His fielding anywhere close to the wicket is of commendably high standard, and his batting is by no means to be despised. Indeed, I should imagine that the biggest disappointment of his career came when he failed by only two runs to achieve a century in a Test match, though I daresay later reflection gave him the appropriate consolation, for 98 is itself a noble score.

Next weekend Larwood takes his benefit when Nottinghamshire play Yorkshire at Trent Bridge. If ever a man deserved reward for all his achievement, that man is Larwood, and every cricketer must wish him well.

July 15, 1936

Harold Larwood was born in Nuncargate, Nottinghamshire in 1904. In 21 Test matches he took 78 wickets at 28.35 including 33 in the Bodyline series of 1932-33. He died in Sydney in 1995.

Chapter Three:
THROUGH THE DECADES

The Horse-Drawn Roller

CRICKET writers of the 1930s found the seasons running in happy continuity. The framework was the county championship in which meetings of the half-dozen leading teams acquired national significance and the occasional upsets of form created a three-day wonder. Test matches retained a scarcity value. Five-game rubbers were played when Australia and South Africa toured England, but South African Tests were three-day matches. West Indies, New Zealand and India challenged in three-match rubbers and their visits decorated the domestic season without being allowed to dominate it. Howard Marshall gave running commentaries on sound radio, but there was no television to draw spectators away from county games during the playing hours. Yorkshire's home matches attracted a crowd ranging in numbers from the 20,000 expected on occasions of outstanding appeal to the few hundreds who would attend a third-day formality. Through the

1930s, when Yorkshire were champions seven times in nine seasons, the average daily attendance was about 8,000.

With such a following the cricket always had an air of importance. Morning approach to a ground was through streams of people and busy road traffic. Intervals in play were a release of tension and the stretching of limbs for a multitude. Homeward journeys demanded recapitulation and assessment of the day's events. Silences of attention, murmurs of anticipation and the applause of satisfaction were a positive contribution to the play. Yorkshire crowds contained three main elements of composition. Members came for the day, arriving early in search of a 'favourite' vantage point and forming a recognisable community, match after match, year after year. Only considerations of transport drove them away before the last over had been bowled.

Turnstile spectators arrived in bulk for the afternoon and evening sessions, except on public holidays or for a particularly significant occasion when the queues awaited the arrival of the gatemen and youngsters suffered agonies of apprehension lest the promised land of boundary edge should never be reached. The third crowd drawn by Yorkshire cricket could be discerned most readily on those grounds with some standing room near the refreshment bars. This crowd became noticeable in the hour before the players left the field for lunch and again in the day's last session. It was composed of cricket's young men, probably players themselves on Saturdays, who could not give a mid-week day to watching but who gave their lunch hour or hurried to the county match when the office doors closed.

Membership subscriptions stabilised Yorkshire cricket; gate receipts measured its prosperity; support by attendance rewarded its presentation. Yorkshire cricket, for both players and spectators, conveyed a sense of citizenship in no mean city. Between players and crowds there was necessarily a vast gulf in cricketing knowledge, but there was a common outlook from both sides of the chasm. The cricket won admiration because of achievements and popularity because its virtues and purpose could be recognised. Playing principles and practices made cricketing sense on the field and round the boundary edge.

Yorkshire cricket was satisfying because it was essentially logical. There was no mystery in its methods. The techniques of the time were accepted and exploited to a degree beyond the capacity of most opponents, but the spectacular was a consequence of policy, not a conscious appeal for attention. As we watched we knew that we could never command the artistry and effectiveness of Sutcliffe and Leyland and Hutton at the crease, of Bowes and Verity with the ball, of Mitchell and Turner and Sellers in the field, but we knew they were speaking our language. They were doing what we could only try to do, but they were not isolating their game from our game. We could always understand the point of their procedures. They had our sympathy in their endeavours and our admiration in their attainment.

Yorkshire made their cricket fascinating because they made it relevant. Their manifest aim was advantage over a day, victory in a match, supremacy through a championship. In tactical details of play they often advanced beyond the understanding or observation of the casual spectator, but strategy was simple and consistent, which gave the followers of their cricket a sense of sharing. Standards attempted and standards desired were the standards of classical cricket.

Orthodox batting was supposed to provide ready scoring and big totals when the pitch was firm and true; skilful defence when conditions were difficult. Bowling was supposed to be based on accuracy of length and direction, with an appropriate division of labour according to the playing conditions. Fielding was to be regarded as a positive virtue in the game with a significance of its own collectively and containing a direct responsibility for every individual. Yorkshire's cricket tried to be translatable cricket, specifically related to first-class requirements and talents but applicable in principle to all levels. It was a public entertainment but it was an education for anyone interested in learning. The cricket of the period was played and seen in an accepted code of purpose. Ethics were not variable according to standards of performance. First-class cricket was assumed to be a game with all the implications of that title and it was assumed to be the same game, in essence, that was giving recreation and artistic expression to the thousands whose setting was the school field, the village green and the town ground. It was assumed to be played with pleasure to give pleasure. Wet days were recorded as disappointments for the teams as well as for deprived spectators and in nine cases out of ten they really were disappointments, though, of course, a conclusive thunderstorm in August could offer relief to sore feet or break routine like an unanticipated half-holiday at school.

First-class cricket was full of professional players and was dependent on them for its presentation, but it was not regarded as being played for the purpose of providing professionals with a livelihood. The understood purpose of first-class cricket was the projection of cricket at its highest level of skill and endeavour. It was public entertainment only in the sense that it was cricket raised to a degree attracting public attention and arousing public favour. The professional was a paid player not through a conscious assessment of comparable financial rewards but because there was no other way of exploiting his cricketing talents and satisfying cricketing longings. The presumption was that all cricketers played cricket because that was what they passionately wanted to do. They all played in the literal meaning of amateurs, some requiring pay because without it they would have been unable to fulfil their desire to play. The basic professional satisfaction was not in being paid but in being able to play. The professional responsibility was in demonstration and development of the arts of the game. The pride was not in extraction of the maximum financial reward but in applying skills to the highest degree conceivable. In this conception the cricketer who declined an engagement because he considered the payment inadequate was less 'professional' than, say, George Hirst when he accepted his coaching appointment at Eton without even mentioning remuneration.

In this conception, too, there was no basis for resentment in conventional distinctions between amateur and professional players. Amateurs sometimes enjoyed superior dressing-room or hotel accommodation but they were also required to undertake representative obligations for the general benefit. The professional accepted the amateur in management capacity but only proof in practice on the field gave the amateur a standing in the cricket interpreted by professionals. All games begin as amateur pastimes. A professional element is introduced for the benefit of the ambitious enthusiast. The professional develops beyond the range of the amateur and eventually drives him out. Under financial pressure the nature of the game turns from entertaining recreation to commercial promotion. Self-supporting and self-governing play becomes business and draws in extrinsic influences. Every art-form shows the same sequence and sooner or later reaches the same conclusion which, in sport, is the separation of the professional performer from the unprofessional player. Cricket has enjoyed two outstanding periods of public favour and playing prosperity. The first was the Golden Age in which the professional was called in and cultivated to support the amateur organisation. The second was the Silver Age between the world wars when the professional carried the burden of presentation for a game that remained self-contained in playing and public attraction. To play successfully in the Golden Age professionals had to be technically superior in the amateur context. To compete in the Silver Age amateurs had to match the professionals in skill and dedication.

When amateur competition fails, as eventually it must, a game divides. Professionals adopt one version for themselves and in self-preservation seek viability where they can find it. They may devise prosperity in commercial terms and set new standards of accomplishment for themselves alone. They may isolate themselves from public concern and so defeat their purpose. The great tournament golfers have done one thing; the great billiards players did the other. Professionals have moved away from the game of Association football to promote a business with techniques and customs and an ethical code designed to meet specific requirements. Cricket in the decade preceding the Second World War was both a game and a public entertainment of rising standards and increasing popularity. From a contemporary viewpoint there were, of course, frequent glances into the glories of the past. That is the nature of mankind in advancing years. With Trumper and Ranjitsinhji to be seen lament could be heard for Beldham and Brett. Had Francis Thompson chosen to 'repair to the matches of the Southron folk' he could have watched Hobbs and Hayward in the flesh instead of the shades of 'Hornby and my Barlow long ago'. The principal complaints in the cricket of the 1930s were founded on general placidity in the pitches which was held responsible for an excessive number of drawn matches. The aim of the groundsman was solidity in the turf and a grassless surface that would resist the wear and tear of playing traffic and groundsmen took a competitive pride in their work. Leonard Hutton gained world-wide renown – and a small fortune – from the Oval Test of 1938, but his satisfaction could not have been greater than that of 'Bosser' Martin who observed when England's score reached 730 for five wickets, 'That's beaten the Lord's record'. He was remembering a Test match total of 729 for six by the 1930 Australians.

In pitch preparation the heavy roller, often moved by man or horse-power, gave the firm foundation and individual fancy concocted a binding agent with animal blood and dung among the ingredients. Some pitches did not require inspection by sight; they could be identified and evaluated by smell. Used to excess the top dressings gave a rubbery texture to the pitch surface and tended to exasperate both fast and slow bowlers. Fast bowlers complained that they had to drop the ball unduly short to make it bounce more than stump high and spin bowlers were deprived of rightful reward after rain because the spinning ball was liable to skid through instead of biting into the turf and so both jumping and turning. The highly prepared pitch also tended to become impermeable, holding water on the surface or allowing it to run off to the surrounds and thereby causing delays that irritated waiting crowds.

For special occasions such as Test matches the pitches undoubtedly were doped to excess, but in county cricket the conditions were generally logical in relation to weather and location. High scoring and hard work by fast bowlers were expected in dry weeks; slow bowlers took their profits after rain unless defensive batting could be raised to the highest standard. Teams therefore had to be constructed to meet a variety of circumstances and spectators were attracted by anticipation. They could calculate the sort of cricket they were likely to see. Grounds and districts also had marked individual characteristics. The Oval provided comfortable batting and was hard on the feet for bowlers and fieldsmen. Essex had left Leyton and played their home matches mostly in public parks where clay promised a pitch of exceptional pace when it was dry and a harvest of spin-bowling wickets when it was wet. At Hove the time to be batting was between lunch and tea because the first and last hours of the day brought a dampness into the air for the delight of swing bowlers. Maurice Tate liked to be beside the seaside. Worcester wickets rolled out to batting perfection after winter flooding by the Severn, and Ted Leyland, father of Maurice, could guarantee scope for a match of 1,000 runs whenever he so determined at Edgbaston. On one historic occasion such a match was his intention. In the early weeks of the season he had suffered much frustration in wet weather, with day after day occupied in mopping-up operations. At last an anticyclone developed and skies became cloudless for a week. The patient horse pulled the heavy roller until a pitch of perfection had been prepared and on the first morning of the match Ted Leyland was content.

As he waited for the captains to toss he sat in the sunshine on a pavilion seat, smoking his pipe and at peace with the world. The final rolling before play was a formality; the roller was on the square, the horse ready in the shafts. Edgbaston made a beautiful picture for Ted Leyland's eyes. In this moment of supreme satisfaction the horse cascaded liquid relief in large quantity all over the gleaming turf.

Thanks to Cricket

What isn't Cricket

BETWEEN the wars, from 1919 to 1939 that is, first-class cricket changed in detail rather than in principles. The experiment of two-day County matches was no sooner tried than it was abandoned and the pattern of the seasons thereafter remained virtually undisturbed. The substance of summer's play was in the championship, with variety provided by such traditions as Gentlemen v Players, a Test Trial and the end-of-season Festivals. Cream cakes were represented by Test matches for national consumption and engagements with the touring side for local feasting. Only Australia, coming to England at four-year intervals, and South Africa, visiting less frequently, were accorded the status of five-match Test series. Throughout the whole period the course of cricket seemed to require no fundamental revision. The public appeal of the game remained constant, its prestige stayed high and continuity of high-quality recruits was preserved. To follow Sutcliffe, Hendren, Tate, with Hobbs and Woolley in autumn glory, came Hammond, Larwood, Verity and at the interruption, which proved to be a watershed, the young

Hutton and the young Compton were taking up the torch of splendour in tradition. First-class cricket was certainly not falling in quality when Hitler's hordes began to ravage Europe.

There was, of course, contemporary criticism and there were changes in outlook and technique. Essentially, however, the game expanded from a fixed centre. The conduct, the intentions, the ideals of cricket were not in question as bowling strategy and legislation sought counters to the challenge of pitch-preparation, as pastime veered towards professional entertainment accepting a public responsibility. Inter-war cricket was not all sweetness and light. It included bodyline, it included sharp disagreement between Middlesex and Yorkshire, between Nottinghamshire and Lancashire, between Sussex and Nottinghamshire and it included controversy deriving from the spoken word of Lord Hawke and the written word of Cecil Parkin and ER Wilson. In the peace interregnum cricket was not entirely peaceful. Yet conflict, even at the most acute stage, was not revolutionary. The disputes were not over standards but over interpretations of ideals and principles held commonly by the disputants. England and Australia both thought the well-being of cricket a fundamental consideration and in that belief they first argued and then settled the bodyline problems. Nobody wanted to change the underlying purpose of cricket, the meaning of the game enshrined in a conception implied by the negative 'It isn't cricket'. In the county quarrels the point was not so much a difference between right and wrong as whether or not certain behaviours were within the bounds of agreed right.

In cricket – and, for that matter, in all sport – there was a 'right thing'. It was not always done by individuals or representative bodies, but it was known and it was the yardstick for reference. The immutable measure has been challenged in present-day philosophies of cricket, which, of course, respond to current social, political and economic philosophies. The very definition of 'right' has been brought into question. 'It isn't cricket' has tended to become 'That is cricket' within a revised morality. In a transformation of outlook on acceptability there can be no precise moment of change. The undesirable of yesterday does not become the permissible of today between dusk and daybreak or at a stroke of the pen. Influences are cumulative and their pressures are frequently unappreciated until they have become effective. That acceptabilities have changed is beyond argument and can be illustrated from almost any form of sport. In tennis it is now so commonplace to make public questioning of decisions by umpires and line-judges that such incidents pass without remark. In Association football the deliberate foul to save an impending goal receives positive commendation. In rugby football an international coach has advocated superior cheating to overcome cheating. Athletes make no secret of drug-taking. These practices and equivalents in cricket have passed through phases of being overlooked, excused, anticipated and approved.

The behaviours of cricket in the mid-twentieth century have been more revolutionary than the revisions of cricket presentation and techniques. What once would have been regarded as taking or seeking a mean advantage has been reinterpreted as justifiable service in a cause. Deliberate waste of time is technical expertise. Exhibitions of lost temper illustrate dedication. Dressing-room privacies are legitimate material for profitable revelation. Self-concerns come before loyalties – for the player to the team, for the team to the club, for the club or organisation to the game. Attitudes on the field are reflected in attitude round the field and in commentary. Where means are claimed to justify ends and the essential end is winning, not for victory's own sake but for rewards of cash and aggrandisement, means come to be seen in pragmatic context.

Acceptance of deliberate obstruction and harassment on the field inevitably gives rise to jeering outbursts from spectators, designed to upset playing concentration. The competence of referees and umpires publicly questioned by players becomes rejection of authority from the terraces. Platforms for the controversial are increasingly available. 'Why not?' tends to be recognised as a standard of judgement. Why should footballers not crowd round a referee in protest against a decision with which they disagree? At best they might secure a reversal of the decision; at worst they will gain the sympathy of committed followers and managerial support. Why should cricketers not throw down a bat or a ball to express amazement and discontent? Why should tennis-players not appeal to high heaven against fancied injustice?

To be sure, an older conception of sport would be harmed by such attitude in innumerable extension from the trivial to the basic, but the revolution is constructing a new conception. Yesterday's what 'isn't done' can be and manifestly is being abandoned. Whether or not the abandonment will prove to be for good or ill depends on viewpoint.

One outlook sees sport as a satisfaction of particular artistic talents, with social significance in the promotion of health, community interest and recreational benefit; as a controlled channelling of energy, ambition and the competitive urge. This sport is an education in physical development, in self-control of temperament, in appreciation of responsibility. This sport is a classroom accommodating pupils and teachers. At first-class level this sport is tutorial by precept and example and it is promotional in its research into techniques. First-class cricketers attract a following by their entertainment, inspire by their demonstration and initiate development by their experiments. They are the graduates of the game.

It is their privilege and responsibility to set standards in 'pure' science, in 'art for art's sake', in satisfactions that are self-sufficing. Their aim is to practise cricket to the limits of its known range and then to seek expansion of the range - to the advantage of cricket. Derivative benefits of pleasant living, fame, prestige and social consequence are supplementary to the essential cause. Thus academically conceived the first-class element in cricket assumes a morality of service. The question posed in every contemplated action becomes 'Is this for the benefit of cricket?' as distinct from 'Is this for the benefit of me?'

The code of conduct derives from an implied notion of service to intrinsic satisfactions of the game, which is a voluntary contest of skills within agreed rules. Opponents are equally entitled to satisfactions if they can earn them, therefore breaking the rules and advantage gained by cheating come under disapproval. Breach of rule incurs a stipulated penalty; cheating incurs opprobrium. The morality of cricket has said that protection of the wicket with the pads is, in certain circumstances, illegal and subject to a punishment of law. The batsman is out lbw. These were terms on which batsman and bowler undertook the contest. The morality of cricket has also said that to derive advantage by misrepresentation of the law is cheating. Punishment for claiming catches the claimant knows to have been picked up on the half volley is a reputation for poor sportsmanship. The terms of participation assume equal opportunity to both sides, or contestants, for achieving the game's satisfactions.

In summary, everybody is expected to 'play fair', to the benefit of the game and all its players. Human nature being what it is everybody did not play fair all the time, but lapses were forgiven rather than defended. Principles can change with purposes. Ploughshares can be turned into swords. Once the function of sport as an end in itself comes to be questioned the values and acceptable conduct of sport tend to be reassessed. The 'done thing' may cease to be done; sportsmanship may need a revised definition. Advance the argument that sport at first-class level is more than sport; is a commercial venture; is a political concern; is a personal promotion and you instigate different concepts of the permissible. Art, you could proclaim, is properly a handmaiden to advertisement; success is the heart-beat of survival; the rewards of talent are measured by the bank account. From this viewpoint sport is not its own justification. It acquires ulterior motives. First-class cricket and League football are business propositions. The Olympic Games are exploitation of national assets. Players are essentially making a living for themselves. Sport is a means to ends beyond itself.

Given such premise, to prevent an Association goal by a rugby tackle is not cheating; it is a business necessity. Drug taking to run faster or jump higher than anyone else becomes dutiful in a country's cause. Controversial behaviour induces profitable notoriety. Sooner or later irreconcilable philosophies must part company and isolate themselves in separate territories. In some games the division has apparently taken place. Principles and practices recognised at first-class level are not principles and practices applicable to lower levels; the superior few have moved into a rarefied atmosphere. The first-class players, managements, exploiters do not live in the general world any longer; they could, no doubt, step down occasionally to join us but we cannot visit them.

Cricket, I feel, has still to experience the vital severance. A hazy borderland remains. The higher reaches are clearly moving towards a commercial and political environment, with county cricket shaped as an advertising package and international cricket commanded by a government department. Individuals, guided by professional agents, are leaning towards an attitude that asserts the game should be devised and directed primarily to meet their requirements. To this end there is a players' organisation and there are demands for the widest freedom of action in contracts that are unenforceable by one party. On the one hand is the security expressed in a long engagement; on the other is the impracticality of an unwilling player.

It is easy enough to envisage first-class cricket of the future being entirely commercial, presented and paid for as an advertising medium. In that event, publicity-value would be the criterion of success. The cause to be served would not be the cause of cricket as a game but the cause of promotion, just as the cause of televised cricket is, basically, not cricket but a television show. For cricket the game and cricket the commercial concern different sets of values are raised. In one context an explosion of temper on the field is bad for cricket and therefore to be deprecated, but in another context it may be good publicity and therefore accepted. A match won by

FS Jackson: Kilburn wrote of him: 'No one ever came closer to illustration of the complete cricketer'.

Lord Hawke: The most significant voice of his cricketing age – and the influential echo of it continued long after he turned from player to administrator.

Wilfred Rhodes: The 'wisest cricketer of all,' was Kilburn's verdict on Rhodes, who became a bowler 'by the light of nature' and a batsman 'from accumulated experience and persistent experiment'. Above, he bowls one of his typical deliveries – nearly always with his cap on. Below, he passes on the flame to Hedley Verity.

George Hirst: He was the Golden Figure of the Golden Age, according to Kilburn – a bowler whose philosophy was 'length and line' and a batsman who based his approach on the 'soundest principles'. Left, he addresses the crowd from the balcony of the pavilion at Scarborough, where he retired from first-class cricket. Below, Hirst the coach passes on a life-time of gathered experience.

Jack Hobbs: The Master, a gentle and unselfish man, who made 'every innings a text-book of batting with illustrations entirely his own'.

Harold Larwood: There was no faster bowler and his classic, fluent action, like a bolt of silk, proved awe-inspiring to anyone who saw it.

Jack Hobbs and Herbert Sutcliffe: One of the outstanding opening partnerships in Test history. If one didn't score runs, the other did. Usually the two of them managed to punish the bowling simultaneously.

Hedley Verity: A bowler of such spin and guile that baffled batsmen used to say to themselves after getting out: 'Couldn't help it; it's quite impossible to play the man today'.

Herbert Sutcliffe: A portrait of a batsman who demonstrated both perfect temperament and technique. 'To watch one of Sutcliffe's innings,' wrote Kilburn 'is to have complete understanding of his power'.

A daunting sight for bowlers: Sutcliffe, left, and Holmes, go out to bat at Scarborough. Swift footwork made the hook and the late cut Holmes' characteristic strokes and 'all his batting carried an air of briskness and eager anticipation'.

The figures tell the story. The indomitable pair of Holmes, left, and Sutcliffe celebrate a record opening stand of 555 against Essex at Leyton in 1932 with a simple, brisk handshake.

Blowing away the winter cobwebs. This trio of Arthur Mitchell, left, Wilf Barber, centre, and Herbert Sutcliffe use sweaters for scarves on a damp, cold spring morning before the beginning of the 1937 season.

The lost team. The Yorkshire side of 1939 – Champions again – was broken up by war.
Back row: B Heyhirst (masseur), C Turner, EP Robinson, H Verity, WE Bowes, L Hutton, TF Smailes, W Ringrose (scorer).
Front Row: A Mitchell, H Sutcliffe, AB Sellers, NWD Yardley, M Leyland, W Barber.

Bill Bowes: A 'huge fast bowler', observed Kilburn, who is capable of making 'the ball lift sharply to the obvious dislike of all but the most accomplished batsmen'.

Opposite, Bill Bowes: After his late call to the England tour of 1932-33 – the Bodyline series – the Yorkshire bowler is measured for his blazer and flannels.

Farewell to the Don. Bradman – complete with deserved guard of honour – walks on to Headingley for the final time on the Invincibles tour of 1948. He harvested 173 not out on one of the grounds that his genius claimed as his own.

Studies in greatness. 'If he is to play a big innings,' Kilburn wrote of Bradman 'the signs are there from the first; without any delay or preamble he is hitting the ball in the middle of the bat and scoring runs with contemptuous ease'.

Len Hutton is trapped in this inelegant pose after an attempted drive goes horribly wrong: the bat flies higher than the ball during a Roses match at Old Trafford.

Left, Hutton and Jim Kilburn set off from Leeds railway station – the first leg of their journey on the 1946-47 Ashes tour of Australia.

blatant sharp practice would be of little satisfaction by some canons of cricket but could, through the result, be of deep commercial significance. In simple illustration, deliberate time-wasting in a friendly game of club cricket would please no one and would be frowned on because the purpose of play is lost to players and spectators alike. The same tactics employed to win a Championship or a Test rubber could be defended as justifiable means to a profitable end.

This is not academic theory. It has happened and it is happening. It has been seen in Test and County cricket. It is seen week by week in Association football of first-class standard. It is seen in tournament golf when a slow competitor takes five or six hours to complete a round, to the frustration of the playing partner and the fury of those waiting behind. Where the commercial becomes completely separated from the recreational differences in approach and conduct are created. The unacceptable in one can become tolerable, even approved, in the other. Difficulties arise in the period of separation, when the differing moralities are not crystallised and impinge on both areas. The recreational golfer, taking a lead from the tournament golfer, assumes slow play to be meritorious and exasperates a whole membership. Committees have to issue a directive and those reproved are probably both indignant and puzzled. First-class cricketers find themselves confusingly applauded for victory in matches that also provoke reprimand for misconduct. The schoolboy footballer notes foul play by his hero acknowledged as virtuous and, naturally, reproduces it without shame in his own context.

The individual player finds himself struggling with divided loyalties. His heart may tell him to 'play the game', scorning any unfair advantage, but his head reminds him that not only his own immediate welfare but also that of a team may be best served by the end-product of, say, winning or protesting or even declining to play. Similar reaction is transferable to spectators and followers. Satisfactions derive less from the play than from the ultimate success of a player or a team supported. Distraction and disruption directed against the opposition or the controlling authority comes to be regarded as both customary and laudable. Cricket, I think and hope, is not yet irrevocably committed to the final division between recreational sport and commercial entertainment. The trend is obvious enough because the first-class level has grown increasingly dependent on commercial sponsorship and government subsidy and the presentation of play has been adjusted to meet requirements. Leading players have indicated changing views on self-exploitation; crowd response and behaviour have been re-chanelled. There are, however, signs of recognition that the ultimate separation would be self-destructive. Cricket as commercial entertainment is a selling proposition to sponsors, to television and to the public only when it displays first-class cricketers. It is their skills and their reputations that form the attraction and it is becoming realised that unless the skills and reputations can be acquired the supply of goods for sale will be reduced.

The chain of development linking all cricket is logical. Club cricket can produce only club cricketers; the best of them want the 'something more' that is first-class cricket; the best of first-class cricketers become the Test players, renowned and respected as ideals for all cricketers. If ever the attraction of the stage beyond club cricket should lose its appeal to all cricketers the binding chain would break. I believe the chain would break if cricket at various levels became imbued with different aims and purposes and codes of conduct. The separate sections might exist and flourish each in its own environment, but the commercial entertainment section would be highly vulnerable to fashions in finance, political influence and the aspect of public fancy that favours material success above all else.

My hope for the future of cricket lies in those cricketers who will always seek widening satisfactions from the game itself. They will ensure the common purpose at all levels of play; they will seek dissemination of common principles from inspiration and example at the top; they will insist on cricket independence.

Overthrows

In the 1950s

THE division of cricket between the wars and cricket in its present guise is to be found in the 1950s rather than in the war years themselves. The resumed cricket of 1946 was cricket of 1939 in conception, eagerly and happily taken up again with an awareness of shortcomings expected to be temporary, but with no anticipation of fundamental change. For a few years the game blossomed in nostalgia. Crowds were never bigger, public interest was never higher. Touring teams took home unparalleled profits and Old Trafford had to close gates when Yorkshire were the visiting team. Bradman became Sir Donald and international development spread with no more disturbance than occasional pin-pricks on surface harmony.

Cricket was seen in the light of its 1939 character; a game presented as a public entertainment.

In the first seasons of resumption satisfactions of relief glossed over inescapable inconveniences and improvisations. England was still on utility standards. Food was rationed; petrol was rationed; materials were in short supply. Most of the country, certainly its cricket grounds, looked shabby and most of the people, including newcomers to county cricket, had of necessity to look makeshift in attire. Travel between engagements was slow and uncomfortable because train services were inadequate and the use of private cars was restricted. Coach journeys frequently extended far into the night, elongated by diversion to widely scattered homes within a county. Sleeping and eating raised problems, with hotels crowded to compel room-sharing and dinner tables were rarely able to offer more than a statutory five shilling meal.

Spectatorial amenities had deteriorated under wartime neglect and damage and though county authorities were willing to spend they found frustration in building regulations and priorities. Houses were needed before dressing rooms, schools and hospitals required the timber and steel and paint that cricket clubs sought for pavilions, enclosures and seating – to say nothing of refreshment rooms and toilets. Yet cricket flourished. It was relished thankfully by those who had known it before the interruption, approached eagerly by a new generation of the ambitious and accepted as a social adornment through the exceptionally warm and sunny summers of 1947 and 1949 and the exciting season of 1948 that brought Bradman on his farewell tour.

The time stays typified for me in recollection of an August afternoon in 1947 at the Dean Park ground in Bournemouth.

The match was of little significance in the Championship, for neither Hampshire nor Yorkshire could reach the head of the table, but the golden weather, the holiday period and the presence of great players had drawn a crowd too big for the seating capacity but uncomplainingly spread across the grass, among the marquees and in the shade of trees and high boundary hedges. There was a little folding of the hands among the senior spectators, occasional restlessness among the sun-bronzed juveniles who had long since disposed of sustenance brought for lunch and tea, but a general air of attentiveness and appreciation for the polished performances on show. The cricket and the occasion were being enjoyed. I had come across an Australian journalist, Tom Goodman, who was making his first visit to England on a year's commission to cover Australian interests in Rugby League and cricket tours. At Bournemouth he was an uncommitted spectator, observing and absorbing the practices and atmosphere of county cricket. We stood in the crowd, considering the general scene rather than details of play; our panoramic view ranged from the little pavilion on our left to tented enclosures on the far side of the ground. The weather was warm enough to meet Australian requirements, but the essence of the occasion was wholly English. The huge arenas of Sydney and Melbourne, with their towering stands and railed-off, regimented sections of spectators, were literally more than half the world away. The cricket, for all the schoolboy cries, the ripples of applause, the ceaseless murmur of comment, had a restfulness of routine understood and appreciated. In one hour of one afternoon Tom Goodman enjoyed an experience that all the scorecards and the record-books could not have given.

This enjoyment was not lessened for me by familiarity. In a

long association with county cricket I have been granted innumerable days of quiet satisfaction in the routine of the game, days without dramatic incident, days on which the quality of play and the patina of place created a pleasurable background to events without any historic significance. Such days I counted the essence of first-class cricket, a conglomerate impression to be treasured in memory and desired in anticipation. Happily for me, in my particular professional assignments, I could indulge romantic reverie as readily at Bradford as at Brighton, at Middlesbrough and at Maidstone. I certainly passed happily and hopefully into the cricket of the 1950s. As far as I knew at the time the cricket I cared for was re-creating itself in an accepted pattern. Observation could not avoid a deterioration in standards of technical expertise and professional responsibility among recruits, but there was sympathetic regard for players who had been deprived of basic cricket education at school and club level and allowance had to be made for time lost to compulsory military service.

The critical misgivings of the 1950s were not directed towards standards shown by the leading players, but towards a widening gap between the few and the many and the apparent complacency of the many in their lower estate. Among the few there was evidence of exceptional talent and its development was exciting. Sometimes it was over-exciting and the history of the period is littered with geese briefly mistaken for swans, but a decade that brought to the mature splendours of Hutton and Compton and Washbrook an infusion of Bedser, Evans, May, Cowdrey, Trueman and the meteoric Tyson could not have been a degradation in cricket. The 1950s gave me enthralling experiences. They were the years of Bedser's magnificence in bowling and I, brought up on Barnes and Tate, had standards for the recognition of greatness and for rejoicing in it. I have never been more absorbed in an art, more enchained in the atmosphere of an occasion, than at Trent Bridge in 1953 when Bedser took seven wickets in each Australian innings. Each time the need was pressing and the achievement was dramatic. In the first innings the Australians fell from 237 for four to 249 all out under the second new ball. In the second Australian innings Bedser was bowling to an England overdraft of 105 runs. In his first effort Bedser kept England in the match; by his second effort he gave his side a chance of victory.

On the two afternoons of his tremendous attack the setting might have been designed for Wagnerian opera. The sky was overcast, the air was heavy with moisture and the bowling successes raised a tremble of wonder and anticipation in the crowd. The most casual and unsophisticated of spectators could not have avoided involvement. The cricket was to be felt as well as seen. When intervals came the relief from tension was needed by watchers as well as by players. The silence of absorbed attention carried Bedser through his run-up of balanced stride and rocking shoulders. Sigh or sharp cry of acclamation pursued the consequence of almost every stroke. Over by over swelled recognition of the impossible being realised. Fielding was inspired to hold swirling catches even when they had been misjudged. Bedser was captain of his soul, master of his fate and, apparently, director of the cricketing fates themselves.

All through his career, in days of triumph or frustration, Bedser was manifestly a bowler of quality. He never neglected the basics which proclaim that a straight, good-length bowler is a good bowler. Bedser invariably maintained length and direction. To make himself outstanding he mastered swing and 'cut', presented, or inflicted, at lively medium pace. His leg-cutter which reversed the in-swinging line of flight was virtually beyond counter by orthodox practices of batsmanship. It was delivered to perfection in the Trent Bridge Test of 1953 and Hassett, bowled when his score was 115, claimed high skill in 'getting a touch' before his off stump was uprooted. Bradman, clean bowled for 0 at Adelaide, acknowledged that he had never been more comprehensively defeated in his batting experience. Bedser made three tours of Australia as a player and in the second one he took 39 wickets in the five Tests. In the home series of 1953 he took the same number and, even against the challenge of Lindwall, he could fairly be rated first among the great bowlers of his time. Dethronement, in Test-match terms, came during the third tour. Few bowlers have been able to sustain success over a third tour, but on the outward voyage of 1954 there was general anticipation that Bedser would be the mainstay of England's bowling, as he had been for almost a decade. Suffering from shingles he missed the early matches and when he played, perhaps not fully fit, in the first Test at Brisbane he shared the bowling discomfiture reflected in an Australian total of 601.

He was dropped for the second Test – logically enough by current form and performances, but controversially in the particular circumstances and manner of omission. The first morning of the Sydney Test provided an atmosphere of high humidity and a pitch with dampness in it, the precise conditions to suit Bedser's type of bowling, though in fact he would have been denied opportunity because Australia won the toss and made England bat. Hutton and the selectors had already decided on a policy-revision in which there was no scope for Bedser, as there had been none for Tate in Jardine's design of 1932-3. The conditions of the Sydney morning raised a complication that left Hutton open to criticism, but he was giving precedence to a policy over an improvisation and events justified his judgement. In the details of his omission Bedser may have been rather tactlessly treated. A story circulated that only publication of the team-sheet told him he would not be playing and if this be so, I think Bedser deserved kindlier treatment. His service was too long and honourable for its end to be indicated without consolatory explanation. All cricketers are overtaken when their stride begins to flag in the march of time, but the fall-out of the great ones should surely be eased whenever possible.

The 1950s gave more than a model of fast-medium bowling in Bedser. They gave splendid illustration of almost every type of style of bowling and batting. In English cricket no left-handed batsman of the highest rank emerged – though one ought to have done under the name of Brian Close – and there was little leg-break bowling of quality, but all the other arts of cricket were on show. Principles of classical batsmanship were handed on from Hutton and Compton to May and Cowdrey. Comparisons of merit would be fruitless and irrelevant, but few observers of the period would deny a blood brotherhood of the four in batting quality. They all wore the purple and would have done in any age of cricket. Cowdrey in self-confidence evoked pictures of Hammond with majesty on the off-side and time in hand when the ball was turning. At his best he was the most easeful batsman of his time and even in his introspective innings he never looked less than an England player. May, I shall always believe, came close to being a director of cricket as Grace and Hobbs were directors. Grace put fast bowling in its place. He broke its threatened dominance, left it an essential part of the game but not the controlling influence. Grace's batting widened the scope of batsmanship and consequently of cricket.

Hobbs also took batting a step further than he found it. But for his swift and masterful response, googly bowling might have spread an overwhelming infection. There was fast bowling after Grace, there was googly bowling after Hobbs, but they were aspects of bowling, not the whole of it, because Grace and Hobbs demonstrated the batting counter and those who noted were able to follow.

Had May stayed a little longer on the field I think his example could have established a school of batting attitude to turn the tide of in-slant bowling that flooded first-class cricket and left it a more restricted game and a less attractive public entertainment. May was a batsman of wide range, but more than anyone of his period he ventured into the on-drive against in-swing or off-break bowling. Accurate footwork and confident approach enabled him to force the ball between mid-on and mid-wicket where so many of his contemporaries were reduced to a cramped defensive stroke or a tentative leg-glance. May hit the leg-side half-volleys from an upright stance and with a full swing of the bat that gave both power and beauty. I hoped he would be followed by eager young batsmen inspired by his method and achievement, with the ultimate result of bowling patterns changing simply on grounds of unprofitability. I think he might have been, but for the sad shortening of his own career and but for the spread of one-day cricket that has stultified first-class thinking and development.

Whatever my fancy and reasoning, Peter May would certainly not have considered his own batting as evangelistic. His talent and his career thrust greatness upon him but he accepted it more from a sense of responsibility than a desire to command and rebuild his cricketing world. His most magnificent shots were followed by a downward gaze, as of embarrassment; when he had been beaten or forced into hasty defence he made acknowledgement with a shy smile for the bowler. He crowded enormous effort into a short first-class career, carrying the burden of England captaincy, at home and abroad, through forty-one Tests in six years. He was the foundation and much of the superstructure in Surrey's batting during an unparalleled run of championship success. He was under pressing demand for festival and benefit matches. His failures made headlines and his successes invaded the personal privacy he desired so earnestly. Exhausted, he left cricket too soon for cricket's good, but he could not be accused of desertion. He had given of himself without stint and left an unfading glory. Nobody playing or watching in the period of Peter May could complain that the time was without greatness. May himself would no doubt agree, but he would point the finger elsewhere, insisting that the 1950s were primarily bowling and fielding years. The records of his country and county support the thesis. In England selection committee meetings the hours were spent in finding batsmen but choosing between bowlers. Statham, Trueman and Tyson were contemporaries and Loader went twice to Australia. Lock and Wardle were alternatives in left-arm spin and Laker was not the only off-spinner to be considered – though on technical merit his claims were surely indisputable. Appleyard had attributes of greatness, but was granted too little time to exploit them.

Bob Appleyard's potential was no sooner seen than it was confirmed. In his first full season for Yorkshire he took 200 wickets. In the next summer, 1952, he fell ill and was compelled to undergo extensive sanatorium treatment before returning to cricket to take 141 wickets for Yorkshire in 1954 and earn himself a place in Hutton's team touring Australia. With limited opportunity he took eleven Test wickets on the tour, but ill-health and injuries forced him out of cricket all too soon. Appleyard's bowling was basically off-spin at medium pace, but he cultivated pace variations that made him uncommonly difficult to play, or to define. Time and again batsmen in forward defence found themselves bowled with the stroke half-completed. Appleyard was tall and bowled with a high arm and because of the 'bounce' he obtained he made forcing shots speculative. In manner of bowling he was patently antagonistic and he was never satisfied with himself. After he had reached Test status I chanced upon him at Headingley one April afternoon. He was alone in a net, bowling earnestly at unguarded stumps and teaching himself, he said, to master the leg-cutter. He had, I am sure, the ability, the desire and the application required to be one of the great bowlers of all time, but the physical capacity to establish a claim was denied him.

Trueman, in contrast, enjoyed full blessing of health and freedom from prolonged injury and constructed an astonishingly extensive career for a fast bowler. He played for Yorkshire from 1949 to 1968 and in Test cricket from 1952 to 1965. In his first season, as a youth of 18, he had to be carried from the field at Bramall Lane with a strained back and, inevitably, he was occasionally troubled by the temporary consequences of his occupation, but to the end of his playing days he could, if he chose, commit himself to the full vigour of his youthful bowling action. He never suffered the creaking shoulder or the untrustworthy knee as a permanent consideration. 'Look at him,' Bill Bowes once said to me in envious admiration when Trueman, after ten years of fast bowling, squatted on his haunches having completed an over. 'If I had tried that I should never have got up again'.

The particular attitude of rest is characteristic of the coal mining community from which Trueman derived and presumably heredity did contribute to suppleness and strength, but Trueman's major cricketing fortune lay in his natural bowling action. It was consciously developed and adjusted in detail as advice and experience accumulated but essentially it was a gift from the gods, recognised and admired as soon as seen. Trueman looked a bowler whenever, and whatever, he bowled. He was unquestionably great not only because he took 307 wickets in Test matches and 1,745 wickets for Yorkshire, but because of the impression his bowling created, the imaginations it stirred, the hearts that it warmed. He brought splendour to the cricket of his time. He also brought controversy through some eccentricities of behaviour, but there was universal agreement that cricket in the 1950s would have been poorer without him. He was always a promise and frequently a presenter of the dramatic. He alerted spectators, as he alerted opposing batsmen. Bumper and yorker and magnetic away-swinger mingled like electric shocks to make both batting and watching a continuous adventure that began with a toss of the head as preliminary to a long, accelerating run-up leading to a wide delivery stride, a beautiful sideways presentation and a flowing follow through. Culmination was often enough a stare, or glare, of disbelief in the batsman's survival and sometimes an uninhibited comment on the luck of the enemy. Trueman always had breath to spare for an expression of opinion.

From a shortened run Trueman could be a high-grade technician in swing and 'cut' at fast-medium pace and in this manner he determined the course of a Headingley Test against Australia; but in my memory his full glory was epitomized at Lord's in 1956 when he strove through an afternoon to restore hope in a losing battle. He bowled from the Nursery end, at his best pace and with impressive control. In this attack he created and dominated the atmosphere of play. There was admirable bowling from the other end, but it was background to the battle between Trueman and the Australians. There was no swift batting collapse; Trueman had to wait for wickets and work for wickets and he did not take them all, but the batsmen knew and the spectators knew who carried the banner of England's desperate challenge. The appropriate acknowledgement was made by Miller. Playing his last Test innings at Lord's he came in when five wickets had fallen for 79, scored 30 in sturdy defiance and was finally compelled into a catch to the wicketkeeper. Before he turned for the pavilion he looked down the pitch to the triumphant Trueman and waved a gesture of appreciation for the fine out-swinger that had conquered him. A great bowling spell could not have been more spontaneously or more generously rewarded and I count the moment among my treasures of cricketing experience.

In the 1950s I came to my own fifties, which is a time of life with sufficient past to induce consideration of the future. With, hopefully, much still to come there is a desire for the preservation of known satisfactions among future changes that must come to a living and developing game. The enthusiasms of youth give little thought to the future; present delights carry a promise of eternity and there is no need for misgiving, because ample time and inexhaustible strength will right any wrongs. Middle age is inclined to more uncertainty, in realisation that if things are wrong or may go wrong there is less time left to right them. Some disturbing trends in the cricket of the 1950s came to the surface to create an urgent problem requiring immediate solution. Wardle challenged customs of behaviour and was rejected by his county and MCC as a touring authority. Illegal bowling actions were condemned and forthright action was taken to eliminate them. These were cricketing aggravations of the day, demanding major surgery but likely to have permanent influence on health only in neglect of that surgery. Longer lasting in effect were the drifts beneath the surface. Test matches began to overwhelm the first-class programme, with all the competing countries elevated to nominal equality of status and all Test matches expanded to the limits of significance in publicity. The publicity itself sought self-justification through drama and controversy that had to be assumed or created where they were not inherent. One consequence of limelight is comparative obscurity for the rest of the stage and for supporting characters, and as Tests and tours proliferated the daily domestic cricket tended to become a background concern for public and players.

In the thinking of the period the ancient distinction between amateur and professional began to appear anachronistic. The move towards abandonment was not regarded as urgent and never became an acutely divisive issue, but proposals indicated the changing outlook that originated the revolution of the 1960s. The case for a common denominator of 'cricketer', with direct payment for all, was advanced on arguments that the amateur would need compensatory payment to fulfil all the obligations being required of him and that the acknowledged professional was suffering unfair competition in the range of perquisites. The traditionalist could contemplate with equanimity the loss of Gentlemen v Players fixtures and in theory, at least, reclassification offered wider opportunity for the introduction of part-time players, but there was misgiving that change of status would not affect the amateur only. The professional, I thought, would lose a quality of respect and independence difficult to define but long recognised and appreciated in sport. Professional 'standing' is more than a matter of payment. It is a recognition to be earned and guarded. Professional and amateur alike can contribute talent to a game, but a greater contribution is required from the professional because he has committed himself to the preservation and development of his particular art. By this definition professional and amateur – whatever the form of payment – undertake different responsibilities and I think cricket, or any other game, will lose a desirable element in a confusion of functions. Events seem to be confirming this belief.

Overthrows

New Thinking, New Era

A CRICKETING Rip Van Winkle, falling asleep in 1961 and wakening ten years later, would have known all the confusion that fell on the character of the Catskills. The decade transformed the face and philosophies of first-class cricket. A trickle of trends that began in the 1950s swelled to floodwaters through the 1960s. When our borrowed character dozed off, the counties were playing 28 or 32 matches in the Championship. Tuesdays and Fridays were travelling days and Sunday appearances were by personal request and of charitable intent. Summer carried the cricketer through a long-established routine from the net-practice of April to festival farewells of September. For the chosen few there were variations measured in selection for Test matches or Gentlemen v Players at Lord's.

The touring side fulfilled a programme of thirty-two first-class fixtures, including five Tests, with a closing appearance at the Scarborough Festival, which extended over its traditional nine days and, in this particular season, added the bonus of a match between the Champion County and the runners-up. With as many as 50 or over 60 innings available to batsmen in regular occupation, aggregates of 1,000 runs were commonplace. Alley, of Somerset, exceeded 3,000 and 17 others, including one Australian tourist, passed 2,000. Seven all-rounders scored 1,000 runs and took 100 wickets. Commercial sponsorship provided cash awards in the Tests and cash and trophies for five individual performances covering the whole season. The advertising potential in cricket promotion and subsidy was scarcely beyond the dawn of realisation and exploitation. The boundary fence was uncluttered and the public-address systems concerned themselves with cricket or emergency utterance.

Coming to 1971 consciousness Rip Van Winkle would have found a County Championship reduced to 24 engagements for all the teams and a further reduction to 20 three-day games under discussion. Two touring teams were in the land, each staying for half the season and playing three Test matches. They came consecutively, overlapping for only a week or two in late June and early July and they did not play each other. The first-class counties and five minor county teams were involved in a knock-out competition of one-innings, limited over matches, culminating in a September Final at Lord's and the first-class counties also took part in one-innings competition designed in league form for the Sunday afternoons of the season. A third one-innings competition was in preparation.

As the nominal distinction between amateurs and professionals had been abolished no Gentlemen v Players match appeared in the programme; MCC, with two Tests and a Cup Final at Lord's, could have raised no financial complaint and at Scarborough the Festival was confined to a week, containing one three-day match and a single-innings knock-out competition for four invited county teams. In the first-class statistics three batsmen raised an aggregate of 2,000 runs, five bowlers took 100 wickets and there was not one instance of the all-rounder's 'double', as traditionally understood.

Rip Van Winkle would have had to accustom himself to new sights and sounds. Cricket grounds were garnished with eye-catching commercial advertisements and match-endings were followed by the public presentation of cheques for team and individual awards. Commercial names identified the sponsored competitions and television presentation competed with the matches themselves for spectatorial support. The reawakened Rip Van Winkle was in a bewildering new world of cricket. He had slept through a revolution. Its accomplishment had been more rapid and more fundamental than the most rabid of cricket anarchists or iconoclasts had contemplated. The gates of tradition were found to have surprisingly flimsy locks and hinges. Cricket acknowledged a need for reform and stimulus by setting up courts for self-examination, but the outcome of their findings and suggestions extended far beyond their expectation and intentions. Their aim was the preservation and prosperity of county cricket in its traditional form of three-day matches and it was essentially to this end that other forms and sponsorship from commercial sources were cultivated.

The original thinking of cricket administration in recommending some one-innings matches was that variety would be introduced into the county season and that a livelier playing attitude would develop, through infection, in the formal championship. Events overtook intentions. Commercial sponsorship surged through the doorway. Cricket found itself beset by offers of money, with an all obvious possibility that if it were rejected by established authority it might veer towards competing organizations. The Cavaliers of Rothman were countered by the Sunday League of John Player as a children's hour programme of sport on television. To qualify for taxpayer's subsidy a constitutional change to the Cricket Council was accepted. As one-day promotions multiplied, the lifeboat launched to save first-class cricket in the counties threatened drowning by its own bow-wave and wash.

The commercial sponsors of sport were not altruistic. They were paying for publicity and it was important to them that their promotions should receive all possible attention. They sought and stimulated television and newspaper publicity and with presentations and prize-money they compensated players for the sacrifice of principles demanded by compressed cricket. The parties involved, naturally, pursued their own interests, but were not to be blamed on that account. Sponsors advocated one-day cricket as exciting and significant; television was concerned to justify its programmes; players welcomed the enlargement of income; cricket's treasurers were glad of the cash. In the outburst of promotional activity the ostensible purpose of it all tended to be obscured. First-class cricket was certainly not stimulated by the novelties.

It was made more difficult to present because the programme lost continuity. Provision for the one-day games meant that the season contained days without any cricket for watchers and the reading followers. The habit of attention to cricket tended to be broken. Apprentice players were deprived of a rhythm for their development. Young batsmen in form could not transmit the assurance gained from one innings to another because the lessons learned one day might not have appropriate application during the next week or even fortnight. Weeds of frustration and cynicism grew readily in the stony ground of limited-overs. Who among middle order batsmen advanced to greatness, or had chance to advance, in the 1960s? One-day cricket, carried to excess as it was, proved not a stimulant for first-class cricket, but a competitor. It took away from the championship all the Sundays and many of the

Saturdays. It claimed the names and services of players who would not have been a public attraction without reputations gained in more advanced cricket. It involved players in exhausting, not to say hazardous, road travel at weekends. It divided interests and ambitions of both players and supporters, though in exceptional cases the possibility of multiplied success did increase public attention.

More subtle influences also contributed towards the denigration of championship cricket. With the game's publicity concentrated elsewhere, the championship declined as a talking point and in the prestige of achievement. Yorkshire were county champions five times in the decade of the sixties, yet they were not girded with the glamour of their own teams in the 1920s and 1930s, or of Surrey in the 1950s. They were, indeed, vested with disappointment for not being successful in one-day competitions. Technical standards of play declined in the championship because lower technical standards were adequate for one-day cricket and incentive was therefore diminished and because three-day cricket became more and more a professional routine, without manifest concern for the interests of spectators. Players and spectators were not inclined to cultivate the difficult arts and appreciation of first-class cricket when the cash rewards lay elsewhere and Test occasions demanded attention for nearly half the season. All logic implies an inevitable outcome. Without a concentration on first-class cricket there will, eventually, be no home-bred first-class cricketers. Without cricketers of first-class reputation one-day cricket will lose its attraction for spectators and for commercial sponsors. In that event both credit and cash will have disappeared.

My hope is that such an outcome will be avoided by a

reversal of current trends, by a rebuilding from the substantial masonry upset in the period of revolution. I do not want cricket of the future to look backwards or to imitate the cricket of decades departed. The qualities of the Golden Age, of the inter-wars era, of the 1950s were appropriate to the circumstances of their time and would be anachronistic in restoration, if restoration were possible. I want cricket to look forward along a pathway clearly seen and firmly trodden. I want cricketers to be satisfied with nothing less than a full exploitation of their desires and abilities. As I should have deplored the wastefulness of a Hobbs or a Hammond in the chains of a Sunday afternoon knockabout, so I should regret lack of opportunity for future cricketers to find expression of their talents in a game of depth and breadth. It is my wish for cricket that every age of the past should contribute to the well-being of the future; that good and harmful should be recognised and retained or discarded. The past has shown what can be done with bat and ball, with material matters of pitch preparation and playing accoutrement and with spiritual matters of adventure, application and enjoyment. The past has also given warning on gambling and corruption, on illegal bowling, on international disagreement and political interference, on unacceptable conduct and on dreary presentation.

I hope the cricketers of today and tomorrow will be able to accept the desirabilities of yesterday not as glories gone but as legacies in transit, capital for reinvestment. Equally I hope the cricketers here and to come will investigate the misjudgements and misconceptions, their own included, and reject the unprofitable because they are trustees.

I feel that first-class cricket – that is cricket at its most advanced development – will not prosper as an appendage of one-day expressions. It must have a life and a will of its own. It must be wanted for its intrinsic rewards. It must see for itself, speak for itself and pay for itself. Money will not save it because money is not its primary objective. Financial return is no more the driving force of the first-class cricketer than of the surgeon, the painter or the musician. One-day forms are to first-class cricket as lighter magazines are to the classics of literature in educated reading – no more than an introduction. When strength and perception increase, the immature reading loses its appeal. Something bigger and wider and more challenging is sought.

So with cricket. When ability and appreciation develop, the simpler forms of the game are outgrown. Yet qualities in unsophisticated cricket and reading remain qualities of appeal at all levels. Childhood readings have a story, an action, as their appeal; so have the immortal plays and novels. Elementary cricket is hitting the ball and defeating the bat and those fundamental desires and attempts are also the lifeblood of advanced cricket.

Beyond physical considerations in cricket, the enjoyments of vigour, are attitudes towards the game. These, too, are derived from early experience and are transmitted into higher education. The notions of whole-hearted striving, acceptance of statutory authority, rejection of sharp practice, come from first experience of cricket and are implicit throughout its whole range. Should these basic characteristics be lost, or obscured, during a period of change that period will be unnsatisfying, as it was in first-class cricket during the 1960s and early 1970s.

First-class cricket lost favour because it was not played well enough, eagerly enough and with manifest conviction in its purpose. It allowed itself to be swaddled in irrelevancies represented by different forms of cricket, complications of rule and tactics and concern for feather-bedding finance. First-class cricket will, in short, recover esteem when it does itself justice again and when that justice is seen to be done. The soft options of bread and circuses marked the fall of Rome.

Overthrows

Cup Final at Lord's

I AM not a committed advocate of one-day cricket for first-class cricketers. I believe this popular fancy of the present time to be a contradiction of purpose and inevitably self-defeating in its object of attracting spectators to cricket. First-class cricketers, in my belief, need more than fifty or sixty overs or an hour or two in which to express themselves. Cricketers of first-class quality need more scope than the one-day match can offer them. Without scope they cannot develop their potential or, having developed, they cannot maintain the standards of which they are capable. Cricketers who have attained first-class level by playing in first-class cricket – which is, of course, the only way to become first-class – will be the most successful one-day players; but should the one-day form become dominant the first-class player will not be developed and county cricket will not rise above club standards.

When one-day cricket for the counties was first proposed I was lukewarm towards it, fearful of long-term consequences of tradition. I saw in the Gillette Cup competition an attractive and useful variation in the summer programme, to be ranked in status with the festivals or the old Gentlemen v Players fixtures; I welcomed it as a parallel to the seven-a-side tournaments in Rugby Union football. With the institution of the Gillette Cup I hoped for modifications in the county championship programme, but I believed then, as I believe now, that three-day cricket should preserve itself essentially through intrinsic attractions; that it should be first-class not only in name but in presentation. I was not living in the past when I deprecated the extension of one-day competitions and when I regretted attempted reform of the county championship by administrative detail of no basic significance. I was and am looking to cricket's future in my desire for first-class cricketers to play first-class cricket that can be understood and enjoyed by cricket followers.

I find the one-day form of cricket as offered by first-class cricketers unsatisfying mainly because of the inevitable artificial limitations imposed. One-day cricket is the appropriate cricket for most of us because it is the cricket of our capabilities and opportunity. Our techniques and temperaments will not sustain long innings or long bowling spells. Blessed with the advanced skills and disciplines we should want to move into a wider range and given the opportunity we invariably do. The illogicality is moving back again. First-class cricket is an extension and development by the gifted few of afternoon cricket attempted and enjoyed by the many, but the quality of the few has to be diminished or disguised in afternoon compression. One-day cricket cannot be a distillation of first-class essence; it must become either a restriction or a parody. The greater and more complicated the artificialities the more blatant the parody.

In apparent paradox one-day cricket has provided fewer days to remember than single days of truly first-class cricket. Few great innings have been played or can be played simply because circumstances do not permit them. Even in the occasional big score sustained mastery is not required because the bowling challenge automatically diminishes. It is a cricketing nonsense to suppose that five bowlers will all be equally testing on one afternoon. It is a cricketing contradiction of common sense that bowling authority established or close upon establishment should have to be relinquished because of overs limitation. The longer one-day matches – or, more strictly, single-innings matches – do, of course, provide occasional hours of rare splendour, occasional achievements to catch the breath in anxiety and admiration. Lancashire contrived such an hour in their famous victory over Gloucestershire at Old Trafford, and Yorkshire made magic in the Gillette Cup Final with Surrey in 1965.

In both those instances the special quality of the day was influenced by the climatic conditions. Lancashire won when by normal assessment of light they could not see to win. Yorkshire won when all the probabilities were against any play at all. Yorkshire travelled to London for their first Final in pouring Friday rain. The southward miles raised increasing resignation to at least one day's waiting at Lord's – and one idle day would have involved another because there was then no provision for Sunday play. Harder and harder the evening rain teemed down and arrival at King's Cross found London awash. Through the talk of a fully covered pitch and a new drainage system optimism was muted beneath continuing bedtime rainfall.

Saturday morning brought fair weather and an encouraging

forecast but nobody went to Lord's with any anticipation of play before lunch or even of a start much before late afternoon. We were astonished. A first sight of the field presented almost as much sawdust as turf but the ground staff were inspiringly industrious and efficient and the start of the match was put back no more than an hour and a half. This in itself was a joyful excitement. Players and others professionally involved make provision for the extension or postponement of a one-day match but there are thousands for whom rearrangement spells abandonment of direct participation. The decision to play, and so unexpectedly early, created its own atmosphere of eagerness on the Grandstand, on the Mound and in front of the Tavern.

Yorkshire won the toss and batted first, but their beginning was timid and tremulous. Taylor was clearly uncomfortable and Boycott was resolutely unadventurous. Time and, more significantly, overs passed without any establishment to the innings. Without a wicket falling the bowling looked better than the batting and Surrey looked like assuming command of the match. Taylor's dismissal when his score was nine was not unexpected but it was, by the proof of events, unfortunate for Surrey. It brought Close to the crease in a revision of the published batting order. The Yorkshire needs of the moment were obvious enough and Close, never short of self-confidence, came to give a captain's inspiration by example instead of by exhortation. He challenged the throttling bowling with speculative pull and square cut and he bustled the suffocating field-setting to a more respectful disposition. He breathed urgency into the batting by his approach and he stirred Boycott from inactivity. The run-rate was raised from below two an over in the first hour to an overall three an over by the end of the second. Bowling changes compulsory under rules of the match would in any case have been enforced by the batting. Surrey looked to be the struggling side.

The afternoon play carried Yorkshire to complete authority and great glory. Boycott took the popular fancy with his innings of 146, which mounted to thrilling domination, but the source of Yorkshire's batting inspiration was Close, who scored seventy-nine and directed the course of the decisive second-wicket partnership. Boycott's batting was technically flawless from the stern defence of its beginning to the wonderful show of mastery in its later stages; Close played some sketchy strokes and always seemed at risk, but he was the leader of the counter-attack. His was the flourish without which Yorkshire could not have burst from bondage. He turned the Yorkshire morning from gloom to gratification; Boycott brought untrammelled joy to the afternoon.

Once their hands had grasped the match Yorkshire never relaxed grip. Boycott's magnificent boundaries were followed by supererogatory addition from the carefree hit-or-miss batsmen. Lord's echoed a continuous roar of Yorkshire approbation and as the total grew to record levels identification of loyalty was plain on faces of assurance and resignation. Surrey's only hour of optimism in the match was the first. Once the avalanche that descended on them was moving destruction could be seen as sure and overwhelming. Theoretically, no doubt, Yorkshire's total of 317 from sixty overs was within reach, but in practice the Surrey batting had no hope. September evenings bring an early twilight; with enormous capital resources bowling and fielding enterprise can afford to be speculative; the feeling of the meeting was essentially of 'when' rather than of 'whether or not'. From my corner of the press box I watched the Surrey innings with a selfish eye. I wanted to be back in Scarborough on Sunday morning, not I must confess to attend the traditional Cricket Festival church service, but to play in the traditional Festival golf match at Ganton. My prospects as Surrey began batting ranged from the Gillette Cup Final extending into a second day to a train leaving King's Cross at 7.30, with an all-night journey and bleary-eyed golf as a possible alternative.

Edrich and Stewart discouraged my hopes of golf in a watchful opening partnership. They took the total to twenty-seven and indicated Surrey intentions of compelling Yorkshire to bowl 60 overs. I waved a metaphorical good-bye to the 7.30 from King's Cross and began to wonder about hotel accommodation for the weekend.

The total was twenty-seven when Trueman, bowling with the shadow of the pavilion behind him, dismissed Edrich, Smith and Barrington in the space of four balls. Nobody, thereafter, contemplated match-extension, though the last-wicket batsmen were good-naturedly obstructive after Illingworth had helped himself to three wickets in one over. From near the Main Gate I saw the last wicket fall and, excusing myself from the presentation scenes and ceremony, I travelled north by the 7.30 to York. In one day I had seen the completion of a match that might well have failed to begin, that brought a record total and a record individual score; that ranged spectatorial responses from anxiety to delirium of joy or, alternatively, from anticipation to disappointment in a degree of disbelief; that, unwittingly, influenced a game of golf 250 miles away.

Thanks to Cricket

Yorkshire 317-4 beat Surrey 142 all out by 175 runs.

The Sunday League

SUNDAY League cricket for the counties is an experiment to be viewed with anxiety. As a failure it could be costly in time and money; as a success it could defeat its own object. County designers of the Sunday League regard it as an adjunct to first-class cricket. They have noted public response to one-day cricket in the form of the knockout cup competition. They have seen signs of a market for Sunday play. Balance sheets indicated only too plainly that the County Championship in its traditional form is not financially self-supporting and has found survival only through supplementary income from Test match profits, ancillary fees and donations from extraneous funds. One-day cricket, presented on Sundays, is thought by the county authorities to be another way of raising money and stimulating public interest for the benefit of three-day Championship.

In this experiment the line of thought does not seem to have been pursued to its logical conclusion. If one form of cricket can be preserved only by the success of another form of cricket is there any justification for attempting to maintain the unsuccessful?

The knock-out competition has its appeal, which is undeniable, in the excitements concentrated by the assurance of a significant outcome. Interest lies in the winning and the losing. One-day cricket carries appeal for a public with limited opportunity to attend. A match or an innings can be seen in its entirety for the expenditure of one effort in time and money and inconvenience of travel. In one-day cricket the consequences of success and failure are immediately apparent. The significance of each over, each hour, each innings is emphasised by simplification. Paradoxically, that very simplification, that focussing of interest, makes one-day cricket an unsatisfactory expression of the highest talent. First-class cricketers spoil one-day cricket rather than improve it. They are too good to accommodate themselves to its scope.

One-day cricket by county teams will draw crowds – given fine weather and appropriate setting – because county cricketers are appearing with the glamour of reputations acquired in another form of cricket. No doubt the leaders in pop music would draw a crowd were they to indulge themselves in a one-day cricket match. Footballers playing cricket nearly filled Old Trafford. Spectators for such occasions will not become the spectators wanted for first-class cricket. Theirs are different, almost alien, interests raising different demands for entertainment. Emphasis on one-day cricket, by publicity and commercial promotion, cannot widen the market for first-class cricket. The taste for smoked salmon and well grilled steak is not stimulated by a diet of candy-floss and fish and chips. The only way to popularise first-class cricket is to make first-class cricket attractive in its own right, to present it where and when it can readily be obtained by the customer and to bring it within the range of educated understanding.

First-class cricket needs, or thinks it needs, the by-play of 'instant' cricket because it has been neglecting these fundamentals of its own salvation and well-being. It has become remote, withdrawn into a tight circle of technical accomplishment offering satisfaction only from within. Most days of county cricket are dull for spectators because spectators are not being encouraged to participate. They can see the end, when there is an end, sharing victory or Championship: but more often than not they are excluded from enjoyment in the means to the end. One-day cricket by county cricketers can save first-class cricket only by indicating that the game has more to offer than one-day limitations permit. First-class cricket can preserve its future only by being a form of the game more desirable than any other to players and spectators. Without this assurance there would be no purpose in maintaining first-class cricket in its county organisation. The Sunday League and its equivalents would have proved not a help, but become an executioner.

November 1968

The Championship

NO game is more conducive towards sentimental reflection than cricket, and any consideration of its future is bound to raise some signs for its past, but county cricket cannot live on glories gone and cannot turn back to prosperity enjoyed in conditions that no longer exist. For present and future success as a form of public entertainment county cricket must adapt itself to the available market. It must assess and create demand and contrive matching resources of supply.

No clear signs point to one-day county matches as a major satisfaction of today and tomorrow. Certainly, the Sunday League has attracted crowds; but before inferences lead to an irrevocable conclusion they need examination. Is the public response to the limited-over form of cricket or is it to the availability of cricket on Sunday? Could a multiplication of one-day fixtures develop cricketing skills to satisfy the player and satisfy the spectator with knowledge of cricket's wider ranges?

A further pertinent question to be posed concerns the amount of novelty-value in one-day cricket played by county teams. The form could be self-destructive because of its limitations. Commercial sport has known many burnt fingers, as deserted speedway tracks and bowling alleys will testify. Equally pertinent to planning is the question of justification for the traditional county championship. County cricket has no claim to be a charity. It is a service, founded on private recreation but now presented essentially as commercial entertainment. Unless it does entertain its purpose becomes indefensible. This point is not always appreciated by players. They have been inclined to isolate themselves from their public behind a screen of complicated technique and concentration on their own immediate welfare. They have not played – perhaps have not been encouraged to play – the type and quality of cricket the public enjoyed.

Players hold any game in their hands. By their attitude and activity they make play interesting or unattractive to spectators and to themselves. If players want, as they say they do, the more sophisticated versions of cricket as a career they must make those versions appealing. Cricket needs spectators not only to pay wages and maintain grounds but also because it is an art-form and artists are stimulated by appreciation. Playing inspiration derives from audience reaction. Observation suggests that cricketers, as players and supporters, will always seek the most advanced form of the game obtainable, providing it is within their understanding. Logic would therefore seem to indicate a promotion of county cricket beyond the level of club cricket; of county cricket served by eager and ambitious players meeting the basic spectatorial demand of high-quality performance, competitive significance and accessibility.

By this reasoning a re-modelling of the first-class programme would involve greater, not less, emphasis on the Championship. The competition would have precedence at weekends when attendance is most convenient for most spectators. It would be extended in competitive significance by such additions as divisional sub-championships to give meaning to more of the matches. It would open itself to new playing units representing local desires and resources.

It would cultivate publicity that encourages attendance rather than offers a compensation for staying away. It would design itself to be an inviting career for the player who rated professional satisfactions higher than entry into a commercial rat-race. In this conception of first-class cricket the Test match would not put its prestige in peril by over-familiarity and the variation of a one-innings knockout competition, perhaps with simultaneous subsidiary, would be acceptable as the equivalent of a picnic lunch. In this conception a continuity of cricket development would be preserved.

1971

Preserving Cricket's Future

HOW watchfully cricket must tread in the immediate future to remain cricket. Change of circumstance, change of form and presentation have hastened in with revolutionary speed and in the collisions of opinion not only the structure of the game, but its beliefs and purposes have been challenged. Within a decade the County Championship has been rushed to the edge of extinction, international cricket has been made a political issue and the soul of a pastime and a recreation has been offered in auction for commercial exploitation.

The road to these disruptions has been paved with good intention. One-day county cricket was introduced in an avowed effort to sustain three-day cricket. Crocodile tears have been shed over cricket's misfortune in being the subject of protest on issues beyond cricket. Commercial patronage has been cultivated in the assurance of altruistic outcome. Good intentions have proved basically disastrous for first-class cricket. The one-day game has been developed as a rival to the three-day form instead of as an adjunct. The County Championship has been weakened, not strengthened, by reduction of the fixture list, by extraction of its most profitable days, by burdensome requirements of travel and concentration from its participants and by the diminished opportunity for higher education in young players. International cricket has lost all meaning as a representation of simple sporting challenge and enjoyable experience in sport. Cricketers cannot play where they wish or against whom they wish because politicians and demonstrators object, not to cricket but to forms and principles of government.

In domestic difficulties cricket has turned to the money-lenders. Seeking to live beyond its means it has pledged capital assets and may well find them to be diminishing security in an age of inflation. The assets are public interest: membership subscriptions, gate receipts, donations. The moneylenders are commercial sponsors and television. They charge interest. The interest is compound and cumulative and the ultimate alternative to payment is bankruptcy. Cricket is suffering and will suffer from wounds inflicted, deliberately or unwittingly, by agencies outside the actual playing of the game, but these wounds are not necessarily mortal. In course of time players and spectators will insist on a form of the game giving greater satisfaction than the one-day match designed to produce victory and defeat, even artificially. In course of time cricketers will find a way to play with and against whom they please. In course of time cricket will prefer to stand on its own financial feet, counting independence preferable to sycophantic affluence.

A greater and more pernicious threat to the ultimate health of cricket could lie in a change of attitude towards the game by its players and its public. The loss of good name would leave cricket poor indeed.

Cricket took a long time to earn a good name. Its early history is besmirched by ill-will, riotous demonstration and corruption. Strong leadership and unwavering faith were needed to carry the game through its dark ages into the light of public favour that gave it the most respected reputation in all sport. When 'It isn't cricket' has become an anachronism and a sneer, cricket will be close to its deathbed. The customs and behaviour in cricket are not static. They reflect current thinking. The acceptable of one day can become the scorned of another. Sharp practice is always current and always will be where a chance of profit appears. Cricket is not and never was exempt from the human frailties.

Anxiety grows when the misconceptions and misdemeanours of cricket are condoned and encouraged; when the manifestly unfair and unwelcome is defended. Cricket loses credit with cricketers' public denigration of each other, in loss of temper without subsequent sign of regret, in complaint against circumstances and dissent from umpires' ruling, in a mean-spirited approach to play on grounds of expediency.

The greatness, the appeal, the joy of cricket come from more than centuries scored, wickets taken and catches held. Cricket more than anything else is a way of playing a game, of thinking a game, of caring for a game – of being cricket. It is not a livelihood, but a living; not an exercise nor an entertainment, but an experience. Unless the leaders of today, the captains and the kings, the players and the watchers and the critics, direct us to the truth of cricket, tomorrow's cricket will be an empty shell, a lifeless relic. It cannot live by bread alone.

I am optimistic enough to believe that cricket will find means and masters to eliminate the tendency to sourness and selfish approach now evident, that the mean and meretricious will be rejected by players and public. I am realist enough to recognize that cricket will always have problems of finance for which all possible solutions deserve consideration and that cricket at its highest level will be exploited beyond its purpose and desires. I am anxious that cricket should see its line of development not as a commercial enterprise, not as a political weapon, not as a synthetic concern of ulterior motivation, but as a form of stability linking a way of life through yesterday, today and tomorrow in practical idealism. To know what 'isn't cricket' we must recognise and preserve what is.

The Cricketer, November 1971

Chapter Four:

QUIET HOURS BENEATH THE SUN

Soft Air and Orchards

IT is a pleasant fancy, if no more, that the cricket counties reflect something of their environment in their play, and one argument in the case for limited 'special registrations' and preservation of birth or residential qualification is a wish that cricket teams should be representative in more than name. Most county sides still do indicate traces of their origin, though in these sophisticated times local enthusiasms and regional differences are tending to disappear and cricketers seem inclined to accept a common mould. In any denial of native talents and resources cricket would lose an attractive feature. Sussex and Lancashire, Somerset and Surrey play by the same rules and with much the same techniques but they need identification by character, easily perceived and readily relished.

Covered pitches threaten even Yorkshire and Lancashire with loss of individuality. In the mind's eye and by tradition Northern cricket is based on spin bowling with an accompaniment of creative fielding and on resolute batting. It is expected to be hardheaded, reluctant to concede a point, quick to seize an advantage, tenacious of grip. It thrives on crisis because it has been nurtured in difficulty. Take away the turning wickets on which half the home matches of Lancashire and Yorkshire would be played under natural conditions and Lancashire and Yorkshire must lose some of their special skills, with cricket in general losing some of the variety that is the spice of its life.

Middlesex cricket has long carried a metropolitan flavour. Its character is an acquisition more than a birthright. It is the polished cricket of self-assured establishment. It seems to be played against a back-ground of Lord's wherever the match may be. Middlesex teams are always expected to be strong teams because their public image is of affluence and well-being. When Middlesex visit the provinces they represent not a county but a capital city. They form the provincial conception of London life. Surrey are seen as a batting side despite all the accomplishments of Bedser, Lock and Laker and innumerable bowling predecessors. Rain admittedly and demonstrably falls on the Oval, but Surrey play in a context of hard wickets and high scoring and long days in the field. Surrey, so splendidly served by a long line of great amateur players, carry an air of professional competence. They look, or we feel they ought to look, businesslike and well-organised in their chocolate-coloured caps. In the West Country cricket has the warmth and rounded maturity of soft air and orchards. Cricket in Gloucestershire, Somerset and Worcestershire sometimes seems a long way from cricket in London or the North. For all its improved and improving amenities in urban settings it remains rural cricket, for observation from the shade of a tree or by leaning on the fence with the harvest outlook to be mentioned in the same breath as a maiden over.

Grace and Hammond came appropriately down the pavilion steps at Lord's to play a Test match innings, but Grace and Hammond were in their spiritual cricketing home disentangling themselves from a deck-chair to pick up bat and gloves on a sunny morning sweetened by a westerly breeze. The polish of Palairet, Fosters and Graveney form sheen on the essential jollity of West Country cricket. Gloucestershire, Somerset and Worcestershire will always be welcome in Bradford or Blackpool but if ever they cease to feel themselves 'foreigners' there they will have lost their cricketing heritage.

Hampshire and Sussex have the salt of the sea and the wind of the Downs in their cricket. However studiously they may pursue and however honourably win a championship the achievement will seem a by-product in their season's play. Sussex and Hampshire cricket is, of course, purposeful and their loyalties run high temperatures, but there is always the feeling that centuries scored, wickets taken, catches missed and ducks endured will mingle happily in the melting-pot of draught ale when evening falls. Hampshire and Sussex assimilate more easily than most counties the exotic skills. Ranji and Duleep and the present Pataudi chose Sussex; Hampshire readily absorbed the South African Llewellyn and the West Indian Marshall and made them happy to be playing there.

Kent cricketers, with their noble motto and challenging crest, cannot escape marquees and fluttering flags and high festival wherever they play. By strict truth they are less romantically housed on some of their own grounds because the garden of England has had to find room for a garage, but Kent cricket contains lawns and parks and strawberries for tea. It preserves, like Essex, an air of improvised day-to-day existence through its admirable underlying organisation.

I have followed my fancy far enough. Character in the cricketing counties will not bear too exacting a scrutiny without revealing contradictions and illogicalities. Places, like people, have a private and a public face and teams, like individuals, are mostly what we see in them.

The Cricketer

The Charm of Lord's

FEW of us like idle hours upon a cricket field, and particularly unhappy are those enforced by rain and unkind weather; but sometimes a ground itself has attractions that are independent of the cricket that is being played, or should be played, within its boundaries. Only the familiarity of the longest of acquaintanceships could make Lord's dull, for instance, cricket match or no cricket match. Lord's stands alone as a home of the game. No other habitation of cricketers is quite like it; some may be more pretentious, some more luxurious, some have greater beauty of setting, but none has superior attraction to this, the most famous cricket ground the world knows.

Chief amongst the charming characteristics of Lord's is its

dignity. This you feel even outside the walls in St. John's Wood Road; to arrive breathless and dishevelled at the main gate would be an offence almost beyond forgiveness, and would certainly spoil your appreciation of the day's play. Once I recommended an Australian visitor to go to Lord's and immediately he referred to it as 'the place where you take your hat off as you go in'. No gesture could be more appropriate, for Lord's does command respect, and, in return, it has to offer the most delectable prospect cricketers can know.

Few other places so happily mingle formality and comfort. Not only are you permitted to walk upon historic turf; but ritual bids you do so at each and every interval. Tradition lingers without dispute even in this casual age; there are seats where smoking is forbidden; there are portions strictly reserved for masculinity. The pavilion is jealously guarded against the unauthorised, yet everywhere there is thoughtfulness and convenience. There is no cheapness, no makeshift arrangement at Lord's. All round the ground rise adequate stands with fresh white paint gleaming always upon seats and railings. Paths are kept in faultless repair, lawns neatly cut and trimmed, and flower-baskets brighten every dark corner. To sit at Lord's is to share in substance and so become a man of substance yourself.

The pavilion is surely the most magnificent of all pavilions. Others may be larger, more lavishly equipped – that I do not know – but Lord's stands for me as the ideal. Graciously the stones have mellowed with age, majestically the outline, flag-topped, stands against the sky. Before is an enclosure, halfway up there are balconies, and on the top is the very perfection of grandstands. Within, the Long Room, from which the play can be watched through wide windows, is a storehouse of cricketing treasure. Here exploration could take a week, and would require the most enthusiastic and knowledgeable of guides, for the exhibits are both many and incredibly varied. You may gaze upwards to oil paintings of past legislators and players or old scenes of cricket, you may note in the glass cases bats that bear but the remotest resemblance to the modern implement, stumps made from the wood of HMS Australia, ancient MCC caps and ties, the original urn and ashes of dispute, a solid ball of the notorious Bulli soil, menu cards of historic occasions, and even torn and broken coins that became entangled in the cutting machine. Some of the relics will mean little to you, others will strike sharp chords of memory, but no man calling himself cricketer could stroll the Lord's Long Room without interest. Even the stairways that lead to the balconies cannot be taken hurriedly, for the walls are covered with photographs and notices, old and new. Groups of teams that sailed the seas beneath MCC colours in search of cricket fame; Australians, South Africans, Indians who have visited this country; score-cards of matches played long ago yet remembered clearly, all are here to be seen. And on the balcony itself you may sit, surrounded by tradition; you have only to keep quiet to be transported into yesterday. On your right the Eton and Harrow match of goodness-knows-when comes under review: 'Fine game, that, sir! Fine bowlers and fielders those lads were. Reminds me, I saw So-and-so the other day – Africa, I believe – no cricket now – by gad, he's out. Beautiful catch, beautiful. I remember – ' On your left. 'I don't know; these modern cricketers seem to take things very easily. Not the enthusiasm of our time, what! I've seen the day when I've made a hundred – I think it was a hundred, big score anyway – and then carried my bag four miles to the station.

Let's go and have some lunch. Shall we?'

The needs of humanity apart from cricket are well catered for at Lord's. Service and food are good and adequate. Full luncheon or a sandwich and a drink are equally easily obtainable. The appurtenances of the game are in keeping with everything else. Scorecards are always ready and up to date; the scoreboards go beyond bare adequacy, and everything is done with dignity and efficiency. Even the wheelbarrows are rubber-tyred. Lord's is more than a cricket ground; it is an institution, a place where cricket is the very breath of existence, and it stands as an example to all its brethren of the game. That it should ever take second place is inconceivable; its example may be followed, should be followed, in many of the practical aspects, but none other place on earth can have the atmosphere of Lord's. As the years go by and new generations come to read its blessed turf they, too, will come under the spell; they, too, will feel the irresistible; they, too, will know beyond question that they have been within the royal palace of the kingdom of Cricket.

In Search of Cricket

Pleasures of the South

I WILL try to give you some idea of how we 'barbaric invaders' enjoy our various excursions into the cricket of your more amiable South country. Our cricket atmosphere here must, of necessity, be businesslike, and though we are mightily proud of the solidity and efficiency of our Bramall Lanes, our

Old Traffords and our Trent Bridges, we freely admit our enjoyment over excursions into what amounts to practically another cricketing world. Of London I do not speak; Lord's stands alone, incomparable, and the pale sister the Oval is essentially Metropolitan. But now that Essex have left the vast acreage of Leyton there is cricketing delight indeed to be found upon their various playgrounds. Once Yorkshire played at Colchester, and, for my part, I was enchanted; of the cricket I remember little save that I had my first sight of the enthusiastic acrobatics of Stephenson*, but the beauties of the ground set in its park, with the pale green of the trees providing a backcloth for the fluttering marquees I shall never forget. I may say, incidentally, that the marquees did more than flutter at one point, for the Press tent gave up the ghost altogether and collapsed with fine confusion upon its startled and distressful occupants. Even so, I would not complain if Yorkshire played Essex at Colchester every year, though that would deprive us of a sight of the equally captivating enclosure at Westcliff, where again there are tents and gay banners and trees.

I suppose Kent must be acclaimed the most festive of all cricketing counties; to us Northerners, accredited with little sentiment or fancy, the Brotherhood of the Cheerful Sparrows represents a spirit that we cannot capture. I am not so sure, of course, that a surfeit of tents and cheerful sparrows would not be easily come by, and when skies are grey or breezes making mischief amongst my papers, I have been known to long for the less inspiring but more appropriate structures of the Northland.

Perhaps most touching of all to the Northerner on cricket adventure bent is the freedom on the grounds of the South.

*John Stephenson (1907-1982) Essex.

Where we must remain strictly within our pens, allotted according to the depth of our purse, in the South we have the freedom of the ground and are excluded only from the pavilion itself (even there, let it be whispered, a confident air and a cheerful 'good morning' will sometimes serve as a membership ticket). We are invited to stroll the grass at the luncheon interval, to make a picnic holiday beneath the trees at tea and hold deliberations near the sight screen all day through. Stroll the grass at Bramall Lane or Headingley and the world would fall about your ears.

This sense of freedom probably means nothing to you of the South; it has always been yours and consequently passes by unnoticed. Your Northern visitors feel it, though, and gather from it a spirit of holiday that is hard to define but very real for all that. Perhaps it is this constant intermingling of spectators that leads to another strong impression I have of cricket in the South. Walk through the crowds in Lancashire or Yorkshire at lunch and the conversation will be cricket; the morning's play, the afternoon's promise, the probable course of the match or some individual achievement. Walk through the crowd anywhere in the South (save always the cosmopolitan London) and the topics are as numerous as the speakers. Farming, the weather, the local flower show, the particular feature of the district, 'my rheumatism,' the price of petrol, all are cast from tongue to tongue. Cricket talk seems invariably prefaced by the 'I remember . . . ' of the reminiscently inclined. I have spent an afternoon at Bath when brilliant cricket was displayed and I heard all the ramifications of farming discussed around me with but occasional interruption for acclamation of the cricketers.

Cricketing days, in short, are not your life; the purpose and the meaning of your existence. The rights and wrongs of the question I will not attempt to discuss, saying only that for one at least, from the North, your Southern ways form very pleasant contrast now and then.

The Cricketer, May 1937

Kentish Men

FOR centuries Tonbridge has lain quietly dreaming in the enchanted garden of Kent. Even now in this bustling twentieth century it is only in the main street, where the through traffic comes hurrying through, that movement is other than leisurely and contemplative. Summer days are sweet and shining with peace in Tonbridge, and cricket week is the crown of the year.

There are prettier cricket grounds than that at Tonbridge, for although there are trees and cool tents and fluttering flags, dull cottage roofs can be seen on two sides and the pavilion's sole beauty lies in its utility. Yet Tonbridge sees and is essentially part of true Kentish cricket. There the boundaries are not so far distant as to suggest their attainment being beyond mortal consideration, and a well-hit six can drop with a thrilling crash upon hard slates. Forbidding railings do not separate all the spectators from the players, and it is possible to watch cricket in that most delectable of ways, seated on the grass and willing and anxious to save perspiring and beaten fieldsmen a certain amount of toil. Years ago there must have been a time when there was no cricket in Tonbridge; then, perhaps, there would be dancing and merrymaking and the pleasant jostling of crowds upon the castle green, over which you can still walk in the cool of the evening and dream, and dream of men and maidens who strolled there long ago.

When cricket was in its swaddling clothes, Tonbridge came to know the game, and today it is a nursery for Kentish cricketers of promise and ambition. To learn cricket at Tonbridge is to come very near to earthly paradise, for every breeze that blows and every sun that glows brings the spirit and tradition of the game. The science of cricket has perhaps to be taught even in Tonbridge, but the life of the game needs no telling; it is part of the air of the place, and to be born in Tonbridge is to be already half a cricketer. Woolley was born at Tonbridge and born in the month of May; how much of his genius, how much of the magic that is within him, and which he has called forth for our delectation these thirty years, is dependent upon those two simple facts? Would Woolley, a Lancastrian, and seeing the first light in a dreary December have been the Woolley we treasure so dearly? It is impossible to separate the place and the men. There can be no grimness, no dour fighting when the environment is all mixed green, and blue and gold. Other counties, stern and points-wary at home, become transformed in Kent, and even Yorkshire scored more than 160 runs before luncheon on the first day when once they came beneath the spell.

Kent cricket is invariably an adventure; think of the Kentish men of cricket immortality, and at once you picture them in their own setting, batting with a smile upon sunburnt faces or bowling with smooth rhythm and gentle courtesy. Dillon, Day, Woolley, Hutchings, Seymour – the very names are poetry in themselves, and as for their achievements, was ever more perfect a living poem than dark-haired Kenneth Hutchings at the wicket or in the field? One name, perhaps above all, means Kent and means Tonbridge. If, at the close of the day's play, you leave the ground and walk along the main street, crossing the almost motionless stream of the Medway, you will come to an alley way leading to the door of the Parish Church. Here you must enter and go down the south aisle to the corner set apart for the children, and there on the wall read these words, graven on a tablet of stone:

IN MEMORY OF COLIN BLYTHE, THE CELEBRATED
KENTISH CRICKETER, THIS TABLET IS PLACED BY HIS
SORROWING WIDOW AND HIS MANY FRIENDS IN KENT.
HE PLAYED FOR ENGLAND AT HOME AND IN
AUSTRALIA AND IN SOUTH AFRICA.
HE WAS THE MAINSTAY OF THE KENT XI, FROM
1899 TO 1914.
IN SEPTEMBER, 1914, HE VOLUNTEERED AND WAS
ENROLLED IN THE KENT FORTRESS ENGINEERS, AND IN A
SHORT TIME PROMOTED TO BE SERGEANT.
IN 1917 HE WAS TRANSFERRED TO THE KING'S OWN
YORKSHIRE LIGHT INFANTRY, AND FELL IN ACTION AT
YPRES 8 NOVEMBER, 1917. AT 38.
AS CRICKETER, SOLDIER, AND PATRIOT HE PLAYED
THE GAME.
"GLORIFY GOD IN YOUR BODY".

And beneath these words is the banner of Kent with 'Invicta' standing clear. Just as tears come to Australians' eyes when Victor Trumper is mentioned, so is the name of Colin Blythe revered through all Kent. He was the darling of his day, supreme master of his art, and, bowling, a sight as beautiful as any ever cricket has known. He will never be matched, and as the years drift by his memory will become more gloriously enshrined in those who knew him by sight and by story. This will be his memorial, deeper and wider and more lasting than a cross in Flanders or a tablet in a Tonbridge church.

As the epitome of Kent cricket, Colin Blythe will never die.

In Search of Cricket

Bramall Lane

TO claim that I knew Bramall Lane as a cricket ground for more than sixty years would be stretching the meaning of words, but there is factual accuracy in saying that I attended cricket at Bramall Lane from 1909 to 1973. In 1909 I was a babe in arms, taken to Bramall Lane because my father was playing there; in 1973 Bramall Lane ceased to be a cricket ground. Before I could distinguish between a pavilion enclosure and a playpen the family home moved from Sheffield to Bradford, so my first understanding of Bramall Lane derived from *Wisden's* and my father's reminiscence. I knew the flavour before I enjoyed the taste.

The eventual recognition was remarkably like the mental picture and the years of the First World War scarcely changed the outline presented by pre-war photographs I had seen. In my youthful excursions to Bramall Lane from outside Sheffield I went by train and followed the crowd, on foot, from station to ground. The admission gate was where I expected it to be, my money or my credentials seemed acceptable and beyond the enclosing rails stretched the turf of promised land requiring no adjustment of preconception. Considering the matter at all, I should no doubt have satisfied myself that this was Bramall Lane as it always had been and would continue to be. I was much more concerned with the batting and bowling than with the buildings, and simply accepted Bramall Lane as a place where Yorkshire and other teams played cricket.

This acceptance stayed with me through widening aesthetic experience. I have never been appalled, mystified, enchanted or amused, as others have been, by the sight of cricket in a Bramall Lane setting. I can understand varied reactions, particularly in relation to the decades of 1950 and 1960 when Bramall Lane had become a manifest anachronism. A first sight of it on a wet or merely overcast Wednesday might well raise alarm and despondency; it could certainly seem a sick joke that anyone should want to play cricket in a pit of concrete and steel, with the evening shadow of a football stand putting half the outfield in blackness and even encroaching on the pitch. In its last years of cricket Bramall Lane had ceased to look like a cricket ground with adaptations for football. It did not look like a football ground, either. It must have looked, on first sight, like nothing on earth.

Because I had known Bramall Lane all my life and had absorbed its changes year by year I was neither shocked nor sentimentally dismayed by its ultimate reconstitution. In commercial sport a Bramall Lane trying to serve both cricket and football had no chance of survival. As a joint accommodation it was only half a football ground and a travesty of a field for cricket. That there should be no Bramall Lane in cricket was a saddening thought; that a Bramall Lane long known and respected should have lost character and quality was wistful reflection; but that Bramall Lane as last seen in cricket had any claim to preservation outside the history books made no argument for me.

Within the history books Bramall Lane holds a high rating. It was as familiar in cricket as Old Trafford or The Oval and as personalised as Lord's. Cricketers the world over are familiar with the name of Bramall Lane and thousands who have never been there carry a firm impression of the place and of its people. This character derived from history and crystallized in the twenty years before 1914 and the twenty years between the Great Wars. Bramall Lane was created essentially for cricket by enterprising cricketers. In 1855, when it was rented from the Duke of Norfolk, it was a field among fields on the outskirts of commercial and industrial Sheffield. Heavy steel manufacturing was concentrated in the Don valley with the lighter cutlery and tool-making factories scattered along the banks of the Sheaf. From commercial Sheffield ran a country lane to the file factory and adjoining residence of David Brammall and the Brammall's Lane of conversational usage became Bramall Lane as a thoroughfare and as the identification of a field enclosed for cricket and other sports in 1855. When the ninety-nine year lease of the paddock was under discussion its advantage in 'being free from smoke' was emphasised and its usage was conditional on cricket matches being 'conducted in a respectable manner'.

Cricket in the middle of the nineteenth century was an expanding game and an increasing public entertainment. It had emerged from a tawdry period of betting and bribery to become a socially accredited pastime for amateur players and a widening opportunity for professionals. Michael J Ellison and his fellow promoters wanted Bramall Lane for the betterment of their own cricket and needed the promotion of

Bramall Lane to justify its existence and develop its potentiality. Within a decade of taking the ground they had established the Yorkshire County Cricket Club.

Bramall Lane and Yorkshire cricket grew up together. Yorkshire cricket was never confined to Sheffield nor was it supplied with playing resources predominantly from Sheffield; but for forty years it was governed from Sheffield and Bramall Lane was its spiritual home.

The ultimate in cricket ground honour was accorded in 1902 when England met Australia in the third Test of the series. The accolade was mistimed. It came too late if Bramall Lane were to be considered as an attractive setting for cricket; too soon if financial considerations were to be paramount. By this time the ground had conceded all pastoral pretensions. Houses and paved streets, factories and service industry had covered the neighbouring fields and gardens and, though cricketers were still granted sight of the sky, no tree, no vegetation except the playing lawn, soothed the roving eye. Bramall Lane provided cricket – and Association football in the winter – to watch, but little else for inspiring contemplation. Its origins had been completely obscured. As a commercial arena its potential was still unfulfilled. It could accommodate enormous crowds, but not in any great creature comfort or with appropriate financial return. In 1898 management and ownership had changed into the form of a limited company, with freehold purchased and funds allocated for ground development. The Test match came before the development could be completed.

Bramall Lane's first and last Test match was full of disappointment for the England team and the Sheffield authorities. Australia won the game and the public reaction to the occasion was discouraging. A total attendance of 40,000 over three days was far below expectations and receipts were reduced by lack of stand seats to be sold. The early July weather – of a notoriously rainy summer – was damp and gloomy and play was harassed by showers and light so poor as to create a lasting reputation. Bramall Lane had to confess a failure. It knew success at county level and preserved it for fifty years. Bramall Lane spectators rejoiced in Yorkshire's cricket before and between the wars and developed a character that was both fascinating and forbidding. Bramall Lane came to epitomise a Southern conception of Northern cricket that was acceptable, because beneficial, to cricketers of the North; if visiting teams felt strangely circumstanced in the grey of stone and steel they might lose a wicket or two or drop a catch before they became acclimatized. If the rough humour of the watching thousands seemed difficult to understand and liable to misinterpretation a temperamental weakness might be exposed to Yorkshire's advantage.

Throughout the cricket world Bramall Lane grew synonymous with smoky skies and biting comment. The characteristics were exaggerated from a foundation on fact. Sheffield skies were smoky and Sheffield wit was incisive, but, of course, there were sunny days to help the batsmen and reproof was directed on friend as well as on foe. Bramall Lane could praise or plague with some approach to impartiality, though it would be true enough to say that the visitor usually had to overcome an initial prejudice applied against any stranger or challenger. One evening in the 1920s I paid my shilling to take a place in the 'Grinder's Stand', which was the seating on the Bramall Lane side of the ground. Sussex had been dismissed and Yorkshire had to meet Maurice Tate with the new ball for an hour or so before close of play. Tate, bowling from the pavilion end, was in magnificent form but completely out of luck. He beat both Holmes and Sutcliffe and shaved the stumps; he had each batsman palpably missed by the wicketkeeper, who was playfully strangled at the end of the over. Tate's bowling was worth three or four wickets and he took none, but he was honoured by the 'Grinders'.

Holmes and Sutcliffe won applause for their scoring strokes and acclamation when their partnership reached fifty (in less than an hour), but Tate was acknowledged at the end of every splendid over and his performance was the talking point of the day, though there was nothing to show for it in his analysis. That was the personification of Bramall Lane, the distinction of its 'shilling' spectators. Of course they relished records, of course they were delighted by Yorkshire success and the downfall of opponents, of course they wore hearts of loyalty on their sleeves, but they were knowledgeable enough to recognise outstanding cricket from any source. Bramall Lane may not have been able to sustain the presentation of Test cricket, but it subjected every match and every player to a test of its own devising and awarded unfading 'caps' of acclaim or humiliation.

The traditional Bramall Lane crowd was not representative of Sheffield alone. Spectators flocked in from the city and its suburbs but they came also from Rotherham and Doncaster and Barnsley and all the townships of South Yorkshire. They came by train and tram and bus and they claimed Bramall Lane as theirs in Yorkshire cricket. Assembly was part of the day's excitement. The railway 'cricket ticket' filled the local trains; trams and buses ran 'special' services. Along the two approach roads to the city Bramall Lane and Shoreham Street, pedestrians spilled from pavement into roadway, reducing the traffic flow to their own pace. Raincoat and lunch-box, in one form or another, made a uniform and the first sight of a turnstile queue inspired a hastening stride.

Inside the ground disposition was hierarchical. County and local club members with pavilion and enclosure privilege were invariably established hours before the start of play. These were, so to speak, the occupational followers of cricket, practised in finding favoured seats and in guarding possession against all-comers. Their characteristic accoutrement included raincoat, rug or cushion and refreshments carrier. These were the avid newspaper and brochure readers, the self-appointed authorities on dressing-room and committee intimacies. They knew Herbert Sutcliffe's batting average and the colour of his motor-car. Among themselves they were severe critics of Yorkshire performances, but they tolerated no denigration by 'lesser breeds without the law'.

Opposite the pavilion ran the long football stand, raised above concrete terracing. Here the seating was slightly more comfortable than in the pavilion enclosure, but the cricket was only distantly in view and a sense of isolation was discouragingly strong. The 'popular' sides of the ground gave witness to cricket's fascination and spectatorial hardihood. The Grinder's Stand had wooden seating but on the Shoreham Street side the embankment, which was primarily a football service, offered only concrete steps and iron crush barriers. A day's cricket was a day's endurance. From discomfort and devotion the Bramall Lane crowd originated a world-wide reputation for sharp wit and shrewd comment. At its best the expression of opinion was pointed without being offensive. Rebuke was for the misdemeanour rather than for the perpetrator and the same player could experience condemnation and acclaim on the same afternoon. Judgement, on the whole, was equitable and Bramall Lane knew cricket as well as the game can be known from an onlooker's viewpoint.

Occasionally there was misinterpretation and consequent misbehaviour. Disrespect towards the umpires led to an MCC inquiry in 1924 and a threat by Middlesex to refuse further fixtures with Yorkshire. Patriotic fervour once or twice stepped beyond the bounds of good humour, but few cricketers, from any part of the world, counted playing at Bramall Lane an experience better to be avoided. In the 1930s particularly, the cricket itself assumed a characteristic pattern based on the qualities in the pitch and the features of the enclosure. First mornings were frequently found to be helpful to swing bowling and a batting struggle could be expected until lunchtime. When early moisture had gone from turf and atmosphere the conditions eased to encourage high scoring and remained, in fine weather, favourable to batsmen for the rest of the match.

In persistent dampness swing bowlers could keep their authority and first-morning drama spread into second and third days, as in that memorable match between Yorkshire and the 1938 Australians when Bowes, for the only time in his career, had conditions to his liking in bowling to Bradman. A comparable engagement of abiding memory came later when Trueman and May met as protagonists for their counties. Bramall Lane was buffeted by German raiders in the Second World War and the years following saw its gradual decline as a stately home of cricket. The physical ravages of war, in which both turf and stands were damaged, remained in evidence long after war had ended and the reconstruction of the stands was more beneficial to football than to cricket.

Spiritual restoration was never accomplished. Sheffield shared the booming public interest in cricket revived, but, when the first-class game began to lose some of its quality in the 1950s and Yorkshire was not the champion county in a period of ten years, Bramall Lane illustrated the decline. Crowds became smaller and noticeably less knowledgeable. The famed comment of tradition degenerated to myopic crudity. Character took on the shoddy appearance of the property. Bramall Lane could not live for ever on a reputation created in a different age.

For me the inevitable ending was engraved one afternoon of interrupted play. On the Shoreham Street embankment a few spectators, dispersed in groups, waited for a possible return of the players. The air was damp, the skies were grey and a melancholy inconsequence pervaded the whole scene. On the embankment a solitary youth occupied himself with kicking an empty beer-can from top to bottom of the concrete terracing. He followed the can to the lowest step, took a hand from his pocket, picked up the can and threw it back towards the top of the terracing. He climbed the steps and set the can rolling down again. When it stopped he kicked it – tinkle, tinkle, tinkle. He repeated the exercise a dozen times and more, the irritating jangle echoing through the cavernous emptiness. Nobody attempted to stop him, nobody offered rebuke. Bramall Lane had reached a resignation of spirit.

Within ten years the cricket turf was torn away. Bramall Lane could no longer justify a cricketing existence, but it has, at least, left a name and a memory beyond obliteration.

Overthrows

Cardus's Home: Old Trafford

NATURALLY the attractions differ according to the different demands. For some, Old Trafford's chief virtue is its accessibility. It is three and a half miles from the centre of Manchester, an eight-minute journey by electric train with the station close to the gates. There are exceptionally good bus services. Car parks are spacious and easy to enter or leave, and police traffic-control near the ground is highly efficient. In fact, it is possible to organise an hour's cricket into the Manchester day's business diary, though, of course, the diary must risk the consequences of that hour's cricket being particularly exciting. Mr. Neville Cardus has confessed to a reversal of such proceeding. He found it possible to slip away from Old Trafford to be married in between two sessions of play.

Something of Old Trafford's rurality still lingers. Fields are gone, and the skyline tends to be broken by cranes and elevators, but the immediate environs are open, and the cricket gains by the good light, which is an outstanding characteristic of the ground. Circumstances favour the preservation of this natural advantage, for Old Trafford is one of the few big grounds with the pavilion running parallel to the pitch. Sightscreens can therefore be used at both ends, and to avoid any glare on sunny days they are painted pale blue instead of the more customary white. Good light also helps the fieldsmen, who rarely have much difficulty in sighting the ball except at deep square leg against the pavilion background.

In addition to a sight of the ball, players are also privileged to superb turf. It would be possible to pitch wickets almost anywhere on the ground and, indeed, minor games are often played off the 'square'. Fielding is a joy, and so soft is the grass that the ball keeps its shine longer than usual, because the cover is not lacerated as it would be on a rougher surface, or one of coarser texture. Batsmen derive their benefit from the speed with which the ball skims away to the boundary.

The wickets are interesting, and in recent years have been changeable in character. The only feature common to the various preparations has been the height at which the ball comes through. There has never been much danger of the shooter and batsmen have always had opportunity for making shots. It is not just coincidence that Cyril Washbrook, for instance, has developed the hook and the square cut as his most profitable strokes.

In the seasons immediately following the Second World War the pitch, in fine weather, helped bowlers only on the first day. There was plenty of juicy grass to make 'greenness', but as this passed away conditions grew easier and easier and in the later stages of a match the batsmen usually found themselves in perfect circumstances. Even after rain the wicket was not normally difficult unless the drying was accelerated by strong sun or high wind. The Lancashire committee felt that the best interests of cricket were not being served by this type of Old Trafford wicket, so they instituted a season of experiment during which rolling and watering were severely limited. The results were immediately apparent. The ball turned from the very first over, spin bowlers had a wonderful time and despite much interruption from the weather few matches went far into the third day in 1950. One of them could not even stretch into the second, Lancashire beating Sussex by an innings and 87 runs on 12th July. Afterwards the Sussex captain, James Langridge, asserted that the pitch was unsuitable for three-day cricket, though he was careful to emphasise that Lancashire were in no way favoured by the conditions, except in having players better equipped to use them.

In this same season the West Indies suffered their only Test match defeat of the tour at Old Trafford, and they, too, had some comment to make on the wicket, though it is doubtful if they actually had the worst of it. For the following season less drastic instructions were given and the character of the wickets changed again. Some of the 'greenness' has gone and the pitch does tend to break up towards the end, but in general the favours have gone back into the pockets of batsmen.

Spectators, too, have had cause to notice changes in the past few years. Old Trafford and the Luftwaffe were not on the best of terms and bombing damaged the pavilion and some of the stands. Complete rebuilding has not yet been possible and the renovations have left the ground with an unfinished appearance far from satisfactory to the Lancashire planners.

The playing area covers about four and a half acres but the whole property is perhaps three times that size. It includes big car-parking space behind the pavilion and alongside the practice ground (which is itself used as a car-park during Test matches), and a wide approach, containing flower beds, from the main gates and ticket office to the pavilion. For a most satisfying first impression, Old Trafford should be entered from the Warwick Road station end, because from there, looking north, the full form of the pavilion and main stands can be seen. This entrance, which is close by one of the two scoreboards, leads to an area of open terracing flanked on the right by an uncovered stand behind one sightboard, and on the left by covered stands facing across the ground to the pavilion. Beyond these, at the practice ground or Stretford End, is more open terracing with a small sheltered step behind, and topped by a separate building which contains rooms now used for the President's guests and a scoreboard. In the north-west corner a half-moon of stands partly covered, partly open, serves lady members and visitors and all members. The ladies are also given a refreshment bar of their own, under their stand, and here they have the privilege of inviting guests – for whose expenses they are responsible.

The pavilion, though damaged during the air raids, is the dominating feature of the ground, and a building of some distinction. Constructed mainly of red brick in the solid Victorian style it occupies much of the length of the north side of the ground, thus facing almost due south to catch all the available sunshine. The design follows the usual custom of large pavilions, with the central feature of a ground floor Long Room, flanked by dressing-rooms and committee rooms, and with a central balcony on the upper storey.

Players' needs have rather outgrown the dressing-rooms which are too small for modern standards of comfort, though their private balconies offer a good view of the play. In front of the pavilion is an uncovered enclosure separated from the turf by white-painted railings. Through the spectators in this enclosure the players pass on to the field making the picture fixed for ever by Cardus's 'white waterfall' metaphor. It was down these steps that Walter Brearley used to bound on his way to the wicket, and leap the railings instead of bothering to open the gate. The story goes that Brearley once laid and won a bet that he would leave the pavilion, complete his innings and be back in the pavilion in the time it took the clock to strike twelve.

Old Trafford is another of the grounds where spectators are allowed on to the grass to circle the whitewashed boundary edge. In this way crowds of 38,000 can be accommodated and the full ground makes a particularly memorable sight from the pavilion balcony or the higher seats in the stands. In 1946 so many people wanted to see the second day's play of the Lancashire and Yorkshire match that the captains agreed to a shortening of the boundaries, and an inner ring was drawn for use during the remainder of the match.

Homes of Sport

William Clarke's Vision

TRENT BRIDGE is more than the headquarters of the Nottinghamshire county club. It is one of the stately homes of cricket. It is a ground with more than 100 years of history, with features so mingling the ancient and modern that much of the story of cricket itself can be traced there. Trent Bridge became a cricket ground through the shrewd enterprise of William Clarke, a cricketer by interest and by profession a bricklayer turned innkeeper who married the landlady of the Trent Bridge Inn. Old William Clarke saw a fine future for the field that lay behind the inn, and one of his hopes was for an indoor practice shed, but all his imagination could scarcely have drawn the picture of the ground as it stands today. He would not recognise the approach to the ground from the city of

Nottingham, for this Trent Bridge is a new Trent Bridge. He would not recognise his old home close by the south bank of the river, for this Trent Bridge Inn is a modern building, though still attached as closely as ever to cricketing interests. His field is changed, too, and the buildings round it, but it is in essence the same field and its usage, at least, has remained constant. There is more than a photograph in the pavilion to maintain the direct link between the Trent Bridge of today and the Trent Bridge known to William Clarke.

The present-day visitors can come in thousands and find seating accommodation — a good deal of it under cover. The biggest crowd to watch any day's play was the 30,000-odd of the 1948 Test match between England and Australia, though many of these had to sit on the grass round the boundary line. The ground is admirably adapted to this improvisation, for the whole playing area extends to about six acres which is more than any cricket match requires. The 17,000 seats are mostly above ground level in the various concrete and wooden stands that surround the turf. The older stands, the wooden ones, are low and somewhat shallow, but behind the bowler's arm opposite the pavilion, and to right and left of the pavilion are two-storey stands giving an excellent view of the play. The pavilion, facing northwards, looks down the wicket and has a stepped enclosure at ground level and a central balcony on the first floor. Essential additions have destroyed the symmetry of the building, for the President's rooms at one end do not balance the dressing-rooms at the other, but much more has been gained than lost by the alterations, and Nottinghamshire have good reason for pride in their pavilion amenities. The four dressing rooms are too small for any one of them to contain a whole team, so for convenience the old arrangement is still preserved whereby the lower rooms are divided between the home and visiting amateurs and the upper rooms are given to the home and visiting professionals. For touring teams or Test matches the sides share the pairs of rooms. All the rooms open on to covered balconies from which play can be watched in comfort and privacy. Players like the Trent Bridge arrangements because the dressing-rooms are easy of access from the field or the dining-room. There are times when a quick lunch and a long rest can be a blessing, and the Nottinghamshire custom of serving tea in the dressing-room has its advantages.

At the administrative end, where the front entrance door is almost exactly in line with the Test match wicket, there is a dining-room for the use of the President and committee and guests, and a smaller room, with glass doors opening on to a balcony, is also used by the President for receiving visitors and watching the play. Here is housed the Nottinghamshire library, one of the finest collections of cricket literature in the country.

For members there is a dining-room behind the pavilion and a snack bar and garden refreshment space with sun-shaded tables near the main entrance, where the gates record appreciation of the services of JA Dixon, county captain from 1889 to 1899.

These gates were formally opened in 1933 and the memorial inscription, composed by EV Lucas, reads:

These gates were designed and erected to honour the memory of John Auger Dixon, J.P. (1861-1931), a member of the Nottinghamshire County eleven from 1882 to 1905, Captain from 1889 to 1899, a Member of the Committee from 1895 until his death, the promoter of schemes for the improvement of this historic ground, and for many years a valued adviser at Lord's. Apart from cricket, at which he excelled as a batsman, as fieldsman, as bowler and as a vigilant commander, he was a sagacious man of affairs, a faithful citizen, a philanthropist, a wise magistrate and a true friend.

In the pavilion itself a Long Bar runs behind the Long Room, as at Lord's. The Trent Bridge Long Room has some of the features made famous at Lord's, with historic bats in show-cases and pictures of Nottinghamshire teams and individuals and important Trent Bridge occasions on the walls. Unlike Lord's, however, players do not have to pass through the Long Room on their way from dressing-room to field because the doors leading to the open are at the side instead of in the middle.

Almost in a line with square leg at this side of the ground is all that remains of an ancient elm which became known in the mid-nineteenth century as 'George Parr's tree', because of the frequency with which that enterprising batsman used to rattle its branches with his hits to leg. When George Parr died, in 1891, a branch of this elm made a wreath for his grave and another piece of wood from the tree has been shaped into a bat by the well-known manufacturers of sports equipment, Gunn and Moore, and now forms one of the items of interest in the pavilion Long Room. In the Long Room are bats once used by such tremendous Nottinghamshire characters as George Parr, Alfred Shaw, Richard Daft, Arthur Shrewsbury and William and George Gunn. Covering the three inner walls, the photographs, sketches and cartoons tell the Trent Bridge story almost from its beginning to the present day. The older pictures are mostly posed portraits which give a clear enough idea of the appearance of the men, but what a pity it is that action photography had not been developed to make comparison possible between the bowling styles of the early players and Larwood and Voce, Nottinghamshire immortals of our own times.

The club has so many pictorial treasures that they flow out of the Long Room into other rooms and the stairways. In the players' entrance there is a set of the famous 'Spy' cartoons, more animated than any photographs of their day.

Trent Bridge's latest building is a scoreboard, unmatched in this country, constructed on the Australian pattern. Electrically operated, this board gives complete details of the match as it progresses. One section lists the fielding side and indicates those who are bowling and those who have bowled, giving the current analyses. The fieldsman in action is identified by a light glowing against his name. Another section accounts for the batsmen dismissed and the fall of the wickets, and the running details of total and individual scores occupy the centre of the board. Inside the board operations are not as complicated as first glance might suggest. There are three storeys or platforms, each approached by steep ladder-stairways amid a maze of wires and pulleys, and the most convenient working is by three operators, though two could actually keep up a supply of vital information. The principal manual labour required is the making up of the names of the players on the two sides and fitting them into frames. When a wicket falls a frame has to be transferred and another substituted, but other information is presented at the pull of a lever, or the pressing of a button or the turning of a dial like that on an automatic telephone. Alertness and accuracy are demanded of the operators and, of course, they must be able to recognise the players without hesitation. This type of scoreboard is to be found on all the principal grounds in Australia, but Trent Bridge has been the innovator in this country and there can be no doubt of the approval of the cricketing public.

Most things at Trent Bridge are well done. Perhaps some things have been done too well. In recent years there has been great discussion on the quality of the wickets, and a state of such placidity has been attained that half the county matches tend to be written off as drawn before ever the captains toss for innings. Trent Bridge wickets have been notably good since the days when 'Fiddler' Walker* first used marl in their preparation, but these last few seasons have seen a serious change in character. The earlier good wickets had pace in them; the latest ones have had no attraction for any type of bowling – or batting either, for that matter – because all responsiveness has been extracted from the turf. Sometimes, in favourable climatic circumstances of a misty morning or heavy atmosphere, there is temporary encouragement for swing bowling but early greenness is invariably succeeded by even more than normal easement as the match progresses. With bowlers so handicapped it might be thought that batsmen would be contrastingly happy, yet they, for their part, find stroke-making restricted by the tendency of the ball to keep low. The light is rather as it is at Lord's: difficult against the

---

* *'Fiddler' Walker, the elder, was third in the line of succession among the great groundsmen who have tended Trent Bridge. His nickname had no significance in the modern debasement of the word, but arose from frequent attendance at the country dances where he played his fiddle. The first Walker was succeeded by his son, and the second Walker preceded the famous Walter Marshall.*

background of the pavilion, better at the other end unless the bowler tosses the ball above the top of the screen. After rain the pitch is seldom really awkward, for if the ball does not skid through it turns only very slowly and maintains an even height. Only the fieldsmen are really comfortable; they can rely on the good behaviour of the ball on the flawless turf, and run in and pick-up in absolute assurance, though, of course, pursuit is usually a formality in the fast outfield.

The characteristics of the wicket have given great concern to the Nottinghamshire authorities. They have found that the public simply will not pay to watch matches in which there is every likelihood of each side batting only once, and with the whole emphasis of the cricket on defensive batsmanship. They have found, too, that young bowlers are inevitably and quickly discouraged by lack of success in home matches, and consequently do not show the development expected of them. It is unthinkable that Nottinghamshire cricket should be centred anywhere other than Trent Bridge, therefore during 1951 drastic action was taken in an endeavour to produce more acceptable playing conditions. The most experienced groundsmen in England were called into consultation, and on their advice part of the square was dug up and re-laid for experimental cultivation. The results may take some time to become apparent, but they will be awaited with interest by cricketers the world over.

Homes of Sport

Worcester: Bradman's Paradise

IN fine weather the Worcester ground is on the bank of the River Severn. In very wet weather it is underneath the waters of the Severn which does not break its banks every year, but as often as not there is some flooding of the ground and allowance has been made for it in the construction of the permanent buildings. The pavilion is on stilts, for example, and though the story that the heavy roller has to be anchored is doubtless kept for likely buyers, it is true that Worcestershire players have swum from the pavilion steps to the middle of the field. The flooding does harm, of course, in creating damp and litter, but it also does good in renewing life in the turf, and the river can claim some credit for the enviable reputation of the playing area.

The way to the ground from the main street of the town is an easy walk downhill through narrow ways to the bridge across the river. Immediately over the bridge on the New Road which leads to the Malverns are the turnstile entrances to the cricket ground. The first impression after entrance is not inspiring, for the little embankment near the turnstiles is rough and tends to be dusty in dry weather. An undistinguished wooden hut to house the Press and scorecard printers is on the left, with a grounds-man's hut behind. To the right the pathway leads to a wooden stand which backs on to the boundary fence. Wooden benches ring the field as a foreground, and on the far side of the playing area is terracing with open country behind. This is not the view to catch the artist's imagination. For that to be obtained it is necessary to pass along the front of the open wooden stand and enter the members' enclosure. This includes the secretarial offices and the pavilion, both buildings with the floors raised above ground level as a precaution for flood-time. Marks on the door-posts record the various heights achieved by the water. The pavilion itself is an attractive single-storey building with a refreshment bar as the main room at the front and a players' dining-room in the rear. The dressing-rooms, which are of comfortable size, are on either side of the main room and look out over the enclosure on to the field.

It is from the pavilion steps or the seats of the enclosure that the pictures are taken. The foreground is the circular field with the wickets pitched almost at right angles to the line of vision. On the opposite boundary edge is the scorer's box and one of the two scoreboards. Behind are the trees near the bank of the invisible river, and beyond, like the backcloth to a stage scene, rises the glorious cathedral of Worcester, built of a brownish stone that looks fresh and clean for all its years, and towering upon an escarpment dominating the river valley. Cricket field, trees and the cathedral make up the most familiar of all the Worcester views.

From other angles the beauty of the Worcester ground is very much a matter of opinion. To the south, along the river bank, and to the west the environs are open fields, some used as school sports grounds, some as pasture land. Refreshment huts are strategically placed round the ground to add to its amenities if not its decoration, and at the south end space is provided for car parking. Most of the public seating is of the bench type, and uncovered, though for the matches against such opponents as the Australians temporary stands are put up, with protective awning for the more favoured. Worcester cannot accommodate large crowds and is rather uncomfortable with them when they do swarm through the gates. It is at its best on the more normal occasions when there is room for the spectator to move round and watch the play from various points, enjoying the sunshine and, of course, the cathedral view.

Playing conditions are decidedly attractive. The wicket is usually easy-paced and much to the liking of batsmen. Bradman played on it four times and the only occasion he did not score a double century was in 1948, when he 'threw away his hand', as Australians say, for 107. Occasionally there is 'greenness' in the first hour or two, and cases have been known of crumbling in the later stages, but the general experience is of improvement with the progress of the match. The spin-bowlers wait for rain, and the reputations of such players as Howorth, Jackson and Jenkins indicate that the waiting is not without purpose and reward.

Both for batting and fielding the light is excellent. There is a high wooden fence at the New Road end, and there are some trees along the roadway itself, but these seem to cause little inconvenience, and at the south end, the neighbouring meadows make a perfect background. In dry weather the outfield is notably fast, but also notably smooth for the encouragement of ground-fielding, and the playing area is not too big to cause batsmen to abandon all hope of hitting straight sixes. No further tribute to the quality of the outfield is needed than to say that when the cricketers are not in occupation members come out to play bowls. Because of its lack of covered accommodation Worcester must be classed among the fine-weather grounds, and it is perhaps a pity that teams from overseas know it only in late April or early May when cold and damp often reduce its attractions. In the best of the summer a day at Worcester can be a delightful experience, with a lunch-carton bought from one of the stalls, the pavilion-enclosure brightened by flower baskets and a general air of rurality so readily accessible from urban amenities.

Homes of Sport

The Oval: Home of Hobbs

PERHAPS the first point to be noted about the Oval is that the playing area is no more than an approximation to an oval. The name – one of the most famous names among all the homes of cricket – is more applicable to the whole of the ground within the boundary wall, which does circumscribe an oval broken by an irregularity forming the main entrance. The Oval is in the Kennington district of south-east London; unfashionable, unlovely and industrial. It is an oasis in a wilderness of harsh streets and utilitarian buildings, very much an urban playground. Its essential character is of bricks and mortar, and dust and noise. It is a part of London's busyness and bustle rather than a relief from these things. It is not a ground for the reflective hour or the stroll round the boundary edge during the course of a match.

Yet most cricketers, batsmen especially, would as soon play at the Oval as anywhere in the world. They are prepared to accept its romantic deficiencies in exchange for its practical amenities. Players are well cared for in the creature comforts of cricket at the Oval, and if they need inspiration from environment they can recollect in the Oval story some of the greatest chapters in the history of the game. The Oval has known first-class cricket since 1845; the first Test match was played there in 1880 (the first Test match in England, that is); from England's defeat at the Oval in 1882 arose the Ashes, there, in 1938, were made the highest Test match total and the highest individual Test match score; at the Oval Hobbs and Bradman, the greatest batsmen of their day, made their final Test match bow. Nowhere on earth is there more stirring cricket tradition than at the Oval.

The sense of history, then, is strong enough and tradition is powerful, but at heart the Oval still remains a Cockney playground. Its adherents may properly sit in shirtsleeves and braces, and express opinions with all the noise and wit at their command. On some grounds barracking seems out of place (however much it may be justified), but the Oval atmosphere condones, and almost commands, it. The best way to the Oval is the plebeian way, by Tube or bus or tram, and the domination of the ground is not by tree or pavilion or grandstand but by gas-holders, more commonly miscalled gasometers. The Oval gasometers are as famous in cricket scenery as the Worcester Cathedral or the Canterbury tree or even Father Time himself at Lord's.

Trams and buses chattering by are a part of the Oval background, and with a sympathetic driver providing a mobile grandstand for a moment or two and a glimpse of the score for the particularly keen-eyed. Very occasionally the trams and buses come into direct contact with the cricket, though only the biggest of hitters making the biggest of leg-hits are likely to cause any consternation in the passing traffic. The Oval is big enough to contain the vast majority of sixes, and, indeed, it is so spacious that there are probably more fives than sixes in a season. 30,000 people can watch cricket inside the Oval and an incalculable number also watch from outside, because huge buildings, mostly blocks of flats, tower above the guardian walls to east and west. Acknowledgment of cricketing debt is delicately made in the naming of the houses after famous players. The main entrance to the ground, at the southern end, facing Harleyford Street, also has a tribute to a cricketer – to the greatest of all Surrey cricketers and the biggest individual attraction among all regular players at the Oval. Here are the wrought-iron Hobbs gates, erected 'In honour of a great Surrey and England cricketer'.

The Hobbs gates open to admit motor-cars in very limited numbers – but not pedestrians, who must pass survey at adjacent turnstiles, and they lead to an asphalted area that is a rare gathering-ground for London dust as well as for cricketing acquaintances. It is also a notable sun-trap with the afternoon heat and glare reflected from the walls of the back of the pavilion and the east stand. For this discomfort the remedy is at hand; immediately to the left of the entrance is a refreshment bar, which forms part of the building containing ground staff quarters and a public dining-room.

Almost the whole of the southern end of the ground is occupied by the pavilion and the adjoining stands to east and west of it. The east stand, partly roofed, contains the Press rooms and some private boxes at the disposal of Surrey officials. To the west of the pavilion is the stand reserved for lady members and friends. Immediately opposite the pavilion is the Vauxhall stand, offering the only covered accommodation at the northern end. The east and west sides, the long sides of the oval, have terracing, renewed since the devastation of the war years, for the general public, with scoreboards in the north-east and south-west. In the 'popular' parts the accommodation can scarcely be counted luxurious, but it does offer a good view of the play and one rather less remote than from the higher-priced seating. The gasometers, one very large and two smaller, are away to the east behind the 'Cricketers' Arms', which opens its hospitable doors where Clayton Street runs into Kennington Oval.

The pavilion itself is perhaps more impressive from the outside than from within, because the rooms overlooking the field of play, and therefore facing north, are inclined to be rather dark and consequently seem to lack spaciousness. The general design of the building is conventional, with a Long Room occupying the central position on the ground floor, and a refreshment bar behind. Fronting the pavilion an enclosure slopes down to railings bounding the playing area. The first floor has a small balcony for spectators but is mainly given over to accommodation for the players. There are three principal dressing-rooms, one used in the normal way by the Surrey professionals, one by the Surrey amateurs and the third by the visiting team. For Test matches the teams use the Visitors' and the Amateurs' rooms, and the professionals' room is reserved for ex-international players who wish to foregather there. All these rooms have excellent balconies for watching the play, and from which valedictory speeches have many times been made at the close of a Test match series. For the further convenience of the players, bathrooms and showers are handy, and the players' dining-room is close to the dressing-rooms for privacy and the saving of time in the precious intervals.

There was a time when intervals of rest were precious indeed at the Oval. It had the reputation of being one of the most wearying grounds in the world. Not only was the playing area among the biggest in England, but the turf was particularly hard on the feet. The area remains the same, but the character of the turf has changed in the last few years, probably because of increased use of the spiked roller. The Oval looks greener now than it has done for a generation, and it is undoubtedly a good deal easier to walk on.

Changes in the nature of the outfield have been accompanied by changes in the wicket. Before the Second World War the Oval wicket was built for batsmen. The ambition of its famous groundsmen, Sam Apted and 'Bosser' Martin, was to prepare a pitch that would outlast any match scheduled to be played upon it. In 1938 ambition was wholly satisfied. One batsman played an innings lasting two and a half days; one side declared its innings closed at 903 for 7 wickets; and when the match was over only the footholds told of its course. This was, of course, an exceptional illustration of a general tendency. In that historic Test match the Oval caricatured itself. In more normal circumstances the wicket was everything the batsman could reasonably desire, and its qualities of endurance were known the world over. Yet bowlers – fast bowlers, anyway – did not dislike playing on it. There was pace in the turf, and some liveliness, and when the air had a trace of dampness first thing in the morning and in the late evening the ball could be made to swing. Bill Bowes could and did take wickets at the Oval, and Surrey teams contained some of the great fast bowlers in all generations.

Hitler's war wrought more changes upon the Oval than upon

any other first-class cricket ground. Most grounds suffered enforced neglect, many were used for military purposes and a few suffered direct damage. Everything happened to the Oval; cricket ceased to be played there before the end of the 1939 season, the ground was equipped as a prisoner-of-war camp (though never actually used in that capacity) and direct hits were recorded by high-explosive and incendiary bombs. By 1945 it looked as though the Oval would never be a cricket ground again. A photograph in Mr. Louis Palgrave's book *The Story of the Oval*, shows barbed-wire barricades across the playing area, and the outfield contained inset concrete bases for huts and searchlights and guns. Grass had grown long and coarse, and weeds were everywhere.

Yet in the face of this appalling prospect the Oval was prepared for cricket in one winter. HC Lock, a former Surrey player, who succeeded Martin as head-groundsman, supervised the colossal task which involved the clearing and levelling and re-turfing of practically the whole field. In addition to the work on the playing area the west wall and terracing had to be rebuilt, and most of the stands and seating were in urgent need of some repair. Though the new Oval bears, in its essentials, a close resemblance to the old, it is in fact a much-changed home of cricket. Playing characteristics have altered as much as any other feature. Oval wickets are not now full of comfortable centuries, with an occasional hour's excitement for a fast bowler. It is now unusual to find an Oval wicket with pace in it and swing bowlers have to wait for a morning or evening of heavy atmosphere. A 'green' wicket is a rarity. There is, on the other hand, much more encouragement for spin bowling. The ball is inclined to turn from the beginning of a match, though this does not mean that there is no hope for batsmen or that bowlers have no need of skill. It means that cricket matches are better balanced.

After rain the Oval wicket can be decidedly vicious. The ball not only turns but lifts as well, and both spin bowlers and fast bowlers can prove highly disconcerting. Batting requires nerve as well as technical skill. Under the present arrangements batsmen always have one awkward factor to consider, even in the best of conditions. It is always difficult for them to sight the ball. At one end the background is the dark pavilion. At the other the sightscreen has been removed to provide more room for spectators, and the ball now comes out of the crowd or the buildings surrounding the ground. Misjudgment of flight is easy enough for any batsman at any stage of an innings. For fieldsmen, too, the light is difficult. Long field catches tend to be lost in the buildings, and close-in fielding faces similar problems to those of the batsmen. One way or another, in fact, it is easier to be a faultless player from the ring-side than in the middle. That, however, is a commonplace characteristic; in the historic words of Maurice Leyland: 'All the best players are watching'.

For all its difficulties, Surrey and England will continue to hold the Oval in affection. It is one of the world's great cricket grounds, clothed in historic associations and claiming a high place in cricket's story. As the Prince of Wales' feathers represent the Surrey badge, so 'I serve' can fairly be taken as the motto of the Oval. Only briefly do Surrey desert it in their home programme. Two games are played each year at Guildford, one a championship match and one against a University. When Surrey are 'at home', they are at Kennington Oval.

Homes of Sport

Scarborough: Cricket on Holiday

CRICKET has the infinite variety that age cannot wither nor custom stale. It can range from the solemn ritual of a Test match, with half the world aware of it, to a back-street game against a lamp post with nobody concerned at all except the players and perhaps a hard-hearted policeman. In between these are as many grades of cricket as there are of social standing in an Eastern civilisation. Festival cricket, as Scarborough knows it, is first-class cricket on holiday. It is an occasion, for the most part, of artificial enmities. Sleep is lost and 'Enterprises of great pith and moment' are put aside when Lancashire play Yorkshire, or Middlesex meet Surrey, but nobody's breakfast is really the worse because the Gentlemen are in danger of defeat by the Players, or Lord Londesborough's XI have lost cheap wickets against the 'Outgoing MCC'.

It does not matter greatly who wins a Festival match; it is much more important that somebody should win, and by the smallest possible margin at the closest call of time. The principles of Festival cricket do not abominate the draw, for the drawn match not definitely drawn until the final over is as good cricket as any, and half the glories in history are of rear-guard actions stubbornly fought, and attempts to save the seeming hopeless cause. The assertion of SMJ Woods that 'draws are of no use except for bathing' was never wholly justifiable. Neither in Festival cricket nor in any other kind of cricket can there be forgiveness for deliberate acceptance of defeat, but in Festival cricket at least there is grace in risking defeat to provide a stirring finish. Who wants the half-loaf of a first innings lead at a feast where the whole fruits of victory are shared by victors and vanquished alike? Festival cricketers, then, try to bring their matches to a climax and to leave them there, sending us home far too excited to regret any repercussions over being late for tea. This is a consummation not easily to be contrived. The thrilling finish of Friday afternoon may well have had its beginnings on Thursday morning when a problem of declaration had to be solved. With a championship in prospect a captain wants to win as quickly and as comprehensively as possible; in a Festival the victory should be as narrow and as long delayed as the cricket decencies permit. This is not to say that a match should be prolonged merely for the sake of passing time. When it has outlived its usefulness (which is to give pleasure to those who play and those who watch) let it be dispatched with all speed to leave us free for the sea-shore or the swimming pool. Even a Roman holiday would have been poorly served by indifferent batsmen making meaningless fifties against music-hall bowling. The element of earnestness must at all costs be preserved. Perhaps an advantageous follow-on was not enforced on the second day, but the batting must be undertaken with the object of a third day victory. A Festival captain cannot afford to take no thought for the morrow.

Cricket, of course, cannot always be thus carefully contrived. A bowler may excel himself and upset all the calculations; batsmen may get themselves out for the most unexpected reasons, and so a match may hasten to its end for half a hundred unpremeditated causes. It must go. Better the loss of an afternoon's 'gate' than the loss of a reputation for genuine cricket. To take off a bowler who is running through a side, to make deliberate errors in the field or pile unnecessary runs on to a total is to do little service to cricket called first-class, and counted so in the records of the game. It goes against the grain, too, for Festivals to serve primarily the purpose of completing individual achievements. There is every congratulation awaiting the batsman who makes his thousandth run during an innings of value to his side; nothing to be said for altering the course of a match to complete a personal record. An honour to the bowler who achieves ambition against honest enmity, none to the misapprehension that risks a result to guarantee a particular wicket or two. Festival cricket may be an exhibition, but heaven (and the critics) preserve it from exhibitionism.

Festival teams are not always the cohesive units, of, say, the county championship. CI Thornton's XI comes together once a year, and in this type of match there is the advantage of novelty. There is attraction in the sight of normal colleagues for once in opposition, or traditional opponents temporarily in partnership. What a roar of delight goes up when a bowler dismisses his county captain, and what an opportunity for conversational cut and thrust in the middle and in the dressing room. A three-day loyalty is the very least to be asked of all players. How happy, then, the Festival commanding more permanent units. The presence of a touring side, for example, practically guarantees the success of any Festival, and the more the spirit of competition can be introduced the better for all concerned. Dominion sides have, indeed, been known to protest that their Festival experiences are like a supplementary series of Test matches; that so far from being on holiday at the end of a strenuous tour they find themselves up against strong opponents whose very evident intention is victory. This I take to be a compliment to the Festivals; and the tourists, too, might note the compliment by implication: we so respect their abilities that we count them very much worth beating.

Festival matches should be worth winning, providing the victories be cheerfully sought. Festivals are a freeing of the spirit, a casting of work-a-day shackles: Hearnes hit sixes and Meads steals short runs after tea. Yet characters are preserved and the violence done is physical as distinct from psychological. Hearne's sixes would be off-drives and hit politely. A man cannot deny himself even on holiday. Festival cricket, then, is cricket played wholeheartedly but lightheartedly; with ambition, but without recrimination or the fear of it; for its intrinsic purpose but with an awareness of obligation towards those who pay to see. The player untrue to himself and his talents would be no Festival cricketer – indeed, no cricketer at all. The man primarily concerned with his own figures should have no figures for concern. When a player engages himself to take part in Festival cricket he contracts to provide the best within him in the best of spirit. So playing he will have the best of good times.

The Scarborough Cricket Festival

WHEREVER a pilgrimage through the cricketer's England may begin it must surely end, if the traveller have any sense of the appropriate, at Scarborough in Festival time. There are gathered together for ten days in September all who matter in the cricketing world. Today's players come for one last battle together before bats and pads are packed mournfully away for the winter; yesterday's players come to sit in the summer's last sunshine and talk over achievements long since written in history: tomorrow's players come to feed the flame of hero-worship and to cajole inspiration and autographs in the most cheerful cricketing feast of the year. During the Festival Scarborough gives itself over completely to cricket and cricketers. Not to be concerned with cricket in the first days of September is to be an outcast in Scarborough, a stranger in a strange land without reason or justification for existence. There are cricket dances, cricket banquets, cricket celebrations of every possible kind, cricket is first and last in the mind of every public entertainer.

Scarborough Cricket Festival has tradition behind it and would persist now from its own momentum; its patrons are its chief advertisement, for they come year after year to meet each other and to tell the same stories. Yet Scarborough made the Cricket Festival, not the Cricket Festival Scarborough, for the town has attractions outside cricket and unconnected with it. It is no upstart of public fancy, no tinsel town of purely summer satisfaction. Scarborough has life of its own and has had from the days when Norman William came so devastatingly into the North Country. High upon the cliff that separates the bays stands Scarborough's castle, built in Norman times upon the site of an earlier fortification. Today those who climb the steep pathway can find little more than a ruined keep, torn and desolate through long disuse and the ravages of a thousand storms. Within the remnants of the great fireplace birds find sanctuary, and only the narrow windows and walls of enormous thickness tell the tale of the strength and dignity of what was once an important military house. There are many medieval castles in a better state of preservation than that at Scarborough, but few can have more striking setting or be regarded with such affection by those who look upon the sight of it as a sign of a pleasure consummated.

From the castle hill you look north and south to the two lovely bays that make up the town. North, the foreground gives you hotels and boarding houses with the cliff falling swiftly to a crowded bathing beach backed by Peasholm Park and a notable open-air theatre, with the coastline beyond running a scarred way to Scalby and Whitby. South, the bay is wider and smooth, and nestling beneath the protective castle hill is the busy harbour whence come and go the trawlers that seek a dangerous living in a sea of notoriously uncertain temper. Beyond the harbour and the foreshore lies the resort of fashion, the playground of the idle. The Spa has genuine curative waters and to them owes its origin, but the Spa is now the centre of Scarborough's holiday life and the waters are no more than a curiosity. On the Spa there is good music and dance music (these in enumeration rather than in any spirit of comparison) throughout the day; it has pleasant walks upon the cliff-side, a concert hall and theatre, is in fact, a little world of its own. In the morning it is favoured, in the afternoon it is busy, in the evening it has no rival.

Above the Spa, beyond the hotels that look across the sea from South Cliff top, you come to Oliver's Mount, whence, so legend would have us believe, Cromwell once made assault upon the castle. To climb Oliver's Mount on foot is half a day's journey, for the path is winding and steep, but even that toil is amply repaid in the end, for from where Scarborough has built memorial to her fallen you may find as exquisite a view as imagination can conjure. The War Memorial has become a landmark to the traveller; from the inland road long before the smell of the sea has reached you the memorial comes into view, and instinctively your pace increases with journey's end at hand. The first glimpse of Oliver's Mount is both a spur and a sedative, for Scarborough calls urgently and at the same time announces welcome proximity.

Once visited, Scarborough takes hold of you inexorably; one visit leads to another, until the succession has turned to ritual and the spell is laid never to be broken. Always you leave Scarborough with something still to be seen or done; always you return to rejoice in familiar sights and repeat fond achievements. Scarborough is always new yet never changes. The daily business insists upon constant variety, yet the years have brought a stable mellowness. You see the trawlers unload as you have seen them unload hundreds of times before, yet there is novelty in this particular catch; you go to see (and hear) the Scottish herring girls in their annual visit, and note what you missed before. As evening comes you stroll towards the Spa and find the familiar outlines of the castle tinged with new light, clothed in yet another atmosphere. Scarborough, as much as any town in the world, has personality, and it is that personality which brings you again and again to her lovely and precious scenes.

In Search of Cricket

Chapter Five:
THE LONE STAR STATE

YORKSHIRE is the Lone Star State of cricket and Yorkshiremen, like Texans, are all invested with a composite character universally recognized at a level of caricature. It is a character partly self-created, partly imposed and now established by both anticipation and cultivation.

Yorkshire cricket is accorded by the cricketing world in general a quality of its own. The reputation, being of practical benefit, is welcomed by Yorkshiremen, who have come to emphasise and guard it, even to an extent of accepting some of the less desirable by-products. Yorkshire cricket is supposed to be played the 'hard way', with competitive success a primary concern. It is seen as the cricket of championships and leagues, of determined batting and painstaking bowling; as cricket of serious men and an unsympathetic, not to say contemptuous, view of failure and misfortune. Summary is traditionally expressed in the observation 'We don't play cricket for fun', variously attributed to Wilfred Rhodes and Leonard Hutton.

This soft impeachment is acceptable to Yorkshiremen on an

agreeable definition of 'fun'. Yorkshiremen do not find their cricketing fun in a purposeless pastime, in idle occupation with hit or miss experiment involving no consequence. They do find 'fun' in the struggles of cricket, the endeavour towards successful batting and bowling techniques, the outwitting of opponents, the satisfaction of ability displayed and potential realised. The worst failing a Yorkshire cricketer can show, to Yorkshiremen, is the slap-happy, thoughtless attitude. The fun of the game comes from solving its problems, from treating it with respect as a worthwhile undertaking and, of course, from winning. By repute Yorkshire cricket lays too much emphasis on winning. The Yorkshire retort would be 'Are both sides not trying to win then? Was the contest not arranged on an intention to determine who would win?' There is right and wrong in both arguments. No team, no individual, can lay too much emphasis on winning as a desirable and fundamental objective, provided endeavour remains within the legal and moral framework of play. Teams and individuals would be uncomplimentary to opponents, to spectators and to self-responsibility were they competitors without trying to win. The Olympic claim that it is more important to take part than to win needs extension; the greater importance is to take part in an endeavour to win by acceptable means.

In the Yorkshire philosophy of sport it is impossible to be too keen on winning a competitive engagement. The desire to win is a virtue unalloyed, but some practices arising from the virtue can tarnish it. Cheating is an obvious example. Manipulation of the rules and customs to an opponent's disadvantage is another. Instigation and cultivation of a disagreeable atmosphere comes within a grey area of tactical behaviour.

Most of us, I suspect, have stepped into the grey area at some time or other in our sporting behaviour; have sought an advantage by unwarrantable appeal, by wasting time, by a practice honed if not sharp. In the ultimate assessment I presume we shall all seek mercy rather than justice.

The Yorkshire reputation for playing 'hard' cricket is not acceptable to Yorkshiremen as an accusation of approving the grey area. WG Grace was not a Yorkshireman, but he had his little ways. DR Jardine was not a Yorkshireman, nor was 'Bodyline' bowling a Yorkshire conception. It was not a Yorkshire bowler who shouldered a running batsman to the ground in a Lord's Test match. Yorkshire cricket has received public rebuke for misconduct on the field and in the dressing room, but Yorkshire cricket authority has invariably acknowledged error and sought correction.

The Yorkshire hardness, attributed and cultivated, is a defensive quality expressed in the form of aggressiveness. It is resistance to challenge, unwillingness to bend the knee or doff the cap. It is the cricketing representation of independence. Reflection extends beyond cricket to the mill where the owner anticipates being addressed as 'Fred' and where the traveller is given an egalitarian 'luv' with request for the fare. The spirit of independence is, of course, two-sided. 'Fred' is expected to know faulty workmanship when he sees it and to say so in forthright manner. Weak or vacillating management wins no approval. Yorkshire's hardness in cricket stems from self-criticism. The weakest periods of county performance have been those in which players were most easily satisfied with themselves, the strongest those in which the ultimate possibilities of achievement were seen and sought. The directive and cohesive influence exerted by Lord Hawke forged strength into a team that became more than its sum of individual talent. The leadership of professional expertise established by Rhodes and Emmott Robinson brought business-like efficiency. Sellers and his players constructed a close community of ideals and interests. The successes of the 1960s sprang from shrewd observation and cricket thinking by Close and Illingworth.

In its development stage, and at its peaks of achievement, this Yorkshire hardness was admired throughout the cricket world. It lost favour when it blemished the character by being an end in itself. Lord Hawke was seen as putting Yorkshire interests and his own above all other. Efficiency in the 1920s was seen as grim-visaged and short-tempered in any frustration. The self-discipline of the Sellers era avoided criticism perhaps because it had not become oppressive when cricket was interrupted. Close fell from favour because he defended his purposes against unacceptable means of attainment.

That Yorkshire cricket should create a character for itself, or have one imposed, presupposes attention being paid made all the more evident by a close contact in work and play. If you dropped a vital catch or failed with the bat at a critical moment you were likely to be reminded of your shortcomings through the next week's working hours. Equally manifest, however rough the expressions, was prestige accorded to success.

From this foundation grew personal resolve to improvement and collective desire for competitive success; grew the hard fibre in play and the league organisation. Casual cricket was to be deprecated because it did not meet life's philosophy.

Again, the development can be advanced only as a broad

consideration. Yorkshire cricket extended beyond the industrial areas; some cricket in Yorkshire was inconsequential; not all Yorkshiremen were prepared to work hard at their recreation and not all determined cricketers have been Yorkshiremen. The composite character attributed to Yorkshire cricket derived from geographical as well as human factors. Yorkshire is a northern county and the soft, turning pitch is a commonplace – or was before the days of compulsory covering. Spin bowling was rewarded, if spin bowling was accurate; defensive batting skills had to be learned if long innings were to be played. In such conditions bowlers and batsmen taught themselves to wait, to persevere and to concentrate. The decisive point of a match could occur in an hour, in an over, and the successful side or individual was the one ready to grasp and hold the fleeting opportunity.

That is the essence of the hardness characterising Yorkshire cricket in its minor and major presentation. At its best it is illustrated in determination to redeem apparently lost causes, to face difficulties with unflinching resolution, to acknowledge defeat only when the last ball has been bowled. At its worst it becomes an attitude of arrogance, a bunkered view and an irritable reaction. In the one form of expression Yorkshire cricket has won the respect and admiration of the cricketing world; in the other it has incurred dislike.

All the great Yorkshire cricket has displayed the common element in its heritage, but individual exploitation has been as widely different as the personal characters involved. The same theme has produced infinite variations. Far back in history George Anderson's Yorkshire independence was recognised in his reputation as a trusty batsman in time of trouble and as a man of principle in his forthright stand against apparent

THE LONE STAR STATE

injustice. 'Happy Jack' Ulyett was a Yorkshireman in hitting fifty adventurous runs against Australia after his captain had bidden him take care. 'I rather felt like hitting them, my Lord,' was his subsequent self-justification. George Hirst crystallised the Yorkshire hardness in his declaration 'It's thee or me for it', as he took bat or ball in hand. His friendly smile neither obscured nor diminished the challenge. Wilfred Rhodes was always uncompromisingly an opponent, even in net practice. Roy Kilner could murmur 'I'll never learn' when he was caught in slips or covers after waving a speculative bat, but he turned pale and sick in nervous exhaustion after particularly exacting bowling occasions. Herbert Sutcliffe's authority lay in the self-confidence that permitted no consideration of failure. 'I love a dogfight,' he confessed. Australian bowlers appreciated the Yorkshire characteristic in Maurice Leyland, that most placid and contented of cricketers who determined with rare precision the difference between a Test match and a Festival.

Hutton illustrated the Yorkshire hardness in his ceaseless self-examination. 'It's nice batting, when you've made 100' was his concession to himself. Trueman's flamboyance and garrulity disappeared when he brought concentration and his magnificent skills together in his hours of glory. Wardle and Close and Boycott gave offence only because they presented the 'unacceptable faces' of their native zeal.

Yorkshire cricketers have come in all shapes and sizes. They have been grim and gay, dashing and dour, calm and excitable, strong and weak. Their batting has ranged from the speculations of David Denton to the immobilities of Louis Hall. An Oldroyd and a Leyland could bring their contrasting methods into the same team and both be counted typical and unmistakably Yorkshire. The imperturbability of a Sutcliffe was carved from the same millstone grit as the passion of a Macaulay. There is no end to the individuality of Yorkshiremen playing cricket. They reflect themselves in all their variety of skills, moods and temperament, but together they have a common end, born of circumstances and accumulated tradition, that is their hallmark. The belief that England cricket is strong when Yorkshire cricket is strong does not imply that England teams need seven or eight Yorkshire players, but that there are Yorkshire players good enough as individuals to be chosen for England and who will bring to the national team a valuable quality of approach that is characteristic of Yorkshire cricket.

Yorkshire cricket supporters are reputedly myopic and parochial – with a reservation that they are prepared to disadvantage each other. One Yorkshireman, of passionate county loyalty, once observed to another, in praise of Yorkshire rather than in deprecation of a great 'foreigner': 'Hobbs couldn't make runs against Yorkshire'. Provocatively, the second conversationalist, who had been brought up on *Wisden*, murmured: 'I wish I had £1 for every century Hobbs took from Yorkshire bowling'.

'You can have more than that,' came the sharp retort. 'I'll give you £10 for every Hobbs century if you give me £1 for every time he played against Yorkshire without making a century'.

The offer was accepted, though on an understanding that no money would change hands because the acceptor knew he could not lose. Education through argument was reward enough. Corresponding licence to correct is assumed by Yorkshire supporters in their relation to Yorkshire play. They are harsh taskmasters. Let Yorkshire fall from the grace of expected supremacy and internal complaint is registered in manner ranging from annual meeting protest to a slow shake of the head and a bewildered 'Nay, it won't do'.

'It won't do' for Yorkshire supporters, of whom more than 10,000 are county club members, when Yorkshire cricket is not manifestly a powerful force in the land. Promise unfulfilled 'won't do'; a diet of hope continually deferred causes intolerance. Protest is the immediate reaction to the cardinal sin of ineffective cricket. Players in a weak Yorkshire side have found more comfort in away matches than in appearance on home grounds. Comment of complaint remains in years of glory, but there is forgiveness in it; the dropped catch, the batsman's mistiming, are condemned as a failure, but explained as an accident. The strong Yorkshires could afford occasional misfortune.

The weak Yorkshires are viewed with a sense of frustration and deprivation, like an ailing business. Workers are not working and management is not managing properly. 'Nay, it won't do,' applies to a whole concern as much as to an individual. Yorkshire spectators have, or had, the reputation of being more knowledgeable than most in cricket, but the impression probably derives more from environmental influence than from any possession of native wisdom. The truth may be that if Yorkshire crowds did not concentrate on the cricket there would be little else of attraction on their home grounds. Tea and social gossip in the marquee or on the lawns are not features of cricket in Bradford and Leeds. Nobody basked through an idle hour in the shade of a tree at the late and lamented Bramall Lane. It is true that the bars are open all day, but Lord's not Leeds has a famous Tavern; it is true that wool is bought and sold at Park Avenue as well as on the Bradford Exchange; it is true that knitting needles have played obbligato to centuries by Hutton and Boycott; but by enormous majority Yorkshire cricket attendances are for the delights and rigours of the cricket itself and by watching and listening and assuming and believing an education is absorbed.

I doubt if Yorkshire crowds can rightly claim any superiority in appreciation of cricket's more advanced technology and tactics. As many naïve and ill-informed observations on play and players are to be heard in Yorkshire as in other places, but I think the comment, wise or foolish, tends to be more heartfelt. Yorkshire cricket has a strong sense of family association. Playing successes and failures are taken home to influence the domestic atmosphere. A cricket topic is virtual guarantee of appearance among 'Letters to the Editor' in Yorkshire newspapers. Yorkshire shortcomings or dissensions are regarded by Yorkshiremen as a concern for internal consumption only, and outside comment tends to provoke a closing of ranks on a principle of 'my county, right or wrong'.

By this interpretation Wardle could be condemned for disturbing Yorkshire cricket but raise sympathy on his omission from an MCC tour; Close could be acknowledged in error as a Yorkshire captain but still supported as an England leader and Trueman's bumpers for Yorkshire could be given an approval not accorded all bumpers – especially those delivered against Yorkshire. Young players are granted a credit of goodwill on the assumption that without some merit they would not be playing at all. Early inadequacies may be tolerated, but debit entries are soon made against the account. Promise must turn to performance measurable in runs or

Len Hutton 'carried factual achievement beyond the acceptable limits of romance'. He waves from the balcony at The Oval after England have regained the Ashes against Australia in 1953.

Headingley in its finery. Above, the ground is filling up with spectators in flat caps or wide-brimmed hats to protect them from the sun and below, in 1935, with a view of its new grandstand.

'The crowd within and the crowd without' was the title of Jack Hickes' camera work in 1948. Through the sheer force of numbers, pressing to get into Headingley for the 1948 Test, Hickes conveyed the appeal of watching Donald Bradman bat on his last tour of England.

Two of the landmarks of Jim Kilburn's cricket life. Above, Scarborough was one of his favourite cricket grounds. 'Once visited,' he wrote 'Scarborough takes hold of you inexorably; one visit leads to another, until the succession has turned to ritual and the spell is laid never to be broken'. Below, Bramall Lane, viewed from the embankment at the Football End, where he was taken as a baby to watch his father play in 1909. 'I have never been appalled, mystified, enchanted or amused, as others have been, by the sight of cricket in a Bramall Lane setting,' he said.

Standing: HW Dalton (Massuer), MC Cowdrey, JH Wardle, JB Statham, TW Graveney, R Appleyard, DCS Compton, JV Wilson, JMcConnon, FH Tyson, PJ Loader, KV Andrew, C Duckworth (Scorer and Baggage Master).

Seated: RT Simpson, TG Evans, PBH May (Vice-Captain), L Hutton (Captain), CG Howard (Manager), AV Bedser, WJ Edrich, TE Bailey.

Above: Jim Kilburn went on two tours to Australia. This card was sent as part of a Christmas greeting from his second trip.

Opposite: As well as covering the Tests, Jim Kilburn was encouraged by the Yorkshire Post to send it dispatches about the Australian way of life. Above, beside Brian Sellers, left, and Bill Bowes, he poses for a typical tourist photograph which was rather incongruously run alongside the announcement of the Test team. Below, the cricket writers could field a decent side of their own – including, of course, Bowes. Kilburn is second from the right on the front row.

GIBB OUT OF TEST TEAM

England Select from 13

From J. M. KILBURN

Our Special Correspondent with the Touring Team

SYDNEY, Thursday

THE England team to oppose Australia in the second Test match beginning here to-morrow will be chosen from the following 13 players, it was announced here this morning:—

W. R. Hammond (Glos.), capt.,
L. Hutton (Yorks.),
C. Washbrook (Lancs.),
W. J. Edrich (Middlesex),
L. D. Compton (Middlesex),
J. Hardstaff (Notts.),
J. T. Ikin (Lancs.),
N. W. D. Yardley (Yorks.),
D. V. P. Wright (Kent),
Peter Smith (Essex),
A. V. Bedser (Surrey),
W. Voce (Notts.),

Cricketers and Teddy Bears

A. B. Sellers (left), the Yorkshire captain, who is describing the Test matches for "The Yorkshire Evening Post," J. M. Kilburn (centre), "Yorkshire Post" correspondent with the Touring team, and W. E. Bowes, all holding Koala bears in the Koala Sanctuary at Lone Pine, near Brisbane. These curious creatures were described by J. M. Kilburn, in an article in "The Yorkshire Post" on November 22.

Test Writers Field a Team

Cricket correspondents travelling with the M.C.C. team in Australia are playing occasional social matches: This group includes George Duckworth (on the extreme left of the back row), Bill Bowes (second from the left in the front row), and J. M. Kilburn, Cricket Correspondent of "The Yorkshire Post" (second from the right in the front row).

Fred Trueman: Kilburn called him 'the tempest', a terrifying and dramatic fast bowler who was a 'forthright and explosive character too' and became the 'popular personification' of his vicious art.

It's spring, 1962 and Vic Wilson, left, and Fred Trueman stride purposefully towards net practice – and the season that lies ahead of them.

Geoff Boycott holds the Man of the Match award at the end of the 1965 Gillette Cup
final against Surrey. He scored 146, an innings Kilburn thought was 'technically
flawless from the stern defence of its beginning to the wonderful show of mastery in
its later stages'.

Geoff Boycott, a mixture of caution and flamboyance at Lord's, moves along his score on a damp and heavily overcast day at Lord's in the Gillette Cup final of 1965.

The victorious Yorkshire team, winners of the 1965 final. From left to right: Don
Wilson, Doug Padgett, John Hampshire, Ken Taylor, Brian Close, Ray Illingworth,
Fred Trueman, Richard Hutton, Jimmy Binks, Phil Sharpe, Geoffrey Boycott.

Yorkshire CCC May 1966

The champagne moments: Yorkshire celebrates winning the Championship in 1967, above, as Geoff Boycott pours the drinks for his captain Ray Illingworth. Richard Hutton, Don Wilson, Brian Close and Fred Trueman admire the fact that he doesn't spill a drop of it. Boycott, below, does the same again for Illingworth two years later after the England-West Indies Test at Headingley.

A study in concentration: Jim Kilburn poses for two of the photographs which occasionally illustrated his columns in the pages of the Yorkshire Post. The newspaper also used them to promote his writing.

A letter from a legend. A collection of the air-mails that Sir Donald Bradman sent to Jim Kilburn both before and after Kilburn's retirement from the Yorkshire Post. Sir Donald considered him to be one of the finest cricket writers of his generation.

26th April 1968

JM Kilburn

wickets.

After inspection proving satisfactory, the Yorkshire player becomes an accepted member of the cricket family. He receives a treatment of domestic familiarity, which implies a consistent welcome, the muted congratulation that takes success for granted and unquestioning support in time of trouble. The final attribution is to the greatest of individuals and teams; they are given the respect and authority that transcends investigation or analysis. George Hirst going in to bat, Wilfred Rhodes and Hedley Verity going on to bowl, Holmes and Sutcliffe opening an innings, the outstanding teams taking the field received tribute warmed by vicarious pride. They were beyond compare and beyond criticism. They were county possessions, like the Dales and York Minster.

In days before handclap in unison and monotonous chant became the fashionable and moronic comment, Yorkshire crowds could fairly claim to have been both a feature of cricket and a force in cricket. For visiting sides they served as a fourth dimension of challenge, additional to the batting, bowling and fielding. They were another opposition of will, another encirclement.

A young batsman bowled first ball felt the finality of a High Court sentence in the roar of acclaim at his dismissal. An Australian has confessed that he needed all his Test match nerve to await the umpire's decision, which was 'not out', when Bramall Lane with one voice appealed for lbw. The spectators were playing in the match. The harshest criticism a Yorkshire crowd can make is not impolite comment, not adjuration to improve; it is indifference. When Yorkshire crowds cease to care Yorkshire cricket must take deep concern for its health. For their own players Yorkshire supporters maintain a general routine of appraisal. They are inclined to look before they leap.

Recent trends in cricket will, I feel and fear, modify some of the Yorkshire peculiarities. Attitudes and customs are changing with changing cricket organisation and presentation. The Yorkshire belief that if you cannot win there is virtue in striving not to lose must weaken under match conditions that insist on victory or defeat, however artificially ensured. Television has introduced a common denominator into crowd behaviour, suggesting that pitch invasion by small boys and simple-minded seniors can be a practice in Bradford and Bombay alike. Professional techniques and ambitions tend to promote a universal sophistication that diminishes distinctions between Yorkshire cricket and Somerset cricket and Australian cricket and West Indian cricket. Covered pitches and limited overs will – as they are presumably intended to do – eliminate the particular skills and opportunities of locality. In that outcome there would be no advantage or disadvantage in being born and reared to Yorkshire cricket. In that outcome cricket in general may or may not benefit. It will certainly be different.

Overthrows

A Letter from the North

A JOURNALIST from London lamented to me the other day that Yorkshire should be a cricketing county of such striking importance. I offered him polite sympathy and suggested some amplification of his grievance (for he is a strange Yorkshireman who is not eager to talk or to hear of Yorkshire), and I was told that were Yorkshire not so important to cricket London editors would not be constrained to send London journalists to the unlovely grounds where Yorkshire's home matches are played. The point is not without significance, however much Bramall Lane and Headingley and Park Avenue may appeal to those of Yorkshire birth and breeding they must inevitably strike a chord of depression in comparison with the lovely settings of the game in Worcester, Sussex, Hampshire or in Kent. Banners and bunting, deckchairs and striped awnings, with ices and strawberries and cream for tea are precious amenities to cricket which we cannot, or do not, offer you in Yorkshire.

Perhaps our very game suffers from its surroundings. The grim purposefulness that is Yorkshire's cricketing characteristic matches the hard practicality of its surroundings. It is difficult to feel grieved and mournful over a duck, or a follow-on, or a defeat when the game is seen from the depths of a deck-chair placed carefully in the shade of a tree. Championship points seem to matter very little when the murmur of a nearby stream encourages the hitting of sixes from morn till eve. Yorkshire's grounds were built for the business of holding as many shillingworths as possible and Yorkshire cricket is business-like to a degree. I shall be surprised if there exists the means, or the desire, to change it now.

It is, of course, not beyond the bounds of possibility to bring rusticity into an urban quarter. You can, for example, very nearly forget Manchester at Old Trafford and most certainly you can forget Birmingham at the newly garnished Edgbaston. There a paint-pot and a little inspiration has worked wonders and a fortunate few can now watch Warwickshire cricket beneath a sparkling sunshade planted on a pleasant lawn with flower-beds close at hand. If environment means anything at all Warwickshire should be playing unceasingly attractive cricket within a year or two. I am afraid that we shall never have sunshades and tea on the lawn at Bramall Lane. We are not even given a sense of contact with the game by being allowed to stroll upon the grass during the intervals or to throw back the ball to beaten fieldsmen. We are kept strictly to our places behind iron bars and when the crowd is big some of us must sit upon concrete terracing the whole day through.

Headingley offers more scope for decoration and a most welcome improvement has brought about the removal of the fencing that once separated turf and surrounding track. There are trees, too, that will be more noticeable in another generation and there is even a grassy hillock of which by no means the most has yet been made. The guardians of Headingley might profitably pay a visit to Edgbaston one day.

Park Avenue is friendly enough; there you can stroll or sit upon the grass and there is even a marquee, though strictly upon utilitarian principles and out of sight of the playing area. Is it accident that nearly all Yorkshire's most exciting matches take place at Park Avenue?

One exception did the unwitting originator of this theme of mine make to his general plaint. To Scarborough he admitted himself always a willing visitor, for Scarborough, particularly at Festival time, goes far towards making the best of both worlds. There is a comfortable and not unhandsome pavilion, there are stands to accommodate the considerable crowds and yet there is also canvas and colour. You must, it is true, be something of a dignitary to be ensconced among the tents and deckchairs but at least they are there for all to see and to admire. In an idle hour some of us once made a list of our ideal cricketing engagements for the summer and a good many of Yorkshire's home matches were unanimously set down for Scarborough.

They would be good matches, too, for there is something in Scarborough's air that lends liveliness to batsman and energy to bowlers. The cricket at the Festival is naturally carefree and has attractiveness as its primary function, but it was not during the Festival that Sutcliffe and Leyland once dealt so dramatically with the fast bowling of Essex or at the Festival when Warwickshire once won incredible victory. The spirit of place is very strong at Scarborough. We will admit that utility comes a long way before beauty in most of Yorkshire's cricket homes but we do insist upon Scarborough being ranked as an exception, just to show you what we can do when we try.

Before we see Scarborough again though, there is a call awaiting me for a sterner occasion. I must hurry away to Sheffield for the Australians are due and there must be no relaxation from duty; Bradman, for one, will probably be watching the ball too intently to notice the surrounding chimneys.

The Cricketer, July 1938

The Historic Decade

BETWEEN 1931 and 1939 there were only two seasons when Yorkshire were not county champions. In this period they played 260 championship matches, won 153 of them and were defeated 24 times. This prolonged and overpowering success may not have been in the best interests of the competition in one sense, but it was certainly an important factor in county club finance, for so tremendous did Yorkshire's reputation become that the side was the outstanding attraction in English cricket and a victory over Yorkshire became a primary ambition not only of county rivals but of touring teams from overseas.

In 1931 Yorkshire were easily champions. They did not seem so half-way through the season, but they then began a run of fifteen matches which brought them thirteen victories and two draws, leaving all their challengers far behind.

The explanation for their success requires little research. It lay in brilliant fielding, the remarkable form of Herbert Sutcliffe and the complete development of Bowes and Verity. In the whole season Sutcliffe made 3,006 runs with an average of 96.96; in championship fixtures alone he had an aggregate of 2,049 and an average of 97.57; nine of his thirteen centuries were scored for Yorkshire. The bowling figures show Bowes and Verity with over 100 wickets, and only Macaulay among the others approaching this number.

The one defeat of the year was in the widely-discussed 'freak declaration' match at Sheffield where, after two blank days, FE Greenwood and BH Lyon, the Gloucestershire captain, resolved upon an endeavour to extract full match points out of one day's cricket. Yorkshire won the toss and sent Gloucestershire in; Robinson bowled the first ball which went unchecked for four byes; Gloucestershire declared. When Hammond's first ball had also been allowed to go for four byes Yorkshire in their turn declared, and the match was fought out on second innings. Gloucestershire won it by 47 runs, Yorkshire attempting more than they could safely encompass in seeking 172 runs in 150 minutes against Goddard and Parker. A similar arrangement of declaration was also followed later in the season in the Northamptonshire match, but neither this nor subsequent evasions of the championship intentions found favour with the law-makers and regulations were in due course re-worded.

Among Yorkshire victories in this dramatic season it would be difficult to make adequate selection, for wonder tended to obscure wonder. At Headingley a first innings lead of 97 over Warwickshire was enough to provide innings victory, for in 18.4 overs Verity took all ten wickets for 36 runs. At Bradford in Macaulay's benefit match, Yorkshire required only the batting necessary to make 281 for 4; Surrey's totals were 165 and 61, Verity taking 6 for 11 in the second innings. At Lord's Sutcliffe hit the first of four consecutive centuries and in answer to the Yorkshire 302 Middlesex could make only 111 and 126. In their first innings Bowes took 5 for 39; in the second 6 for 63. The 1932 championship provided a closer struggle but it was decided before Yorkshire went to Hove at the end of the season to play the return match against their nearest rivals, whom, in any event, they defeated easily enough.

The two failures of the year came in the early part of the programme. At Bradford Lancashire made 263, mainly because of a splendid 152 by Paynter, and on the second day, after rain, Sibbles returned the remarkable figures of 7 for 10 in Yorkshire's dismissal for 46. There was no real recovery and Lancashire won by an innings and 50 runs. Hampshire won at Leeds when 220 in the fourth innings proved too much for batting weakened by the absence of Holmes, though Sutcliffe made memorable effort in carrying his bat for 104.

Perhaps the most satisfactory occasion of the year was the game in which Sutcliffe made his hundredth hundred. It was at Bradford, against Gloucestershire, and provided three days of unceasingly stimulating cricket. In the first innings Yorkshire declared at 472 for 7 wickets, Mitchell making top score with 177 not out. To this Gloucestershire replied with 404, Hammond following Sinfield's century with 147, made out of 191, and containing six sixes and eighteen fours all in a glorious 130 minutes. Yorkshire, led by Sutcliffe, went at an even more furious pace and reached 240 for 6 in less than two hours, Sutcliffe hitting eight sixes and eight fours in his 132. Yorkshire's declaration left them just time for victory, for though the eventual margin was 133 runs the last Gloucestershire wicket fell in the last over of extra time.

In their very next engagement, at Leeds, Yorkshire declared when they were 71 behind on first innings and Verity, for the second time in his career, took all ten wickets. This time they cost him only ten runs, and included the hat-trick. Yorkshire were left to make 139, and Holmes and Sutcliffe collected them in an hour and a half.

Perhaps of all the counties Essex had most cause to remember their engagements with Yorkshire in 1932. The first of them, at Leyton, brought the world's record first wicket partnership of 555 by Holmes and Sutcliffe who stayed together for seven hours and twenty-five minutes before Sutcliffe uncaringly threw away his wicket. Not altogether unnaturally Essex were left in poor heart for batting, and they lost the match by an innings and 313 runs – precisely Sutcliffe's score. In the first Essex innings, which totalled 78, Bowes took 4 wickets for 38 runs, Verity 5 for 8. In the follow-on Bowes had 5 for 47, and Verity 5 for 45.

This was in June, and in August Essex played at Scarborough. They won the toss and on a beautiful wicket they made 325, Bowes toiling through forty overs, with the unusual discouragement of a dropped catch or two, to take 9 for 121. Whatever he may have felt to be the tribulations of a fast bowler must have been endorsed with complete accord by Farnes and Nichols. In less than six hours Yorkshire made 476 for nine wickets, Farnes at one period paying 75 runs for four overs; in that particular half-hour 102 runs were taken by Sutcliffe and Leyland from six successive overs. Sutcliffe's whole innings of 194 lasted 165 minutes, but his especial hurry was in taking his score from 100 to 194; this occupied him for forty minutes. Essex yielded themselves up to another innings defeat.

For the second year in succession Sutcliffe finished the season with over 3,000 runs (and then went to Australia to make a further 1,318). Twelve of his fourteen centuries of 1932 were made for Yorkshire and his average in championship matches was 87.46. Leyland, Holmes, Mitchell and Barber all passed 1,000 runs, and Bowes and Verity between them were responsible for 314 wickets. Leyland had his disappointments in the early months, but extraordinary form throughout August brought him four centuries and 1,000 runs in the month, and ensured his selection for the Australian tour. Sutcliffe and Verity had been among the first to be chosen and, with Bowes a last minute inclusion, there were four Yorkshiremen in that historic expedition under the captaincy of DR Jardine.

There were two defeats in Yorkshire's final matches of 1933, but they had no influence on the championship which had been assured since mid-August and had, indeed, never seemed in much dispute throughout the season. So strong was the bowling that nine of the nineteen victories were completed in two days, and Bowes, Verity and Macaulay were scourges of the land. Verity with 168, Macaulay with 141 and Bowes with 130, took nearly three times as many wickets as all the other Yorkshire bowlers put together, and each enjoyed some days of breathtaking success. Against Essex at Leyton Verity took seventeen wickets in one day, 8 for 47 in the first innings and 9 for 44 in the follow on, a feat hitherto achieved only by Colin Blythe (though subsequently equalled by Goddard for Gloucestershire against Kent). On the Monday of the Whitsuntide match at Old Trafford Macaulay found the crumbled wicket so much to his liking that when he had returned figures of 7 for 28 (including a hat-trick) and 5 for 21, he was heard to regret that Lancashire could not have a third innings. Bowes achieved perhaps his finest performance of the year against Kent at Leeds when he had to bowl on an excellent wicket for his 6 for 44 and 6 for 73.

Leyland and Mitchell, both averaging over 50, were the outstanding batsmen, for Sutcliffe, by his own phenomenal standards, had a moderate season (a 'moderate season' bringing over 2,000 runs!). Holmes struggled through the summer under the handicap of an injured knee, and at the end of it he left first-class cricket with final figures altogether unrepresentative of the ability he had shown in the rest of his career. His highest innings, of 65, was played against Nottinghamshire at Bradford in the match representing perhaps the most satisfying victory of the year. On the first morning Keeton made a century before lunch and the Nottinghamshire total reached 324, but Holmes and Sutcliffe made 115 together and Mitchell and Leyland, each scoring a century, put on 221 for the third wicket in two and a half hours and Yorkshire's first innings lead amounted to 191. Carr made 97 not out in Nottinghamshire's second attempt, but there was inadequate support for him and Yorkshire were left with only 12 runs to make in the fourth innings.

Middlesex also made over 300 in their first innings at Leeds and with those runs on the board they were given a chance to bowl at Yorkshire on a wet wicket. So completely did they miss the opportunity that Yorkshire, with Sutcliffe making 177, won a first innings lead of 62, and then Macaulay demonstrated what could and should have been done by taking 7 for 52, leaving Yorkshire to make the necessary 53 without losing a wicket.

Another match at Leeds illustrated the tremendous difference in strength between the leading and the lower counties. The wicket was encouraging enough for Northamptonshire to send Yorkshire in, but a brilliant 192 by Leyland led to a declaration at 349 for 7, and when Northamptonshire batted they were utterly conquered by Verity, who took 7 for 35 and 6 for 67 in totals of 63 and 135, Mitchell holding six catches in one of his most spectacular fielding displays.

1934 was a year of Australian invasion and so heavily were Yorkshire taxed by representative calls that Leyland missed as many as thirteen county matches, Sutcliffe and Verity twelve, and Bowes eleven. These sacrifices were, of course, only too willingly made even though they must have contributed to the county's fall to sixth place in the championship, with seven defeats and twelve victories in thirty matches. Two of the best games of the season were with Middlesex, though both were played at Test match times and the sides therefore not at full strength. At Lord's Yorkshire's batting was not convincing against the leg-spin of Peebles and Middlesex were set to make no more than 51 in the last innings. The task was very nearly too much for them for, finding some life in the pitch, Bowes bowled at his best pace and his most disconcerting length and eight wickets were down before the runs were made. Bowes took 6 wickets for 17 runs.

A fortnight later, at Leeds, Middlesex batted first and amid interruptions because of showers could make only 123. Mitchell made a stern century for Yorkshire, who declared at 191 for 4 leaving less than three hours for play. Middlesex could only try to escape defeat and Hearne stayed for almost an hour and a half, scoring only 11 runs, but the persistent Macaulay was not to be denied and his 6 for 22 in thirty overs gave Yorkshire their victory with twenty minutes to spare.

Equally exciting and perhaps even more surprising was Yorkshire's defeat at Leicester. Here there were no signs of the unusual on the first day, for Leicestershire's batting was no better than a total of 94 would suggest. By close of play Yorkshire were 196 for 5 and at that score they declared on the second morning. Expectations of players and prophets were wildly at fault; Leicestershire made 250 in their second innings and an utterly confounded Yorkshire collapsed to be all out for 90 and so lose by 58 runs.

Another defeat where the probabilities pointed to victory came at Scarborough where, in sunshine after rain, eighteen wickets fell in three hours on the first day; Yorkshire were all out for 101 and Warwickshire lost 8 for 25. To their eventual first innings lead of 56 Yorkshire added a further 159, but with the pitch improving and Parsons in most determined hitting mood Warwickshire made their 216 and won by one wicket.

Arthur Mitchell, carrying a good deal of batting responsibility, scored six championship centuries and headed the county averages, and Leonard Hutton came into first-class cricket at the age of seventeen to show clear evidence of that technical ability which was to carry him to the top of his world.

Yorkshire went back to first place in the championship in 1935 with nineteen victories and one defeat. The defeat was the sensation of the season and, indeed, remains one of the most-discussed cricket matches of modern times. At the end of July Essex went to Huddersfield with little in their record to inspire self-confidence, but their fast bowlers, Nichols and Read, found the wicket so full of life that within an hour of the start of the match the Yorkshire first innings had been completed for a total of 31. Nichols took 4 for 17, Read 6 for 11; only Wood reached double figures.

For the remainder of the day Yorkshire were in the field whilst Essex were making 334, with 146 by Nichols, and on the second morning Yorkshire began their second innings. It was over before lunch time, for 99, and again Nichols and Read shared all the wickets, Nichols taking 7 for 37 and Read 3 for 51. Yorkshire's distress was summed up during the astonishing first morning when Leyland splintered his bat. He was climbing the pavilion steps a few moments later, having been bowled for 0, when a lugubrious supporter muttered to him: 'Nay, Maurice, tha's brok' thi bat, tha's brok' thi wicket and tha's brok' thi reputation'. He was unduly downhearted. Yorkshire recovered, and defeated Lancashire in the very next match.

1935 was not one of Leyland's best seasons, and Sutcliffe and Barber were the only Yorkshiremen to average over 50. Barber had such a good run in mid-season that he was chosen for England against South Africa in the third Test, and, because of Leyland's last minute withdrawal, Mitchell was also called upon for that match.

Though the Essex match provided the greatest astonishment, surely the finest contest was in the game with Kent at Bradford. In the whole history of cricket few occasions can have produced such sustained tension as the second day, which brought the match to its end. On the first day each side had completed an innings and Kent led by 51. They began their second innings with Woolley and Ashdown, who put on 107 in 70 minutes before Macaulay bowled Woolley for 73. In another 55 minutes Kent were all out for a total of 140, Macaulay and Verity each taking five wickets. The remaining battle was almost a contest between the individual champions, Sutcliffe for Yorkshire and Freeman for Kent; no other batsman could cope with Freeman for long, but Sutcliffe played with superb assurance and skill and made one of the finest centuries of his career. Six Yorkshire wickets were gone for 120, but Sellers swept some heroic boundaries to square leg and though Sutcliffe fell in the end, lbw. to Freeman, only seven runs were required when he left and Yorkshire won home by two wickets.

This was Macaulay's last season. Rheumatic illness kept him out of the majority of the matches, and although Smailes took 96 wickets in all matches the essence of the attack lay in Bowes and Verity. Bowes was perhaps the more significant because of his ability to remove the early batsmen, and he had notable performances at Bradford where he took 6 for 16 in the Lancashire first innings, and at Kettering where he took sixteen Northamptonshire wickets, 8 for 18 and 8 for 15.

Yorkshire lost fewer matches than any other county in 1936 but, possibly because they lacked quite the forcefulness of other years, they were only third in the championship. Bowes and Verity were far ahead in the bowling averages and Verity, in all matches, took over 216 wickets, yet there was good reason for satisfaction in the work of Smailes who reached his 100 wickets for the first time, and Hutton in his first full season scored over 1,000 runs in his patient apprenticeship. Leyland was clearly the outstanding batsman, scoring twice as many centuries as any other Yorkshireman and easily heading the averages. His highest score was 263 against Essex at Hull, but that brilliant innings was no more characteristic than his gallant defiance for much smaller reward when Worcestershire, at Stourbridge, won their first victory over Yorkshire since 1909.

Whenever the wicket helped him Verity was a sore trial to batsmen. Against Kent at Sheffield in May he took 6 for 26 in the first innings and 9 for 12 in the second, against Glamorgan he had 7 for 35, against Nottinghamshire 8 for 42, and against Essex at Westcliff 6 for 52 and 9 for 48. As he also headed the England bowling averages in the three Test matches against India he could fairly claim to have been the bowler of the year.

In the remaining three years of the pre-war championship Yorkshire were always leaders. They had an exciting struggle with Middlesex in 1937 and the issue was still open in mid-August when Sellers received a telegram from Robins suggesting that, whatever happened in the championship, Yorkshire and Middlesex should play a challenge match at The Oval in September. So much public interest was aroused by the novelty (or, rather, this return to a very old custom) that over £700 went to charity from the gate receipts. Yorkshire were fortunate in winning the toss, and scoring 401 by lunch time on the second day they put themselves beyond much likelihood of defeat. Middlesex began their batting in rather poor light and they were so much troubled by the sustained hostility of Bowes and Smailes that they lost their first six wickets for 63 runs. Rain during the night quenched their last hopes and, following on 216 behind, they were all out for 101 in their second innings, Verity taking 8 for 43.

In the championship fixtures between the two teams Middlesex held a decided advantage, winning by an innings at Lord's and leading in a drawn game at Sheffield. Another Sheffield match brought the only other championship defeat of the year, Lancashire winning by five wickets when Verity seemed to miss an opportunity of using a wicket that suited Iddon well enough for him to take 9 for 42 in the Yorkshire second innings.

One of the most notable home matches was Arthur Mitchell's Benefit at Bradford, where Surrey were beaten by three wickets. Yorkshire had much the better of the early stages, Sutcliffe making 138 of a first innings total of 398 and Robinson taking 6 for 33 in Surrey's reply of 187. There came a remarkable change in the follow-on, for Fishlock and

Gregory put on 215 for the second wicket, and Fishlock's 146 was the leading contribution to the eventual 409. This left Yorkshire to attempt 199 in the final 105 minutes, and though Hutton was immediately run out Sutcliffe and Mitchell hit so splendidly that they made 105 in less than an hour, and Smailes saw to it that the remaining time was properly used.

Smailes played a number of other hard-hitting innings, including his first county century, and in all matches he took 120 wickets as a most useful supporter for Bowes and Verity. An unreliable knee kept Bowes out of many matches and turned him into a medium-pace bowler for much of the season, and Verity was therefore left with a tremendous amount of work to do. He finished in splendid form and by the end of the season had taken over 200 wickets – though in July he had been dropped from the England side.

Among the batsmen Sutcliffe showed excellent figures, but the averages were headed by Hutton who justified all the promise of the earlier years and came to his first experiences as an England cricketer.

In 1938 Yorkshire reached the top of the table in mid-season and never lost the position, though they were strongly challenged by Middlesex until the closing weeks. The results showed twenty victories and two defeats, and the triumph was achieved despite all the calls of an Australian Test match season, and injuries which kept Mitchell, Hutton and Turner away from many matches. The batting was comfortingly solid with as many as eleven players averaging over 25, but the great strength of the side lay in the bowling and fielding which was quite beyond compare among the counties and nearly brought a victory over the Australians at Sheffield. Bowes, Verity, Smailes and Robinson all reached 100 wickets, and Smailes became the first Yorkshireman for twelve years to complete the double. This was one of the very rare years in which Lancashire were twice defeated, by eight wickets at Bradford and by an innings and 200 runs at Old Trafford; and victory by seven wickets over Middlesex at Leeds brought some compensation for the earlier defeat at Lord's when the extraordinary misfortunes of the first day left Yorkshire to play their second innings with:

Hutton, absent hurt	*0*
Gibb, absent hurt	*0*
Leyland, retired hurt	*1*

Leyland tried to bat with a fractured thumb when things were going very badly for Yorkshire, but a further blow on the injury compelled him to give up. Yorkshire also found both defeat and victory in their games with Surrey. At Sheffield in June Yorkshire made 416, Barber and Smailes both scoring centuries, and when Bowes, with 6 for 32, and Smailes, 4 for 16, had dismissed Surrey for 52 the remainder of the match was a formality. At The Oval, co-incident with the fourth Test match, Yorkshire were without Hutton, Leyland, Verity, Bowes, Gibb and Yardley, and Smailes broke down in the course of the match. Yorkshire were overwhelmed by 262 runs, their only satisfaction lying, in some stubborn defiance by Turner who stayed more than three hours for 97 on the last day.

Outside the championship engagements Yorkshire's finest achievement was against the Australians at Sheffield. Sellers sent the Australians in and they were dismissed for 222, mainly by Smailes's off-breaks, Hassett alone showing much assurance. Yorkshire were 17 behind on first innings but they then put out the Australians for 132, Bowes and Smailes bowling magnificently in an atmosphere of rare excitement. On the final morning the Yorkshire batsmen went slowly and grimly towards the 150 runs they needed and at lunch time they were 83 for 3, with Sutcliffe and Barber not out. Rain came and not another ball could be bowled.

Political crisis ran through all the everyday concerns of 1939 and there were times when cricket was played and watched almost in a dream, representing not so much a current performance as a memory of something fading rapidly into the affairs of a different world. When war had become inevitable – indeed, when the troops were actually moving – cricket was still being played because there seemed no way to stop it, and the county programme was completed to leave Yorkshire champions once again. They were four times defeated during the course of the season, but no other county could match their record of twenty outright victories and there was little doubt that honours went where honours were duly earned.

It was, on the whole, a season of wet wickets and Yorkshire's spin bowling and superb fielding served them well. With Bowes to break into the innings, Verity and Robinson were formidable attackers when the wicket was helpful and between them these three bowlers took 433 wickets. In championship matches alone Verity's average was 1269 for 165 wickets and the last three county matches in which he ever played brought him 25 wickets for 248 runs, ending with the incredible 7 for 9 against Sussex.

The first defeat came early in the season when Gloucestershire played at Bradford. Rain washed out the first day, but there followed some forceful batting by Leyland who made 112 of Yorkshire's 253, and by Hammond who made 75 in the Gloucestershire total of 227. Yorkshire then hit 162 for 7 in eighty minutes and declared to leave Gloucestershire chasing 189 in less than two hours. They made them in ninety-five minutes, for the loss of four wickets, Barnett setting the pace by collecting 90 in an hour with four sixes and eight fours.

This was a defeat that could have been avoided by circumspection; but on the other three occasions Yorkshire went down despite themselves. Essex won by an innings at Sheffield when there were Test match calls upon Yorkshire. Gloucestershire won by seven wickets at Bristol when Goddard proved the bowler and B O Allen the batsman of the match, and Worcestershire won by 36 runs at Stourbridge in a match during which none of the four totals reached 120.

To set beside the few defeats were many victories, some of them won by brilliant cricket. The most comprehensive triumph came at Sheffield where Hampshire were beaten by an innings and 129 runs with Yorkshire losing only one wicket. Hampshire batted first and made 174 before Sutcliffe and Hutton put on 315 together. Sutcliffe's departure for 116 - he was, incidentally, the only batsman to be bowled throughout the whole match - brought in Barber who stayed with Hutton until the innings was declared closed at 493, Hutton then having reached 280 and Barber 91.

Much more even was another match at Sheffield when Yorkshire had to meet Derbyshire without their Test match players. Half-way through the Saturday afternoon the news spread across the countryside that Yorkshire were all out for 83 and Yorkshiremen amid the alien corn had to put up with a good deal of chaff. Within an hour there was further news.

Derbyshire were all out for 20, with Smailes showing figures of 4 for 11 and a young bowler named Smurthwaite 5 for 7. Yorkshire's second innings contained a century by Barber and, with some assistance from unreliable Derbyshire fielding, amounted to 310. Derbyshire's fourth innings total was 97, and all the ten wickets were taken by Frank Smailes, for 47 runs.

Lancashire were defeated both at Old Trafford and at Headingley. At Old Trafford Lancashire made 300 in their first innings, but Yorkshire went far ahead and could declare at 528 for 8 by the end of the second day. Sutcliffe and Mitchell put on 288 for the second wicket, Sutcliffe making 165 and Mitchell 136. Lancashire lost heart and Bowes, taking 6 for 43, gave them no encouragement to find it again. Lancashire also batted first in the August match at Headingley and they were in no hurry over the making of 217. They seemed to have justified their deliberation when they won a lead of 54, but Robinson's off-spinners, in an analysis of 8 for 35, conquered them in the second innings and Yorkshire were left with 147 to make. They had to make them in haste because rain was always threatening and Hutton's century and the final runs were only reached because Lancashire stayed on the field as the rain began to fall. The winning hit was, in fact, a skied mishit and had it proved a catch at cover there would certainly have been no time for another batsman to come in; as it was, the players were drenched by the storm before they could reach the shelter of the pavilion.

The final matches of the 1939 season were the acme of unreality. Yorkshire were on the South coast where they defeated Kent and Hampshire by an innings and Sussex by nine wickets. Nobody was in the least elated; a good many people probably knew little about it, for telephones and telegraphs were so heavily engaged that cricket reports were often delayed and abandoned. At Hove there was cricket that would have been sensational in any other circumstances. Cox made a furious 198 in Sussex's 387; Hutton and Yardley made centuries in Yorkshire's 392. Long distance train services were cancelled and Yorkshire had to improvise road transport for the journey home. On the third morning Verity took 7 wickets for 9 runs and Sussex were all out for 33. Yorkshire travelled North and in the early morning of Saturday, September 3, a great cricket team broke up, never to come together again.

The Secret of Yorkshire's Success

YORKSHIRE county cricket does not begin upon the fields of Bradford, Leeds or Sheffield any more than a meal begins with the placing of the dishes before the diner. Behind the appearance of those dishes lies care and forethought and organisation in the kitchens, and behind that there must be enthusiasm and inspiration. So to make possible these games of bat and ball which are so dear to us, there are months and years of trial and error, and whole generations of enthusiasm.

Yorkshire cricket begins upon those fields bare of grass and innocent of any amenity save space, where boys with broken bats and shapeless cricket balls imitate their heroes of another sphere. There was a time when almost every Yorkshire village could show you a cricket match in the street during the dinner hour of the factories and workshops. Then boys and men would forget the morning's cares and the worries of the afternoon in play, and cricket was always the game. Men who played in good club cricket each Saturday would not scorn this elementary practice and boys would treasure for weeks together the memory of an envied wicket taken or a good run scored. Bye-laws and motor buses have removed most of this cricket today, but the spirit remains and seeks outlet elsewhere, with the old ambition unquenched and the old joys merely transferred to another scene.

Almost always the young Yorkshire boy has the county eleven upon the limit of his horizon. With his dream an ever-present companion, he plays for the nearest available team. From school he goes to his church, from church to the second eleven of some prominent club; further promotion brings him into the first team and important league cricket and watchful eyes note his progress and bring him to the attention of the county authorities. Winter nets, spring coaching, success in the Colts, and the end of a journey is at hand and another cricketer wears the beloved White Rose upon his cap. Few counties achieve success without the backbone of good club cricket and Yorkshire is particularly fortunate, if inevitably so, in the. excellence of the leagues that provide entertainment and recreation for thousands of people each Saturday of summer. There club cricket has tremendous strength and force, and is in itself an ideal as well as a stepping stone to higher things. Far more cricketers remain league players than ever go beyond, but few indeed are the men to represent Yorkshire who do not pass through training ground. Indeed, there are cases of Yorkshiremen qualifying for other counties who are sent back to their Yorkshire league each Saturday for the best possible experience during the period of waiting.

Sometimes the training course in the league is long and

anxious and of late years in particular, players have been drafted into the Yorkshire side at a greater age than is customary in a cricketer setting out to make a name for himself. Sometimes a young player comes within the county's sphere of activities without having had league experience; invariably he is then allocated to a league club and his performances there watched and analysed. It is of enormous significance that of the present Yorkshire team, Sellers, Sutcliffe, Barber, Wood and Hutton played in the Bradford League, and Leyland, Verity, Turner and Smailes have had experience in the Yorkshire Council. This league cricket is a testing ground for both the technique and temperament of a young cricketer. Here a man learns the difference between playing for amusement and playing for a purpose; his mental cricket is developed in an atmosphere to which carelessness or indolence are entirely foreign and where the light excuse of 'It's only a game' is scornfully rejected. League cricket is not merely a game; it is a business in the form of a game, and none the less pleasant for the seriousness and responsibility involved, for the greater the earnestness and endeavour demanded the sweeter the taste of success when it comes.

In league cricket the player learns that there are no inconsequent moments and comes to realise that his every action is observed and has meaning. He learns that continual care and concentration alone can bring success, for where the standard is high any defection must of necessity prove fatal. As a batsman he meets professional bowlers who know all there is to be known of guile and cunning and who exhibit invariably the cardinal virtue of length; thus he comes to curb his natural impatience and grows selective in his moments of attack. As a bowler he meets batsmen who rarely fail to take advantage of opportunities and who must be thought as well as bowled out; thus he appreciates the necessity of bowling to his field, and adapting himself to the needs of a particular situation. Where championships and cups are at stake and matches watched by distinctly partisan spectators, tense situations arise, and until the young player has been tested in the nerve-racking fires of close finishes and knotty problems, he cannot account himself in any way experienced. The light of publicity is upon him as a league player; he learns calm philosophy and acquires self-control in times of elation.

From all this it might appear that Yorkshire league cricket is a very grim and forbidding experience, but, in actual fact, it is nothing of the kind, for the lessons are mainly self-taught and follow so inevitably in the course of playing that the learning is chiefly subconscious, and only the sense of responsibility differentiates league cricket from any other kind of club cricket. Yorkshire cricket may have a pronouncedly business-like air, but that is because the Yorkshireman has business-like qualities and prefers his life, even his sporting life, to be run on that principle.

With a few seasons of league cricket behind him, a player has very sound technical and spirited qualifications for the county game and requires only polish and experience to make him a first-class product. It would be idle to pretend that league cricket and first-class cricket differ only in the time element, for there is much to be learned by the county cricketer that never comes within the sphere of the club player; yet, in fundamentals, the game is the same, and it is surely beyond argument that the league cricketer has a considerable advantage over his colleague whose training has been less arduous, when the time comes for the strain and fierce fight of county cricket.

When a Yorkshire cricketer has attained county status, he becomes at once part of a tradition that he has known and appreciated all his life. Consciously or unconsciously, he realises that he is treading in the footsteps of great predecessors and that there is a noble heritage in his keeping. He knows also that the eyes of the county are upon him and his doings; not cast carelessly in his direction in idle moments of leisure, but following him everywhere and appreciating success or demanding explanation of failure. A Yorkshire cricketer is not responsible only to his captain and committee for the charge in his keeping; he is responsible to fellow cricketers all over the county and that responsibility colours his existence and stiffens his determination to deserve well of his friends, known and unknown.

The huge and envied membership of the Yorkshire County Cricket Club comes not only from the appreciation of value for one guinea, but from the earnest belief among Yorkshiremen that the county's cricket must receive adequate and enthusiastic support. It is a point of honour with followers to see as much cricket as possible, not only because there is pleasure to be had, but also because it is a matter of personal importance to watch over the county's cricket representatives. Apart from the general interest in the team as a whole, each district of Yorkshire has a personal interest in its particular contributions to the side. Sheffield rejoices at Turner's success; Bradford has a particularly warm welcome for Wood; all Pudsey knows Sutcliffe and Hutton as its own sons. This interest never flags in good years or bad, and Yorkshire's players, knowing this, find an added incentive to improvement which goes beyond personal considerations.

Great as have been Yorkshire's cricketers as individuals it is as a team that the county has won most lasting renown, and it is because of the realisation by each player of his personal responsibility to his colleagues and to his county as a whole that the team-work has attained so high a standard. Yorkshire cricket, on the field and off, is run primarily as business (certainly as a pleasurable business), and in business little progress can be made without co-operation. To watch a Yorkshire eleven in the field is to find living illustration of cricket co-operation; there is no confused wandering in doubtful positions when a bowling change is made, no hovering in doubtful positions when this or that bowler is at work. Rarely indeed does the Yorkshire attack seem to be at its wits' end; rarely indeed is the side put to rout even in the fiercest blaze of batsmanship. So, too, in batting, one Yorkshireman knows how to make himself subservient to another for the good of his side. Is it not conceivable that Mitchell may have made an even greater personal name under another banner? Yet Mitchell is in the truest tradition of Yorkshire cricketers, placing always side before self and working always to the common rather than the individual good.

It is not by accident that Yorkshire has achieved enviable success in the County Championship. It is through long hours of quiet and unassuming work, persistence here, inspiration there and a perpetual consciousness of a tradition to keep. So long as Yorkshiremen, in general preserve their characteristics of earnestness and enthusiasm and a full realisation that the whole is greater than the part, with the object utterly and incontestably worth the striving, so long will Yorkshire cricket maintain the standard that has brought the admiration of the cricketing world.

The Cricketer: Winter Annual 1935

A Hat in a Hundred

HERBERT SUTCLIFFE is a great batsman. He is more than that; he is a great personality; is himself under any guise or disguise. Today he played a double century innings for Yorkshire, watching the ball for most of the time from beneath the brim of a grey trilby hat, and although he is perfectly entitled to wear a trilby hat or a top hat or pitman's cap should he so desire, it is doubtful if any one other than Sutcliffe in present day cricket could have appeared thus without provoking audible comment from the crowd.

With or without hat Sutcliffe was a very fine batsman today, and he not only laid the foundation of Yorkshire's score but remained at the wicket to do a good deal of decorative work. Once or twice he had disturbed moments when the ball did not behave as expected upon pitching, but for the most part he was a superbly serene Sutcliffe, watching and waiting the arrival of half volleys and full tosses which meant boundaries as surely as they came.

It is generally accepted that he is not a great batsman who must needs wait for his runs to come from bowling deficiencies, but the day's object for Sutcliffe consisted of more than mere run-getting for himself. He might perhaps have made a quick 50 and seen the rest of the day's play from a shady seat, but he preferred to induce in the Leicestershire bowlers that state of mind which looks upon the taking of wickets as something to be read about in the history books and the only rests from toil being intervals of custom – at lunch and tea. That Leicestershire never quite reached this stage was scarcely Sutcliffe's fault, and if wickets did fall it was only at long and irregular intervals and there were many Yorkshire runs in between.

The day's beginning was all Sutcliffe, for that batsman had early fours with a leg hit from a no ball and a late cut, whilst Hutton spent twenty minutes in thinking things over before scoring his first run of the morning. Sutcliffe himself always put comfort before speed, but he left Hutton far behind, and a perfectly placed shot through the covers made him 36 to Hutton's 12 and the total 52 at twenty-five minutes past twelve.

Sutcliffe took off his hat for the first time just before one o'clock to acknowledge the applause in appreciation of his fifty, but in this same over the wicket partnership ended at 79 when Hutton was lbw to Marlow. Hutton, so far as I remember, never made a false shot, but he could do no more than put the ball to the fieldsman, and whatever the bowlers may have thought about him, the spectators were clearly disappointed.

Sutcliffe, too, had a critic in the stand who gave him advice and expression of opinions in anything but a modest whisper. But what effect could one poor voice be expected to have upon a man who has triumphed over the commentary of the Hill at Sydney. Sutcliffe looked once in the direction of the offender and turned back to the game to put up the 100 in two and a quarter hours and swing a full toss negligently to the leg boundary.

Coincidence came into the cricket at lunch-time. Then Yorkshire had collected exactly as many runs as did Leicestershire yesterday, and a wicket again fell to the last ball of the morning, this time Mitchell being bowled when he hit over a ball pitched well up.

Barber brought a fresh mind and body to the treatment of the bowling after lunch, and at once pulled Prentice for four. He was unceremonious and unrepentant, and hit boundaries with or without provocation.

To a certain extent he stimulated Sutcliffe, who, however, was never prepared to forget his dignity in any riotious or ill-mannered swinging of the bat, and more than 70 Yorkshire runs came in an hour. Just before three o'clock Sutcliffe reached his hundred out of 172, and promptly put on his hat which had been neglected since lunch, thus stating clearly as though written in words that one hundred was merely a beginning of the day's labours.

At three twenty five Yorkshire were 200 and the welcome new ball immediately gave Leicestershire a wicket when Barber was caught low down in the gully. A shower of rain gave everyone rest and peace for a quarter of an hour, but the interruption made little difference to Sutcliffe, so that Leicestershire had to wait 81 runs before further success came their way and Turner was beautifully caught low down at second slip.

Wood must see another day before his season's thousand runs can come to him, for wanting twenty he had made eleven when he tried to cut Astill and became a picture of amazed dismay as the ball turned back and bowled him. Even Sutcliffe, guardian of Yorkshire's fortunes, smiled. There was no alarm at the comparatively quick fall of this wicket, for Yorkshire were by this time 321 and three-quarters of an hour remained for easy runs to be taken from a tired attack.

It is not altogether to the batsman's credit that this tired bowling was allowed to keep a length and demand defensive forward strokes. Surely this was the time for number seven on the list to break pavilion windows or perish in the attempt; surely five wickets left justified the possible risk in the long field, but all was quiet and careful until at ten minutes past six Sutcliffe became 200.

When any batsman makes 200 the day must be accounted solely his, and in every way Sutcliffe was Yorkshire on this Thursday of August. Whether or not his work will bring victory remains to be seen, but the glory of the achievement remains independent of result, and not the least remarkable feature of the accomplishment lay in the fact that he was running short singles as well in the day's last minutes as in the morning hours.

Ten minutes from the close, Sellers was caught from a miss-hit to cover, and the players left the field with Yorkshire 109 runs ahead and Sutcliffe (hatless) not out 210.

August 9, 1935

Sutcliffe made 212 and Yorkshire won the game by 10 wickets.

Chapter Six:
AUSTRALIA
AND THE DON

Don Bradman's Finest Hour

AT 11 o'clock this morning a man walked from the pavilion at Headingley; a man clad in flannels and with a green cap pulled down to shade his bright eyes. He carried with him a beautiful white bat and the only trace of aggression about him was the spring in his step. Yet that bat was a terrible weapon which dealt destruction all round it, and at 6.30 this evening Don Bradman ran for shelter, closely guarded by policemen; the long day's battle was over and he stood undefeated, the champion of champions.

Through the hours he stood defiant, with his enemies helpless around him, and in the course of the day he killed England's hopes of victory and spread destruction in the ranks of her bowlers. The story of Saturday is the story of Bradman, and that is doing no injustice to Ponsford, for who could refuse to bat well and stay there with Bradman as partner? Bradman's calm was the herald of nothing, no more than a few careful steps in a steady tramp over the moorland, and when he saw his way clearly again and had paid a moment's tribute to the possible thorns on the path, he laid back and forced a ball from Hammond, a ball only a fraction short of length, away past mid-on to the boundary, and then he placed one tantalisingly out of Hopwood's reach for another four. At 113 Mitchell bowled for Hammond and Hopwood for Verity. Hopwood's first ball, Bradman pulled for a four and the second he placed to leg for a single to complete his 50 after batting an hour and a half.

It was hereabouts that Bradman showed a touch of humanity. He actually missed a delivery from Mitchell and, had Ames been very quick and very clever to gather the ball which came to him low, Bradman might have been stumped. A little later Bradman swept Hopwood to leg and the ball dropped, perfectly safely of course, over Leyland, and this, I believe, was the only time Bradman skied the ball until late in the evening.

Bowes fielded so well this morning that the semi-humorous clapping which usually greets his efforts gave way to genuinely appreciative applause.

There is really no reason why it should ever be otherwise, for there is little justification for believing that Bowes is at his worst in the field. Anyway, he picked up smartly and saved more that one boundary when Bradman played the ball to mid-on. All signs of a possible separation had vanished, and even two missed chances never gave a thrill of expectancy. I use missed chances more or less as a technical term, for had either been held we should have witnessed something approaching a miracle, and the batsmen would have been justified in bewailing their fate.

After lunch Bradman got into his stride again by pulling Mitchell to the square leg boundary and forcing another ball to more or less the same place, and Ponsford fell into step with a straight four off Bowes. After a lovely shot through the covers off Hopwood, Bradman lingered in the by-ways of the 90s for some time, postponing the delicious vista he well knew awaited him to pluck a delicate wild flower of a single or so, and while he was there Ponsford stood with him awhile gazing at the wreck of England's 200 now past. At three o'clock Bradman topped the rise and the broad road lay straight and clean before him.

He never noticed the prickles of the new ball at 200 and went serenely on his way, turning Bowes to fine leg and hitting Hammond viciously past point and then straight. At 20 minutes to four, Wyatt was reduced to calling upon Leyland to bowl, no doubt vastly to that gentleman's amusement. No one expected him to get a wicket (he was neither good enough nor bad enough for that) and steadily and surely the runs mounted up. The batsmen were scoring pretty well as they liked without unduly forcing themselves or taking any risks; here a four, there a single, and occasionally a shot with no result at all. They beat England's score in their own right, so to speak, and went on to set a new record for a fourth-wicket partnership in Test matches (Bradman, of course, was in the other one, too) and it became quite impossible to conjecture how the business would end. At five minutes to five the partnership was worth 300 and when Ponsford put Mitchell away past mid-on for four two gentlemen in the Press box gave up their claim to having shared the biggest partnership in Test match cricket, which took place in the sun of Australia more than 30 years ago.

Bradman after tea was simply magnificent. He played Mitchell (nay, he played them all) with such consummate ease that the man ceased to bat and became a-boundary-recording machine. He took two fours and a single off one over from Hammond to make his score 200 at five minutes past five, and after raising his cap he went on in the same way towards the next milestone. It might be said that Ponsford gave a chance when Wyatt dived forward from silly mid-off to try to take the ball from the bat, but at 5.30, 400 was up. Wyatt at deep mid-off had done some excellent picking up, one-handed and two-handed, and showed most touching faith in Verity's length by standing close in to Ponsford. It is, however, poor consolation to this suffering England to know that her men fielded well. Heaven knows, they had plenty of practice.

After 5.30 Ponsford played a forcing bat shot of Verity, and we watched the ball going its inevitable way to the boundary. But what is this? Ponsford is walking away looking round in mild surprise at the wicket. We look, too, and see a ball on the ground. An absolute silence for one breathless second and then a roar of cheering. Ponsford trod on his wickets in making his shot, and so ended the greatest stand in Test cricket: 159 was Ponsford's share of it, and his whole Innings counted 181, in which there were 19 fours.

At ten minutes past six Bradman thought of another shot which he had not previously used on the day (it must surely have been the only one left) and he tried it out on Verity. He lifted the ball high to long leg where it dropped amongst the spectators for six. Meanwhile McCabe settled down as though he saw no reason why Bradman and Ponsford should be the only Australians to make a lot of runs, and he had three excellent fours before stumps were pulled up and the policemen raced to the middle to protect Bradman from the hysterical crowd. What they would have done to him I really do not know (the policemen won the race) but no honour could have been too high for the incredible cricketer. Look at him from any viewpoint you like; he has all the shots, he is master of himself; his stamina is amazing and his thirst for pure runs seems unquenchable. He is a textbook of batting come to life with never a mis-print or erratum.

Between 11 o'clock and 1.30 he made 76, from lunch until tea 93 and in the final hour and three-quarters 102, and has so far ('so far' mark you, after batting all day) hit two sixes and 39 fours.

From 39 for three the Australians have moved to 494 for four, and there is scarcely an England bowler who dare creep home tonight with the story. And all this before the largest crowd ever assembled at Headingley; let those who would venture on Monday not draw back. There is yet more homage to be paid to the game.

Bradman's innings began on July 31, 1934 – the second day of the Fourth Test. He eventually made 304 – which followed his 334 at Headingley in 1930 – before being bowled by Bill Bowes. Australia totalled 584 all out. The match was drawn.

Two Australians: 1934-35

D G BRADMAN and W H Ponsford, batsmen of Australia, have at least one characteristic in common; they amass huge scores. Fifty to them is merely indicative of the playing-in period safely passed, the century but 'a milestone along the road to progress, the end of the journey lying ever beyond'. Time and again these batsmen have made scores of over 200, not infrequently they have passed the 300 mark, and innings of 400 and more are not unknown to them.

Batsmen cannot make such big scores with such consistency without having something in common in their method, and in the case of Bradman and Ponsford the common factor is their determination. Determination to succeed in their self-appointed task makes them forego the delights of ordinary batsmen, makes them ignore or quell the craving for one wild glorious moment leading inevitably to destruction, and keeps them along the same road all the time. For them there is no wandering in the fragrant bypaths of big sixes and improbably unorthodox shots. They have their limitations, of which they are fully aware, and they never venture beyond the boundary fence of their own proved ability to dabble in the prohibited lands of uncertainty. Thus, and thus only, are great scores made with regularity. But with this much in common, Bradman and Ponsford then diverge widely in matters of detail. Test match spectators have had rare opportunity to study the difference between these two men, for this year they have been together in two stands which developed into affairs in which the only records left to be broken were their own.

Bradman is unquestionably the greater batsman of the two. Ponsford is always a little hesitant in starting; there is always a certain straining of his eyes and tentative pushing of the bat at the start of his innings, and there is always a period when the bowler can delude himself into believing that he might easily get Ponsford out. With Bradman there is no such hesitation. If he is to play a big innings, the signs are there from the first; without any delay or preamble he is hitting the ball in the middle of the bat and scoring runs with contemptuous ease. Nobody who saw those two back shots in the first over on that memorable Saturday at Leeds could help but read the writing on the wall or fail to appreciate its significance.

Bradman deals safely and profitably with balls that Ponsford makes no attempt to master. It is very doubtful if there is any batsman in the world who hits so hard as does Bradman the ball, of whatever pace, pitched only just short of a length on or outside the leg stick. Not for Bradman the swift covering up movement and the bat loosely held lest the ball spring off into the waiting leg trap. He stays where he is in line with the ball and, timing his shot to the last fraction of a second, hooks with all the incredible power in his wrists. Were he to miss the ball he would himself be hit, but that accident occurs very rarely indeed. For this particular ball, Ponsford has no counter. He could, no doubt, play the usual defensive back shot and risk a simple catch to short leg, but he invariably prefers to turn his back and allow the ball to hit him in a manner which has more than once drawn derisive and scornful laughter from the spectators.

Ponsford apparently admits his inability to deal with this

particular ball, and rather than risk losing his wicket in attempting to master it, he prefers to suffer what must amount to considerable physical pain. In view of these methods one can readily appreciate that leg-theory as bowled by Larwood, and as bowled by anyone else, is a distinctly variable quantity. Not that Ponsford is without many good shots; he cuts delightfully and as safely as anyone can cut, but he has this stroke under control and reserves it for the appropriate ball; never will he cut at anything not simply asking to be cut.

Bradman does not cut as late as Ponsford. He requires less time to see the ball and prefers to play it more towards (and invariably past) point, the ball leaving the bat with the speed of a bullet from a gun. Generally speaking, all Bradman's shots are played harder than Ponsford's, because Bradman's timing is so immeasurably superior. Ponsford gives the impression of playing forward more than Bradman; Ponsford plays forward as a defensive measure without any intention of making a scoring shot. To such balls Bradman finds an extra instant in which to play a forcing shot off his right foot, the ball generally going towards mid-on. Bradman goes forward to drive, and drives with a full swing of the bat, hitting the ball with tremendous force through the covers, but rarely straight. Ponsford is more sparing in his use of the drive, waiting patiently for the half-volley, without ever going to look for one on his own.

Bradman, of course, is far and away the more beautiful bat. Where Ponsford crouches at the wicket, Bradman stands upright, creating no impression of tenseness and strain, simply as a monarch surveying his all. Ponsford can become boring to watch, but Bradman, because of the miraculous power and perfection of timing, holds the interest to the end. It may seem that Ponsford does not come out too well from the comparison. Let it be remembered that it is only a comparison, and however superior in technique and attraction Bradman may be, Ponsford must have proved to his own and the satisfaction of everyone else that he knows a thing or two concerning the scoring of runs.

In Search of Cricket

The Farewell

THE 1948 Australians have played their last first-class match and their captain, DG Bradman, has played his last innings in England. The match was drawn at Scarborough yesterday, very much in Australian favour, so leaving the tourists with an unbeaten record, which is a unique achievement; Bradman made a century, which was a proper ending for a genius of batsmanship who has made approximately one century for every three innings of his career. The achievements are almost beyond belief, the methods certainly beyond adequate description. When Bradman has batted, thousands of people, in, and from, all parts of the world, have come to see for themselves.

Nobody, not even WG Grace, has attracted more attention to cricket: his last innings in the country where he has created so many of his most spectacular triumphs was clearly intended to be a century, and until he had reached 100 Bradman played well within himself, eliminating risk and error and scarcely falling from perfection for an instant. The prettiest of late cuts gave him his 13th boundary and took him to 100 in rather less than two and a half hours – after that he was indifferent to sixes or a catch in the long field, and provided both. Barnes, too, evidently felt that the occasion called for a century from Barnes. He spent four hours over it and then made a further 50 runs in 20 minutes, including three sixes and six fours and 24 runs in one over from Brown.

The Australians were 150 ahead at lunch-time, but as they were not concerned with outright victory and the interval extended itself to an hour most of the afternoon was spent in extravagance of hitting, good, bad and indifferent and quite meaningless. One mis-hit was unfortunate. It flew from the edge of the bat into Loxton's face and caused retirement with a broken nose. The tea-time interval, again unhurried, brought Australian declaration with a lead of 312 and the final proceedings while preserving the decencies were of the Festival festive.

September 11, 1948

Donald Bradman (New South Wales, South Australia) – the greatest of all batsmen – ended his career with a Test average of 99.94 runs and a first-class average of 95.14. In 52 Tests (just 80 innings), he scored 6,996 runs. In 338 first-class innings he totalled 28,067 runs with a highest score of 452 (not out, of course). He was born in 1908 in Cootamundra, New South Wales and died in Adelaide in 2001, aged 92.

He was knighted in 1949 and selected as one of Wisden's *five* Cricketers of the Century *in 2000.*

The Unforgettable Miller

THE Adelaide Oval has an easy and pleasant approach from the city's shopping and business area. The way lies across a wide bridge spanning the Torrens river and its embankment gardens and then along pathways through lawn and rosebeds to the main gates of the ground. The bridge links city centre with residential suburbs and carries public transport, thus permitting an improbability to be raised on my behalf one sunny afternoon. At the kerbside on the bridge five or six strikingly attractive young ladies were standing beneath a sign that read: Queue for Kilburn. An envious companion assured me that the girls were merely waiting for a local bus.

The Oval itself is world-renowned for its setting and outlook, though, as at Worcester, the beauty depends on the viewpoint of the beholder. From the seats in Adelaide, the background to cricket is the cathedral spire and distant blue hills, but from the open embankment of the popular side the eye that roves from the play finds little refreshment in severe outlines and garish paintwork.

One February morning in 1955 I gave myself the most uninspiring of all vantage points in the Oval. With my back to the main scoreboard and the cathedral I looked away from the soothing prospect of the hills down the length of the brown field towards the harsh colour and black shadows at the end of the semi-circling stand. My asceticism on this fifth morning of the fourth Test was self-imposed. I went to this unfrequented part of the ground to watch the cricket in a quietness the Press

Box or the crowded stand could not offer, to seek such freshness as still remained in the air of a scorching summer and, most of all I suppose, to relax in detachment. Touring cricketers, and to a lesser extent touring cricket-writers, need occasional recreation derived from wearing the face of personal joy or sorrow instead of the facade appropriate to professional proprieties.

The Test was in delicate balance after four days of careful manoeuvring for advantage – or, more strictly, for avoidance of disadvantage. England, batting second, had led by eighteen runs on first innings and had taken three Australian second innings wickets for 69 when stumps were drawn on the fourth evening. That all these three wickets had been taken by Appleyard after Benaud and Johnson had been the principal bowlers for Australia suggested that spin bowling would direct the remaining course of the match on a pitch that never had lifted the heart of fast bowlers. The fifth morning, by popular estimate, was to be conclusive. If England's spin bowlers, Appleyard and Wardle, could take immediate command England would be spared a daunting fourth innings. If that fourth innings demanded 200 runs or more Australia were probable winners of the match.

My expectations no doubt followed the general and logical pattern of opinion, but in my vigil near the sightscreen I isolated myself from prophet's boom and questioner's pleading. I wanted to avoid anticipation, analysis and argument; to watch in that state of consciousness without concern experienced in the first moments of recovery from anaesthesia. In this 'willing suspension of disbelief' I had no need to wonder why England's opening overs were given to speed instead of the anticipated spin. I merely saw Statham bowling and I felt no reaction of astonishment or elation when McDonald, pushing forward like a man with sleep still on his eyelids, was clean bowled. At the time it never occurred to me that England were winning the match illogically; that Australian batsmen were being overwhelmed by Statham and Tyson when they should have been struggling against Appleyard and Wardle. The Australian collapse seemed natural enough on the simple premise that the bowling was superior to the batting, but I thought I had better make a little bow to cricketing superstition by remaining where I was to keep the spell of desired success unbroken. Australia were 83 for eight when I returned to the Press Box.

I stayed there after lunch and knew no moment of mental ease or physical comfort until the match had ended. The afternoon temperature was not exceptionally high, but Adelaide in February is always hot and sun and sensation made the Oval a cauldron of bubbling emotion. By now some legend will surely have grown of the 'man who slept through it', but such distinction would mark a sorrow, for this was a cricketing experience granted only once or twice in a lifetime.

The Adelaide Press Box is an enclosure in the stand, open to the sights and sounds expressing public opinion as well as generating its own atmosphere. The afternoon uncertainty was in vivid contrast to the morning assurance. I saw formality turned into the fiercest fight. I felt, with every other spectator, the approach of the impossible. I bolstered with reason and recall of history a faith tested close to its limits. Detachment was out of the question and hysteria was a communal threat.

England's need was no more than ninety-four runs. Time was of no consequence; weather and pitch required no consideration; Australia were a weakened bowling force because of Johnson's arm injury. By no extravagance of calculation could an Australian victory have been reasonably devised as Keith Miller bowled the first over. By the end of it one wicket had fallen. By the end of his third over three wickets had fallen and England's total was twelve. Prophecy, prospect and probability were upsidedown.

It is a commonplace of sportswriting to say that some individual 'dominated the play' and the expression has lost its force, but it could have been properly used of Miller on this Adelaide afternoon. For an hour and more he commanded eyes, thoughts, hopes and fears. He rose gigantic in cricketing stature.

To the end of my cricket-remembering I shall know the agonies and ecstasies of that afternoon; feel the heat, shudder to the shouting as wickets fell, tremble with anticipation in the silences. Miller took us all beyond the contest between bowler and batsman, beyond the conventions and contrivances of a game, into the spiritual experience that is claimed as consequence of art and a justification for it. Miller himself would, I am sure, request dissociation from such elevated sentiment. He was not self-sacrificially defending Australia's last bridge,

Facing fearful odds
For the ashes of his fathers
And the temples of his Gods.

Not he. He was bowling in the mood of the moment, taking cricket in its context of the day. If I had spoken to him as I am now writing of him and of the emotions he inspired he would have said: 'Aw-come off it. I was only bowling'. By only bowling he yorked Edrich and had Hutton and Cowdrey caught in the slips. By only bowling he compelled defence of desire by unconvincing logic; the philosophy that says: 'It can't happen here. We must be able to raise 94 runs. Leg-byes, no-balls, edged boundaries, soon mount up. There is plenty of batting to come'. Even as we sought the comfort of such self-assurances May played back to Miller and the ball climbed sharply from the pitch to the splice of the bat. May was surprised and Miller was surprised and though the bowler changed direction in his follow-through and made swift strides up the pitch he could not reach the falling ball. In cold analysis the catch never was the chance of a catch, but in a thousand bedazzled eyes it was a looming reality.

May and Compton, who were not by nature subservient batsmen, challenged Miller only by inviting him to exhaust himself against their defensive shield. Through this partnership of repulse the scoreboard scarcely moved, but the tension scarcely slackened. The contest seemed to be entirely between Miller and the batsmen, with the overs from the other end somehow failing to impinge on the consciousness, but that impression is a measure of a major character rather than depreciation of the minors.

There was no assurance, no relaxation on the field and around it. Initiative remained with Miller until May and Compton played him into a rest from bowling. Miller tossed back his unruly hair, passed a forearm across the waterfall of his brow and moved casually into the covers for Johnston's bowling. May drove, firmly but with fractional mistiming that lifted the ball, never more than waist-high, so that it would have pitched just short of extra-cover and, unchecked, would certainly have rattled against the boundary fence. A catch was a consideration only because Miller created one.

In three floating strides he reached the point of interception, swooped with hands outstretched at ankle height, plunged to earth under his own momentum, rolled over and claimed his prize. England were 49 for four and nobody believed that the match was merely awaiting collection by obvious winners. Miller's catch raised controversy. As I remember, May moved immediately towards the dressing room when Miller took the ball, but Compton checked him with a cry: 'Go back'. A possibility was presented that the ball had been lost and recovered during Miller's fall. I have no direct observation to offer because the fieldsman had his back to the Press seats and his body shielded my view of the ball, but I never questioned the catch in the instant of its making – merely marvelled. I suppose I felt then, as I am inclined to feel now, that whether or not the catch were genuine it ought to have been, like an anecdote revealing character.

Miller could not win the match for Australia, by bowling or fielding, but he made England's victory a convalescence of relief after fever of uncertainty, delight augmented after the gloom of doubt. His was the day, though he held the stage for only an hour of it, though his team went down to defeat, though in technical excellence and effective endeavour he was matched by England's morning bowling and England's final batting. With a five-wicket margin of victory the match clearly reached a predictable end before its last overs, but it never descended to anti-climax. The winning hit was made by Evans, whose catchphrase through the tour had been 'We'll be there at the finish', and before the runs could be recorded arms were flung on high, cheers drowned the conventional clapping and more spectators were standing than sitting to applaud the players from the field.

Overthrows

Keith Miller (New South Wales, Victoria, Nottinghamshire) made 55 Test appearances. He scored 2,958 runs (average 36.97) and took 170 wickets (average 22.97). He was born in Melbourne in 1919 and died there in 2004, aged 84.

Lindwall on the Kill

RAY LINDWALL is a cricketer's cricketer. His major bowling virtues are not discernible by casual observation, and he has not the appearance and character to create a popular sporting figure. The cartoonists can make little of him; neither can most batsmen, though he is one of the easiest of fast bowlers to play – from the ring-side seats.

As his surname suggests, Raymond Russell Lindwall is of Scandinavian stock. But he is a second-generation Australian, born in Sydney on October 3, 1921, and nature has granted him the physique and quick co-ordination of mind and muscle that are the primary advantages of the games player. The young Ray Lindwall was rugby footballer as well as cricketer, and his cricket has lasted him all the longer because of a native toughness carefully cultivated and preserved. Rarely does he begin a spell of bowling without preliminary flexing of the muscles of back and legs, rarely does he attempt any action beyond the limit of his poise and control.

Since the season of 1945-46 he has played in 36 Test matches and withdrawn from only one through injury. No other fast bowler in cricket history can show a comparable record of appearances, and though Lindwall has been fortunate in the wisdom of his captains on tour he has been his own best nurse during his extensive career.

At first sight on the field he is not obviously the fast bowler of the side as, say, JM Gregory was the fast bowler, or Kenneth Farnes. He is no more than 5ft 10in tall, neither bulky nor slim, and without even a swagger in his walk. His shoulders and arms are not noticeably powerful though here, of course, there must be deception in appearances, as there must also be rare strength in the flannelled legs. In action Lindwall's magnificence remains partly disguised. His run-up looks leisurely and has no terrifying flamboyance of final leap to the crease. His arm is low in defiance of classical principles. He could be mistaken, from a great distance, for a commonplace bowler. Batsmen at closer proximity know better, and spectators in careful analysis revise opinions. Lindwall's bowling is in fact superbly designed. Not a step in the run-up is wasted, not an ounce of energy unnecessarily expended. Acceleration is progressive, culminating in a long delivery stride with a marked drag of the right foot. The right arm may not reach the vertical but it makes a wide sweep, fully stretched from beginning of the swing to the end. The head remains steady and the back is arched, though there is never any sense of strain. From first movement to last the whole action is splendidly controlled.

It is in his control that Lindwall's bowling greatness originates. His variation of pace can be properly appreciated only from the batting crease or by the wicketkeeper, but his variation of length, direction and swing are on view for the delight of any watchful connoisseur. Lindwall, as much as any fast bowler who ever lived, knows where he is bowling. If he wants to bowl a yorker, nine times out of 10 he does bowl a yorker. If he wants to remind the batsman that cricket is played with a hard ball his point is usually clear enough. His bumper may not rise so steeply from the pitch as does Millers', but it is no less disturbing to complacency or dignity. Lindwall is perhaps the only bowler whom Jardine would have found acceptable as substitute for the Larwood of 1932-33. Since he came into first-class cricket there have been few occasions when Lindwall looked less than a good bowler. In his casual overs, when neither the pitch nor the state of the game offers him any incentive, he strolls through the formalities with accomplished ease and clear conservation of energy. In crisis he is menace unmistakable, thunderous and thrilling as the crashing surf on Sydney beaches.

With Lindwall 'on the kill' cricket becomes an enthralling, breath-catching spectacle, magnetic to players and watchers alike. Greatness transcends the spirit; drama charges the atmosphere. Lindwall seen in a match without meaning could be forgotten; Lindwall concentrated upon a purpose stays in the mind for ever. When England were 455 for 6 wickets in the scorching heat of Adelaide in 1947 Lindwall suddenly caught and bowled Compton and then took a new ball to end the innings in one swift over. In 1948 at The Oval England were all out for 52 and Lindwall's figures were 6 for 20. His many battles with Hutton, champion against champion, are the pinnacle of current cricket. How much Lindwall enjoys his chosen game or is conscious of his own splendour lies hidden from the general gaze. Only in the fierce appeal when breakback or inswinger thuds against obstructing pads does the inner passion show, though once at Old Trafford in 1948 he was driven out of temper, to judge by the snatch of sweater from the umpire and the haste of his captain to speak soothing words. Without some hardness, some roughness of character, Lindwall could not be the cricketer he is. Great fast bowlers are not of apologetic inclination, and by the very nature of their attack they must live in some isolation of spirit. They must feel a little hate when a batsman faces them.

On the field Lindwall wears an air of detachment between assaults. He holds, or assumes, a philosophy of contemplation, born, no doubt, of slip catches gone astray or the inability of batsmen to touch his outswinger. His gestures of disappointment or satisfaction are few, and becoming fewer with the ripeness of years. The more he plays cricket in England the more he accepts the English disinclination to demonstrate, yet he would not easily be mistaken for anything but an Australian. The stamp of independence, of equality between Jack and master, is firmly upon him. He looks as though he knows how to look after himself. It is Lindwall the bowler who will always be remembered in cricket, and rightly so, but Lindwall is also a batsman above despising. He has taken more than 100 Test match wickets and there is every likelihood of his having made more than 1,000 Test match runs before this rubber is ended. At Melbourne England once found that he had scored a century before the field-placing could be adjusted to cope with his hitting, and at Lord's this season he was a batsman of distinction as well as a bowler.

His fielding is invariably competent in an unobtrusive manner. Ray Lindwall would be a useful cricketer without bowling at all; yet as the world's worst batsman and fielder he would still, for bowling alone, hold unquestioned place among the cricketing immortals.

July 1953

Ray Lindwall (New South Wales, Queensland) played in 61 Tests and took 228 wickets at a cost of 23.03. He was born in Sydney in 1921 and died in Brisbane – aged 74 – in 1996.

Made in Australia

CRICKETERS on tour and attendant recording angels see more of countries visited than the majority of residents, but impressions are necessarily superficial and founded on questionable values. The transient on privileged terms is in no position to offer definitive assessment of domestic concerns. The happiest and most productive travel derives from the preservation of a sense of wonder. I have been fortunate enough to see something of Australia from tropical Darwin to temperate Tasmania, from Pacific beaches to dusty desert, but I am in no position to determine whether or not I should appreciate life in Australia on a permanent and irrevocable footing.

I can and do declare that I enjoyed experience of Australia. Thanks to cricket I had opportunity to go there and because of a cricketing purpose I was granted facilities and comforts to be acknowledged with gratitude and remembered with delight.

With increasing scope for transportation tours for sport have become almost commonplace. Through every month of every year a cricket expedition is being undertaken somewhere in the world and familiarity does tend to breed its proverbial outcome. For the over-indulged traveller satisfactions come to be measured in terms of hotel plumbing, airport efficiency and the view from a dressing-room window or a Press-box seat. Whatever the inclination, there is often no time to stand and stare.

In Australia and on journeys to and fro I was happily enabled to indulge a romantic predilection. I was given time to stand and stare at Sydney Harbour, at ocean sunsets, at the gaunt destruction left by a Victorian forest fire, at the fury of a Brisbane thunderstorm, at the grace of skilful surf-board riders. I knew transcendental moments when I looked at myself in disbelief that who I was should be where I was – an English provincial in the bustle of Sydney's Martin Place, in the dusty main street of Northam pausing before the swinging half-doors that gave access to a saloon whose amenities included a hitching rail for horses. Like the 17-year-old Leonard Hutton finding himself playing for Yorkshire I could relish an improbable reality. Hutton chuckled in his moment of wonder on a journey from Hull to Lord's; I was probably too frightened of falling off the magic carpet to risk a chuckle in Australian sun, but I offered, my silent thanks.

Cricket took me to Australia and was my principal preoccupation there, but in a list of Australian satisfactions I doubt if I would rank cricket first. Cricket in England, to my way of thinking, is a more alluring form of recreation than in Australia because it offers a greater variety of circumstances for play. Australian cricket is, of necessity, founded on an artificial basis. It is not a meadow game because the 'wide, brown land' has few meadows where two or three, or twenty-two, can gather in an evening, pitch the wickets and improvise a contest with bat and ball. The English field gave cricket to England but the Australians have had to take cricket and pursue it under pressures of practicality. From their limitations they have contrived skills of world renown.

The Australian cricketer, or someone on his behalf, has to work before he is able to play. Half an hour with a roller and ten minutes with a whitewash brush will not give him even the appearance of a pitch. To make cricket feasible he must manufacture a surface which might be wood, concrete, composition or clay. The Australian groundsman, who calls himself a curator, is as much an engineer as a horticulturalist. His concern is not so much the cultivation of turf on which cricket can be played as the construction of a surface for a specific occasion of cricket. The leading curator is distinguished by his mastery of the mechanics.

The cricketer in Australia plays in virtually the same conditions at all stages of his career. The pitch is of fundamentally the same texture for his school cricket, his club or grade cricket, his State cricket and his home Test cricket. In Sydney and Perth, 1,000 miles apart, the ball will behave in much the same way, consequently batting and bowling reactions do not need the fine shadings demanded by the infinite variety in the behaviour of turf in England. The Australian cricketer has less to learn and more opportunity to learn quickly. Technically he can become a Test match player at school and Australians can, and frequently do, leap up the ladder from obscurity to fame. Uniformity of playing conditions deprives the Australian cricketer of scope for satisfactions from adaptability. He cannot, in his own country, age gracefully or use his head to save his legs. He comes, he sees, he conquers and he abdicates. He can rarely linger in a supplementary guise that might be well within his capacity but finds no useful sphere of operation. E A McDonald derived more from cricket by joining Lancashire than he could have done by remaining in Australia. He became a great fast bowler in Australia and was an equally great fast bowler in England, but English conditions allowed him additional satisfactions and effectiveness as an off-break bowler that he could never have found in Australia. Australian pitches and weather would have discouraged, if not prohibited, the translation of Trueman in his later playing years from devastating speed to inspiring spells of 'cut' and swing.

These observations are not designed for any deprecation of Australian cricket, which has given me countless hours of enjoyment and cause for admiration. Unusual travel arrangements necessitated by after-war conditions took Hammond's team of 1946 and some attendant descriptive writers to Western Australia three weeks before the official programme of matches began.

The MCC team occupied the time in acclimatisation through net practice and two games arranged at Northam and Freemantle, outposts of cricket not normally intrigued by the sight of international players. The visits were deemed beneficial.

So, too, were the undertakings of another collection of cricketers. Arthur Mailey, once a great Test bowler and later a cricket-writer and cartoonist of uncommon perception and wit, raised a team from the English and Australian journalists assigned to the tour. The object of the exercise was not only to give pleasure to those invited to play but also to stimulate cricketing interest in schools and clubs at whose request matches were arranged.

Mailey's proposal was given practical form in the establishment of a club under the comprehensive and rather grandiose title of *Empire Cricket Writers*. Mailey, modest and inconsequential in personal concerns, liked to bring sentiment and style into his public creations. He appeared on the field in the most disreputable of accoutrement but he gave wholehearted exhibition of the extravagant and bewildering spin bowling that had made him famous in the cricket of the 1920s.

He asked the same approach from his teams. We may have creaked a little in the joints, we may have looked a motley crew with borrowed pads and bats, but we were expected to exhibit our remaining talents without reservation. Some of the talent would have been worthy of expression in any company. In our opening match, played on the Perth ground where MCC were later to begin their first-class programme, we had JH Fingleton to bat for us, supported by the South Australian RS Whitington and Vivian Jenkins of Glamorgan. We had Bill Bowes and Arthur Mailey and EM Wellings, of Surrey, among our bowlers and George Duckworth was wicketkeeper. As the tour progressed and the writers' corps expanded the *Empire Cricket Writers* team gained distinction and strength from the addition of AB Sellers, from Percy Beames, the dashing Victorian batsman, and from an aggressive bowler named WJ O'Reilly. With such players available we came under pressure to exceed our original brief and undertake matches to raise money for charities. The founders' conception of our purpose, which was always preserved, was to take cricket to schools in an attempt by our small means to safeguard the continuity of cricket tradition threatened by the break of war years.

Whatever the outcome, the experience was thoroughly enjoyable. Our three weeks in Perth offered more fixtures than we could accommodate and we engaged ourselves in all the States during days between our professional obligations. With the talent and experience at our command individual responsibility was rarely under severe pressure, but I was impressed by one characteristic of our play that seemed to be based on national differences of outlook. We all tried to play to the best of our ability, but where those of us from England sometimes deployed the ability to offer a concession the Australians usually insisted on asserting their authority. The Australian batsman, for example, would end a dominating innings by retirement rather than through sacrifice by an extravagant stroke. Australian bowlers would appeal against boy batsmen with the fervour and frequency associated with Test match cricket. I asked about this approach and it was readily confirmed. 'You have to be tough with Australian kids,' I was told. 'They can take it'. They certainly could and they reacted with a similar form of toughness. School batsmen invariably came to the crease with every outward sign of self-assurance. During one match in Perth, Bowes was bowling to a field that included a forward short leg. The young batsman was obviously of aggressive intent, but he was given no scope for scoring shots and in his frustration he swished his bat and said to me: 'I wish he would drop just one short enough for me to move you'.

Apart from the Writers' team matches there were many individual invitations to play. These usually took us into the 'bush' where playing conditions were much more primitive than on the carefully tended school grounds. On one occasion Bowes, Duckworth, Sellers and I were taken from Melbourne to appear in a festivity at the little town of Healesville. Most of the morning was occupied in a motor journey from the coastal metropolis towards the forested hills and because our hosts had to make calls on various friends on the way the lunch arranged for players and officials had long been started when we arrived at the Healesville hotel. Our tardiness in no way affected the duration and substance of the meal. When the local players left the dining-room to go to the ground we were not allowed to accompany them. We had more eating to do. 'The others will get the game started,' we were told. 'You can go down later'. We did go down later to discover the Healesville Oval the centre of high holiday and a general atmosphere of fairground noise and bustle. The team to which the four overwhelmed and overfed visitors were attached had begun their innings and by the scoreboard were making comfortable progress, but interpolation of the visitors changed the balance of the game. We were sent in to bat in succession – Sellers, Duckworth, Kilburn, Bowes. There was a sound-amplifying system on the ground and an enthusiastic speaker behind it. Sellers walked to the crease to the accompaniment of a eulogy 'Great player-captain of great Yorkshire team-selector for England-great day for Healesville . . .' and so on until Sellers had reached the wicket and taken guard. By this time the attention of all present had been concentrated. Small boys laid aside their footballs, seniors suspended discussion on the problems of agricultural prices and the injustices of world society, the ladies' committee and helpers stopped preparing tea. Sellers was out first ball – lbw. No prestige appeared to be lost. He walked back to resumed eulogy over the loudspeaker and sustained applause that implied exceptional merit in his performance.

George Duckworth, one of the most popular England cricketers ever to visit Australia, received his elaborate introduction over the public-address system. He, too was out first ball. He edged a waist-high slip catch that was comfortably held. George ignored the incident. He gazed down the pitch, smiling seraphically through the uncertainties of the moment, and then took up his stance to receive the next ball. His second innings was longer than the first but contributed no more to the total and, after the four visitors had concluded their batting with an aggregate of seven runs, credited almost entirely to Bowes, play was suspended for the tea interval. Interval is used as a technical term. Tea was a major feature of the afternoon proceedings. In quantity it was enormous; in variety it encompassed the whole range of local produce and home baking. Healesville residents appeared to find no abnormality in either the timetable or the banquet, but four Englishmen, their appetites still conditioned by years of wartime austerity, watched and shared with barely concealed amazement. Hospitality continued with resumption of the cricket match. Duckworth was required to keep wicket. Bowes as an England bowler, Sellers and I as exponents at a lower level, were requested to bowl two overs each. After that the four of us were withdrawn from the field and replaced by waiting substitutes. 'You've done your share,' we were told. 'It's time you had some refreshment'.

This pressure of hospitality and persistent expression of anxiety for our well-being was characteristic of this tour throughout Australia. Cricketers and those associated with them found sympathy and good wishes everywhere. As the MCC programme advanced and Australian superiority on the field became more and more evident strangers would stop in the street to express a hope that England would win at least one Test. They never did, because Australian cricket was much the stronger at the time, but England's players were given popular support to the end of the series. A cynic might advance the view that England popularity maintained proportion to Australian success and this suggestion has, indeed, been given supporting evidence on other occasions, but I doubt it applied to the tour of 1946-7. Thinking back and making comparison with further experiences I believe that Australians in the immediate post-war period felt a genuine admiration for the endurance Britain had shown under bombardment and the secondary stresses of conflict. Australians seemed slightly embarrassed by the creature comforts of their homeland and were glad of an opportunity to share them. Cricket and cricketers presented one such opportunity and though the tour of Hammond's team was disastrous by measure of playing results, the cricket never lacked public attention and welcome. The crowds were enormous and there was much more regret than recrimination over individual shortcomings. Hammond's personal batting failure in the Tests was an Australian disappointment, and sentiment for these six months was on the side of the inadequate.

In the context of cricket history the MCC tour of 1946-7 was not of outstanding significance. It illustrated a peak of Australian playing supremacy that continued through 1948 and lasted until 1953. The supremacy was emphasised by the rather unexpected continuation of Bradman's career and the decidedly unexpected anticlimax and departure presented by Hammond. In the absence of both these champions Australia would still have been stronger than England in 1946-7 and 1948, but with Bradman in power and Hammond unauthoritative or absent the margin was overwhelming. In golfing terms the rubs of the green favoured Bradman and ran against Hammond. When Hammond arrived in Australia for his last tour his path promised to be rose-strewn all the way. He was an admired leader in the world of cricket, his batting and fielding still gleaming with achievement. His one first-class innings in Western Australia brought him a score of 206.

Bradman in that Australian springtime was an uncertainty in cricket – in the public mind, that is. He was little beyond the stage of convalescence after serious and recurrent illness. So astonishing had been his pre-war performances that anything further he could do was almost bound to represent decline more than advance. To play again, at Test match level, was to hazard health and reputation.

After the England party had travelled by train across the desert from Perth to the eastern States a two-day halt was made on the border of South Australia for a match at Port Pirie. It was a match of goodwill more than of cricketing consequence and remains memorable to me only for the extensive follow-through of one of the Country XI bowlers. He invariably finished his run-through within a yard or two of the striking batsman and on one occasion I was delighted to observe the wicketkeeper hand the ball, not throw it, to the exuberant bowler. Bill Bowes and I agreed that one night in a Port Pirie hotel constituted fulfilment of social and journalistic obligations, so we deserted the match to make early arrival in Adelaide. We called on Bradman at his stockbroker's office. We asked, as all the world was asking, whether or not he would play more cricket.

He said he did not know. We enquired about his batting form. He said he did not know about that, either, but suggested we join him at the Adelaide Oval where he was to have a net. We joined him. To me the experience was worth a hundred days of watching minor matches. It was Bradman's first practice of the season. He was eager and cheerful in spirit, but he looked frail and drawn and immeasurably older than the husky players assigned to bowl to him. As I watched from behind the net I felt I should not have guessed that this was a first practice of the season but would also not have recognised Australia's greatest batsman had Bradman been unknown to me. All the bowling was fast medium, competent but undistinguished. Bradman played a back-foot shot intended to force the ball towards mid-on. He picked up the ball from the side net in the square-leg position and murmured what sounded like 'No-no'. The next half-dozen deliveries all produced fierce flawlessly timed back-foot shots that would have left helpless any mid-on not directly in the line of the speeding ball. I had seen enough to assure me of the return of Bradman and the coming destruction of England bowling. I had seen enough to appreciate the ability that made possible the scoring of a century once in every three innings played throughout a career.

The net bowlers were not 'feeding' Bradman for practice in a particular stroke. They did not offer the ball at a length on a specified line. Bradman made the choice stroke and the satisfaction of accomplishment in those few minutes may well have been a factor in his decision to extend his first-class career. Had he failed to convince himself in practice, and in his first few innings of 1946, that his technical resources remained he might never have played for Australia again. He was convinced. He did play again for Australia and in 23 post-war innings in Test cricket he completed nine centuries and averaged over 100 in an aggregate of 1,903 runs. Fortune favoured him through the closing scenes. A debated decision over a slip catch gave him opportunity to develop an uncertain innings into a masterful one at Brisbane. A weak Indian touring side gave him scope for happy and brilliant batting in 1947-8. He was able to come to England in 1948 as captain of a magnificent team virtually assured of success.

To Hammond fortune showed another face. In his final tour of Australia he led a team that proved to be outclassed. Hammond himself was under a cricketing strain and under personal strain through involvement in divorce. At Brisbane the weather in the first Test gave England's batsmen no chance to match the Australian score and thereafter Hammond was out of luck when he most needed it. At Sydney, having rightly resolved to attack the leg-spin bowling, he was caught in an improbable fielding position. At Melbourne he went to the crease with thunder on his brow induced by real or imagined umpiring injustices. He swept the ball to the mid-wicket boundary with force enough to have sent it twice as far; he drove, with evident passion, low and hard and was caught and bowled in what cricketers recognise as a form of accident. At Sydney, again Hammond was denied a farewell appearance. He could not play because of fibrositis.

Comparisons between Bradman and Hammond as batsmen must be for ever inconclusive and fruitless, but in the manner of their career endings the luck of little things contrasted machination with tribute. Bradman, it is true, finished his Test batting with 0 when the stage was set for his 100, but his departure was not in defeat or in shadow, whereas Hammond's curtain in Australia conveyed a sense of classical tragedy. In cricket there was never any cause to feel sorry for Bradman;

Hammond won sympathy from humans because it was not accorded him by the fates. For those who played and watched in the time of Bradman and Hammond, the memory of the two at the crease is imperishable and the impression they created is almost impossible to convey through analysis, explanation and eulogy. What Bradman and Hammond meant to their contemporaries is in the light shining from a reminiscent eye, in the warmth and tremble of a tone of voice. Their greatness in batting was utterly convincing. From all the thousands of words spoken and written in tribute to Bradman's ability the most telling and definitive of my experience were uttered during the Headingley Test match of 1934. Bradman was at the wicket throughout the second day, his mastery complete. My next door neighbour in the Press box was Wilfred Rhodes, commissioned to supply ghosted comment (not to me), and so far as I remember he offered no word of opinion during morning or afternoon. Shy and busy – for in those days 2,000 words was a common daily stint – I had said nothing to Rhodes beyond the civilised pleasantries of juxtaposition.

Towards the close of play I was writing hard when he turned towards me confidentially and expressed an admiration for Bradman he could evidently contain no longer 'Good player,' he said. Years later – in 1953 it must have been – I had Bradman in the next Press box seat at Lord's. He was an irreproachable working companion, thoroughly professional in his acceptance of conventions. He claimed no privilege, made no complaint over manifest inconveniences afflicting everyone. He was courteously responsive to all approaches, meticulously appreciative of a neighbour's needs for desk space and peace for concentration. How much his match reports were edited before publication I cannot say, but I do know that handwritten 'copy' in adequate quantity was always available for the collecting messenger. Bradman in the Press box was neither a nuisance nor a 'deadhead' and there will be no objection from me should we ever again be allocated adjoining seats.

Thanks to Cricket

Diary of a Cricket Tourist

CONSIDERATION of current affairs in Australia without the mention of cricket would be unbalanced. England's victory in the Test match rubber has not represented all the recent news and conversation but no other topic has exceeded it in general interest, and in the newspapers, the front pages, sports page, and letters to the editor have discussed the whys and wherefores of the Australian fall from high estate at remarkable length and with astonishing diversity of opinion. Many reasons for the Australian defeat have been offered but few excuses. The acknowledgment of England's cricketing superiority at the moment has been wholehearted and widespread; though in praising England the Australians have been perhaps unduly harsh in the censure of their own players, the selectors and the administration. Australian criticism of their own shortcomings always tends to be violent and this is their own business, but there is room for objection to the attitude of English commentators who are currently inclined to offer advice on the reorganisation of Australian cricket.

Advice was less readily forthcoming when the same system

of Australian selection and administration was producing notable Australian success not so many years ago. Len Hutton, England's captain, has been particularly careful to avoid any impression of superiority. He has accepted victory with obvious thankfulness and satisfaction, but he has not overlooked the closeness of the struggle, or under-estimated the virtues in the Australian team. Nobody has more reason to appreciate the force still remaining in Australian bowling and fielding, and Hutton was paying more than a tribute of formal politeness when he said he wished that Keith Miller would concentrate on batting and that he counted Alan Davidson the finest close in-fieldsman in the world.

Precise assessment of Hutton's feelings when the last ball had been bowled at Adelaide is almost impossible, for he has never worn his heart on his sleeve and the self-control that is in his batsmanship has always been evident in his public life. The reserve that is an essential part of his nature may lead to occasional misunderstandings with more forthcoming characters, but throughout this tour his obligations and Press relations seem to have been happily handled. No doubt some variation could be traced between private and public sentiments but he has borne the inescapable publicity with patience and grace and he has been approachable at all reasonable times.

The considerable company of journalists following the tour have been helped more than discouraged and Hutton even provided them with some prophesies that have proved reliable. In the early days he said that Tyson and Statham would no doubt break some stumps as the Australian summer progressed and he placed May and Cowdrey high among his batsmen; and after the rout at Brisbane he gave an assurance of better things for Sydney.

The Brisbane experience was the only dark period of the tour. There is credit due for the revision of technique and the resurgence of spirit that brought the later triumphs. On the whole the touring cricketers have been lucky in their experience of Australian weather. Perth in the spring gave them a comfortable introduction; Brisbane was kind in providing unusually low humidity, and comparatively cool nights; Sydney offered an encouraging breeze; the fearful Melbourne day of searing wind and temperature above 100 chanced to be a Sunday; the Adelaide heat wave broke as the Test match began.

Playing conditions have, of course, been a severe trial to the tourists as Australian conditions must always be, but they have not been enervating to a point of exhaustion. The flies and mosquitoes are increasing their forces for the ultimate assault and the parched brown land urges waves of hot air to the formation of mighty thunder storms. Air passages have become rather rough, particularly when flights are the lower levels. Australia is a sunburnt country of sunburnt people. It is a country of evening parties out of doors – but still with grilled steak or chops on the menu. A country of midnight bathing in pool or sea or stream; a country of shorts and shirtsleeves for the less inhibited male and the brightest of frocks for the ladies; a country of bush fire danger and water shortage in the less fortunate parts; a country drenched in fierce light and gathering its layer of seasonal dust. But the tiring summer days and nights and the momentary disappointments of sporting defeat cannot quench the vitality in Australian life. This is a country where the prevailing philosophy involves a belief that 24 hours are not too many for a day's enjoyment.

February 1955

A Game to Remember

A GOOD many games of cricket will be played in the North and will pass from memory before Yorkshire's recent game with the Australians is forgotten. Test matches or no Test matches, that was, I think, very nearly the match of the season and though topicality is supposed to be the lifeblood of journalism I hope I need offer no apology for this recapitulation.

There would have been a stir of anticipation in the air in any event on the morning of Saturday, July 2, but when the assembled multitude discovered that Yorkshire had won the toss and invited the Australians to bat there were cheers of excitement to be heard around Bramall Lane. Wickets were not pitched until quarter to twelve because of the damage done by the overnight storm and the morning hours, much to Yorkshire's regret were sunless and grey, yet the Australian innings began badly and whilst tribute was still being paid to the virtues of the new ball both Fingleton and McCabe were dismissed for no more than 20 hurried, uneasy runs. When, at 41, Verity was called into action Bradman and Badcock were preserving a perilous existence and the wicket was beginning to show distinct traces of liveliness; Verity, indeed, almost achieved success in his second over for Badcock edged him beyond Turner in the gully, but to the general surprise and to the undisguised dismay of the Yorkist hordes the remainder of the morning, save for the departure of Badcock at 58, was wholly Australian. Bradman drove and pulled and pranced and pirouetted and suggested that he had been brought up from the nursery on turning wickets. He was gone; though, by half past two, stumped off Smailes when he had seen his side beyond 100 and taken his personal total to 59. Such score is, of course, normally accounted failure to Bradman, but it was no failure this day for it answered a problem some of us have long pondered and it announced that the highest batsmanship contains always the quality of adaptability. The most curious feature of this curious day was the uncompromising failure of Verity to accept the throne of domination that had been carefully set for him. During the afternoon he retired to the comparative obscurity of plain fieldsmanship and by Smailes, with his off-spinners, was seized the bowling honour of the innings. The sixth Australian wicket fell at 125, but Hassett took charge of the remaining proceedings and played such skilful and gallant cricket that the knowledgeable multitude abandoned patriotism and gave him unstinted adulation. They roared appreciation of the sixes pulled and driven off Smailes and Robinson and they were genuinely grieved to find him missing a century by six runs.

To the Australian total of 222 Yorkshire had responded with 74 for 3 at close of play, and Sutcliffe had been compelled to interrupt his innings because of a split finger. He returned to the wicket, though, on Monday when Smailes had been caught at cover at 81, but an old trap was once again successfully laid and Fingleton, away on the leg boundary, held a catch off Waite. Only Wood and Robinson made much pretension towards a stand, their partnership for the eighth wicket putting on 42 runs, and shortly after luncheon Yorkshire were all out and 17 runs in arrears.

The remainder of the day was magnificently Yorkist. Bowes

held the early batsman in the most uncomfortable subjection and if he took only two wickets he experienced the dreadful misfortune of having both Badcock and Bradman missed in the slips. It is invariably a characteristic of the major Australian batsman that they are either out or at ease and progressive; this time there was survival in acute discomfort and with little profit.

Rain was responsible for a short interruption just before tea-time, but when sunshine followed, the Australians went rapidly to destruction. Bradman, who can scarcely ever have had to fight harder for 42 runs, again yielded up his wicket to Smailes and the whole innings was over at ten minutes past six for 132.

Speculation on the Tuesday morning was widespread and fantastically varied. Yorkshire, requiring 150 runs for victory, were thought to have no chance whatever, to be certain of victory, and to be likely winners by anything from eight to two wickets or losers by anything between 10 and 100 runs. The actual ending, so far as I can remember, was never even contemplated. The morning was dull when Verity and Wood continued the innings that had known only formal opening and by the time 18 runs had been scored (13 of them in one over from McCormick) two wickets were down: Wood having been bowled and Verity run out. There was high alarm in Yorkshire's camp, but Sutcliffe and Hutton did much to soothe fluttered nerves by batsmanship of gentle persuasion. They served by waiting and took only those runs that were to be gathered in safety.

At quarter to one, Hutton was caught in Waite's leg trap, but Barber held on until lunch time when the scoreboard showed 83 for 3. Sutcliffe, an hour and fifty minutes at the wicket, had played by no means the least meritorious of his innumerable great innings. His every action from the quiet push forward to the determined leg hit suggested a man not only master of his own fate, but of the fate of a whole match as well. The imagination could not have pictured a worthier spectacle of concentrated endeavour. During the luncheon interval came rain and during the afternoon came shower after shower; at four o'clock Sellers and Bradman strode to the middle, looked upon the sodden turf and shook hands in admission of the inevitable. An amazing match had ended in anti-climax. We who saw will never forget; we shall wonder and no doubt argue for the rest of our cricketing days. No sooner do we convince ourselves of Yorkshire victory than we think of hat-tricks and historic collapses; no sooner do we contemplate Australian chances than we remember the calm assurance that was Sutcliffe. For myself, I should not have been greatly surprised over either Yorkshire's or Australia's success, but I should have been astounded had Sutcliffe not seen the game to its end. It would have been against Nature.

The Cricketer, August 1938

Chapter Seven:
EXTRAS

Weather Bound

CRICKETING DAYS remembered are coloured by the weather. Sometimes it is a backcloth, sunshine to a century, heavy atmosphere to a bowling triumph, rain or threat of rain to a dramatic finish. Always it is a significant item. No description of cricket is complete without indication of the weather conditions and the state of the pitch. Somewhere, somehow, the circumstances of play must be conveyed if the picture is to have life and meaning. Without a setting some flavour of the game is lost and some truth. A journalistic joke reflects wisdom when agency representatives are required to report at each day's beginning: 'Weather fine (dull) (showery) (cold). Wicket good (soft) (broken). Hours of play: 1.30 to 6.30 or variations'.

I marvel that cricket writers can cross the world and report a match in Sydney that might have been taking place in Sussex for all the indication given. Time and place, light and shade, heat and cold are factors as relevant as the bowling figures or the sum of boundaries hit. The feel of a cricket occasion may be even more significant and memorable than the facts in the scorebook. I shall always believe that weather changes scarcely mentioned in contemporary accounts were an England ally during the tour of 1954-5. The strong wind that raised Tyson's pace at Sydney has been well recorded but there is little mention of blessings England received at Melbourne and Adelaide.

The Melbourne Test covered a weekend of exceptional heat in which a north wind seared the city. Of the Sunday conditions I have two illustrative recollections. My hotel room had a window which could be opened top and bottom and which ran almost from floor to ceiling. For an hour in the morning I was writing at a desk by the window with the lower pane pushed up to allow breeze, though not direct sunshine, into the stifling room. I was wearing khaki shirt and shorts, but not the three-quarter-length stockings that would have made the attire conventional for outdoor appearance in Australian mid-summer. When I moved from the desk I felt my legs to be stiff and sore and examination showed them to be scorched as though they had been in a flame.

Later in the morning I sought to refresh myself with a bar of chocolate that had been in a drawer overnight. I would have needed a spoon to eat it.

Though the wind had dropped before Test match play continued, the temperature was in the nineties Fahrenheit at breakfast-time on the last morning, when England had to take eight wickets before Australia scored 165 more runs. The state of the deteriorating pitch suggested that chances were about even for batsmen and bowlers. Before the start of play Denys

Rowbotham, of the *Guardian*, and I were taking our customary mid-morning tea in a refreshment bar near the Press Box. The room was airless and sweltering so we moved outside with our drinks, preferring the burn of sun to the threat of suffocation. As we sipped and speculated we became conscious of a sharp change in the air. The sky stayed a brilliant blue, the sun lost none of its brightness and power, but breathing became easier, the skin felt fresher, alertness returned.

In this 'cool change', as Australians name it, temperatures can fall by as much as 20°F within an hour. In this case they fell from summer distress to summer delight and with fast bowling of sustained resolve Tyson and Statham tumbled Australia to defeat by 128 runs. The bowling and fielding were literally inspired. At Adelaide in the same series a similar climatic benevolence was bestowed, though this time over a whole match. In the preceding week normal life in the city had been scarcely tolerable. Daytime temperatures soared beyond the 100 and the dark hours brought little relief; mosquitoes also could not sleep. Road-surfaces melted and policemen on traffic duty needed the protection of a sunshade. Bush-fire smoke crowned Adelaide's circling hills and the sand at Glenelg was too hot for beach recreation.

Test match eve brought the change. Down dropped the temperature, up went the spirits. The game was played in hot weather, but not in a furnace, as it would have been a week earlier. England's players, fulfilling up-country engagements in cooler areas, escaped the Adelaide heat-wave and they won the Test match. The most spectacular climatic interference with cricket in my personal experience was undoubtedly the Brisbane thunderstorm of 1946. I have seen Lord's briefly carpeted in white by hailstones; I have seen Old Trafford submerged in half an hour; I have seen the lower part of Headingley flooded knee-deep, but I have never known anything commparable with the Brisbane visitation.

It began with an ominous calm, with a swift darkening of the tea-time sky. There was no rain as the players strolled from the field after appeal against the light. There was no rain with the first steely-blue flashes of lightning. This was a period of grace for seeking shelter, though the shelter had to be close at hand. The first raindrops made splashes big enough to represent a little pool and whirlwinds spiralled litter ten and twenty feet in the air. Raindrops became hailstones, big enough and hard enough to bounce from the open seats and terracing. In the Press Box, which was at that time little more than improvised accommodation at the back of the main stand, we spoke to each other in wonder at the density of the downpour and the intensity of the lightning. Five minutes later we had no means of verbal communication. Each one of us was cut off from all others in a cacophony that defied the loudest shout. Shrieking wind tossed tarpaulin from the pitch and flattened sightscreens. The downpour of hailstones stretched a curtain across the field and rattled on the roof as though all the kettledrums in the world were being played together. Anyone without some feeling of fear must also have been without imagination.

English weather is less alarming but it can bring memorable discomfort to cricketing occasions. May days can be cruelly cold. Derbyshire and Yorkshire once abandoned a match at Chesterfield in snow that was still lying over the whole field as the players left the ground on the way to their next engagement. Arthur Mitchell once fielded at Fenner's with two pairs of flannels over his pyjama trousers.

I think I touched my nadir of reporting discomfort on the Castle ground at Colchester. The whole day was damp and cold and windy and the Press accommodation was a small tent, sited to face the breeze. In late afternoon the rain came, driving before the wind into every corner of the tent. There was nowhere else to go; the pavilion was on the far side of the ground and the nearer stands were plank-and-scaffolding and unroofed.

A tide of water swept across the trestle writing-table and the grass beneath the freezing feet was liquid mud. There had been sufficient play before the rain to demand at least a half-column account and for some reason, presumably telegraphic, it had to be written at the ground. The desk was useless because paper became soaked and the words illegible as soon as they were written. I was cold; I was wet; I was miserable.

I took a chair to a corner of the tent, turned my back to the field and rain, gave the paper such protection as I could with raincoat and huddled body and used knees for a desk. The substance of the message, its character and its dispatch have long since passed from mind but I remember with gratitude the hotel service that provided a hot whisky to be taken, for medicinal purposes of course, in a hot bath. The next time I was in the *Yorkshire Post* office an innocent and well-meaning colleague asked if I were enjoying my 'summer holiday'.

Overthrows

The End of an Age

A YEAR ago a season of indifferent weather was ending with some show of dignified sunshine while across the metaphorical skies of politics the storm-clouds gathered. Some of us, incurably optimistic and wilfully myopic, spoke of the impossibility of war and, defeated in argument, declared that 'there was nothing we could do about it'. The more thoughtful counted cricket an ephemeral blessing and made preparations. In May Douglas Jardine told me he was 'learning to be a soldier,' and Hedley Verity was another who saw little prospect of a cricket season in 1940.

As the summer ran its course so the situation grew more critical. Cricket was swept from the newspaper headlines during the Oval Test match when Hitler and Stalin signed their unholy bargain. 'That,' we said, 'is the end of Poland,' and for a moment we neglected Yorkshire's Championship position. Yet optimism, or 'ostrichism,' still remained. We went to Dover and found unmistakable signs of military activity. Evening paper reports began to represent so much waste of time, for telephone calls were hours delayed and scores were no longer scores by the time they were sent. At half past eleven one evening a telephone message came to our hotel to inform a colleague that not a line of his morning paper story had been received. There was improvisation, brilliant and blasphemous.

We went on to Bournemouth, in trains packed with troops, and rumour flew fantastic through the air. We spent a weekend of unease in lovely sunshine, with cricket insubstantial yet precious even though it had no heart. We strolled the ground as men about to undergo a serious operation might stroll their gardens. We enjoyed it in sorrow and doubt. The match was over in two days and a Championship borne on to Brighton. Between Portsmouth and London we had the company of a naval reservist who had been recalled to service, and was glad of it. He talked, and talked and went on talking, for he had, as he readily acknowledged, been spending some time among congenial company and in congenial ways. I have passed my days at sea, both with the Royal Navy and with the Mercantile Marine, but I have never been nearer to the heart of the sailor than in that railway carriage. We said goodbye at Waterloo and our friend, for friend he was by then, left me much cheered. God bless him now wherever he may be. In Brighton we spent an afternoon of blazing sunshine on the pier. There was holiday in everything but heart. There was bathing but with an eye, so to speak, on the horizon. There was walking on the promenade, but always with an unconscious hastening from one newspaper-seller to the next. We celebrated the winning of the Championship, and toasted 'next year,' even as we listened to the pot of Poland boiling.

We had planned to travel from London to the North by the 'West Riding Limited.' On the Thursday evacuation of the children was announced and there was no 'West Riding Limited'. Some of us made tentative arrangements for emergency transport, and wondered. There was talk of an abandoned match, which Yorkshire's captain promptly quashed. 'We're public entertainers aren't we?' he maintained, 'then we must carry on'. Friday promised a meaningless day's cricket with a gentle draw in sight. Yorkshire led on first innings by five runs. Within an hour Sussex were all out for 33 and Verity in six overs had taken seven wickets for nine runs. Shortly after lunch the game was over, only Hutton losing his wicket in Yorkshire's second innings. In normal times the story would have filled the sporting pages and the Yorkist day been accounted blessed. As it was, the wonder did not seem to matter. There were no signs of triumph as we stepped into the motor coach that was to take us home. We headed North, almost in silence, each man heavy in his thoughts. The Sussex lanes were lovely in their autumn glory, and peace curled from the village chimney pots and through the trees and across the Downs. Near London we returned to war. An endless stream of cars, laden with luggage, perambulators, bedding and minor necessities of life, swirled away to the West. We stopped for evening papers and were not encouraged by their stories. (There was no word of Yorkshire's victory, which in itself suggested evil things.) We hurried on. Hurried into a night that was thrice night because the earth was darkened against the terror from the skies. In Leicester we stayed and when Saturday's light came into the sky, went on again. And so to Yorkshire. Unshaven, weary and unhappy so came we home. We took our bags, we turned and said goodbye and then 'good luck'. We went our several ways. We had come to the end of an age.

The Cricketer, August 1940

Sir Neville Cardus: Lord of Lancashire

VICTORIA was Queen and AC MacLaren was batting when a boy named Neville Cardus introduced himself to first-class cricket and to Old Trafford with sixpence paid and a 'hard push with his stomach against the iron turnstile'. In 1971 Sir Neville Cardus will pass through the main gates of Old Trafford as Lord of Lancashire cricket, President of the County Club. The man will remember the boy with the sophisticated irony that is born of affection.

From his memories and observations and professional skills in writing Cardus has created a world of cricket. Much of it is a world of imagination, seen through 'a light that never was on sea or land,' but its reality is sharper and less disputable than all the minutes of committee meetings and all the lists of batting and bowling averages. Cardus came to cricket with a poet's eye and extracted the essence of the game for presentation in glowing prose. The opportunity he took was adventitious. The young Cardus played cricket at club level and as assistant professional at Shrewsbury School, but neither cricket playing nor cricket writing was the ambition that burned through boyhood. He endured poverty, frustration and the distractions of ensuring existence to qualify himself as a writer acceptable to the *Manchester Guardian* of CP Scott. At the age of 29 he had reached the *Guardian*, had fluttered apprentice wings in reporting and features, but had written not a word on cricket, or, at least, no published word.

After a winter illness Cardus was casually assigned to

cricket at Old Trafford as a contribution towards recovery of health. He assumed the engagements to be temporary and his first reports were formalities in the customary style of the day, factual and uninspired, but the cricket revival following the First World War demanded increasing newspaper attention and Cardus the convalescent became 'Cricketer,' an accredited correspondent of privilege and responsibility. Cricket journalism, the *Manchester Guardian* and Cardus were never the same again. They were all enriched as 'Cricketer' became a cricket writer of self-expression and self-fulfilment. Daily essays developed into a revelation of character, philosophy and romance presented with wit, erudition and craftsman's care.

'Cricketer' was the transmutation of Cardus the writer with boyhood dreams and adolescent resolve. Through 20 years he followed the summer round of the cricket correspondent, his original anonymity uncloaked as reputation grew and platforms widened. Morning after morning he presented Lancashire and England cricket with astonishing sparkle and novelty of perception. Year by year through books and periodicals he enlarged his kingdom as an essayist. He revealed new aspects of his subject, and sometimes from his own wonderland he created cricket and cricketers that no-one else could have conceived. In one he destroyed his function by his adornment of it; he came to be read for his writing as distinct from his cricket and he emerged as the writer, the distinguished writer, he had always longed to be and had laboriously trained himself to be. He was not consulted, or wholly approved, in the councils of cricket but he was ushered into literary halls. The career of Cardus the cricket writer came to an end with the outbreak of the Second World War and the suspension of first-class cricket – and first-class music – in

England. The cricket writer became redundant; the music critic was invited to Australia.

There, with 'emotion recollected in tranquillity', he began the distillation of Neville Cardus, cricketer, musician, philosopher and romantic, into *Autobiography* and *Second Innings*. Cricket was part of his theme, music another part; the dominant was self-examination, boy, man and writer. 'Cricketer' and 'N C' were fused, integrated and defined under a writer's compulsion.

Those books carried Cardus beyond claim to be a distinguished cricket correspondent or music critic. Since their publication he has written again about cricket and about music. He is still to be seen at Lord's and at London's Festival Hall, but he has no need to be identified by association with cricket or music writing. He requires no noun in apposition. The institutional years have been accepted with modesty and grace and, to all appearances, a vast contentment. A saving sense of irony prohibits all possibility of arrogance or pomposity. Living and continuing the practice of writing form the essential satisfactions, warmed by the creature comforts of London club residence, routine and pipes and tobacco of high quality. The honours of society have been accorded and accepted with due propriety. Sir Neville Cardus trips as readily from the tongue as Sir Walter Raleigh, and the later knight is unlikely to be beset by envious intrigue. He has found his El Dorado and distributed it for universal welfare.

He found it through the accident of an opportunity to write about cricket, but cricket-writing was his ship and not the treasure itself. That he has defined as 'music and the savouring of life by a free and civilised mind'. The savouring has been extensive and enjoyed and shared and the quiet man, frail in physique but tough in constitution, ascetic in features, brisk of gesture, bright of eye behind his spectacles, has made the world a more civilised place for his contribution. In the medium of his talents he could not have done more than he has done or been more than he is.

The Cricketer 1971

The Ghost in Cricket's Machine

CRICKET produces more writing than any other game. Its reading public seems insatiable and there is apparently a market for everything from verse to statistics, from the scholarly to the sensational. A library of cricket could extend to thousands of volumes and whenever England play Australia, Post Office preparations have to be made for the transmission of millions of words. Amid such quantity of literary outpouring, quality must necessarily be variable, and both understandably and acceptably so. All readers do not demand the same standard of writing; levels of appreciation differ widely; there is room for an infinite variety of style in presentation, of outlook and of purpose. There is also room for a great deal of deception. First-class cricket, especially international cricket, is public entertainment and those who play quickly become public figures whose names have commercial value. Exploitation takes many forms of which the most common are personal appearances at functions where the organisers are anxious to gather a crowd; endorsement of advertised products; and expression of opinion in books and newspaper articles. For benefits received, or expected, sponsors offer remuneration and it is common enough for people of exceptional prominence to draw a far larger income from side-issues than from the essential source of their popularity. Very few players of games win the luxuries of living by direct payments from the games they play.

No sooner has a player achieved some measure of distinction than he is invited into print; by his own composition, by expression of opinions, or by the mere loan of his name. Public interest in the distinguished – or the notorious – is never-ending and any achievement from the climbing of a mountain to the commission of a lurid crime guarantees readership. A gifted few have the power of scoring Test match centuries and also of describing experiences and emotions in acceptable prose and their writings are treasures in any library. A greater number find the dual talent denied them because as playing improves with practice so does writing, and one lifetime is rarely long enough to attain more than competence in both exercises. Some games-players eventually turn to writing as a full-time occupation, blessing the name that gave them an opportunity, but accepting the obligation to master the basis of a new trade and finding both financial recompense and intrinsic satisfaction in accomplishment. The majority of games-players, on the other hand, have no desire to learn to write and no intention of attempting the craft. All they want is the income from books and articles bearing their name. This is not necessarily so unreasonable an attitude as it might appear at first glance. If every book or article had to be written by the person whose name it carries there would be a great less writing and a great deal more honesty in publishing, but there would also be decreased satisfaction of a public demand.

There is a perfectly proper interest in the opinions and reflections of celebrities and those opinions and reflections may be worthy of publication even though they cannot be satisfactorily presented by the holder. Writing an article, or making a speech, involves a technical ability that can be acquired only through instruction and practice. The ideas of most first-class cricketers and footballers and golfers would never be expressed at all in any coherent form if the expression depended upon the abilities of the players themselves, yet those ideas could have value and interest and it is arguable that their presentation offers a public service. The 'ghost' writer (he who writes on behalf of another) is no more reprehensible in principle than the disc that records the voice of a singer.

Deception enters when the contribution of the ghost is denied-usually by a sin of omission. Nobody is deceived over the straightforward purchase of a gramophone record, but there would be justifiable complaint were a hidden gramophone to be offered as the actual presence in performance of a singer. A concert audience attracted by that promise of a personal appearance by a singer would quickly demand the return of admission money on the presentation of a recorded recital. A publisher who offers a 'ghosted' book or article is left open to the same charge of substitution. Defensive argument might be that 'ghosted' writing does nobody much harm and does many people much good. The reader is content in the mistaken belief that the work was created by the celebrity whose name it bears; the celebrity enjoys both cash and credit; the 'ghost' and the publisher take a share of the profits. Who suffers?

Morality, of course, has a ready answer and there are more mundane effects also to be considered. Authorship and journalism suffer because unless the young writer can find an honest market for his wares and scope for his apprentice years he will turn elsewhere for his satisfactions and his development. He will abandon his devotion to writing on sport when he finds that all he can anticipate is 'ghosting' a celebrity who will be paid twice, three times, ten times the amount of his own remuneration for doing the work. The reading public will suffer because in course of time individuality will disappear from writing as fewer and fewer 'ghosts' are left to present more and more celebrities. Even now, it would be difficult to distinguish between several cricket books but for the illustrations. The 'ghost' can change his cloak but not his characteristics except in reduction towards featureless nonentity and when, as in so many cases, he is left entirely to his own resources he cannot even concoct novelty in subject matter.

Sooner or later, presumably, the over-exuberant publishers will spoil their own market and find that their vast outlay is not returning compensatory dividends. At the moment the top figures paid to cricket celebrities approach, in fees and perquisites, £10,000* for a season's employment. Much of this is recovered by the syndication of a newspaper series and the serialisation of books, a process hastening its own destruction the more widespread it becomes because names have not the same significance everywhere and because reading tastes cannot be bludgeoned to a common level. Absurdities are increasing. Books are being compiled from the lightest of contacts between the writer and the nominal author suggesting in some cases that even the responsibility of proof-reading has been shelved. The same personal anecdotes are being transferred from subject to subject. Applications for Press Box

*£10,000 is worth more than £560,000 in 2008.

seats are being made for 'our representative and his editorial adviser'. One newspaper has found it necessary to remark that one of its 'Big Names' does write his own articles – naively inviting readers to draw their own conclusions about the others.

There would be vastly better feeling among journalists and greater public respect for publishers of books and newspapers in an immediate change of heart over this growing misrepresentation. If the celebrities have something to say, and cannot say it because they lack command of words, let the co-operation of practiced writers be freely acknowledged and their names be given equal prominence with that of the celebrity. Let the pretence that makes cynics of the knowledgeable and dupes of the uninitiated be swept away to leave a cleaner literary atmosphere. Let the celebrities who want the reward of writing either learn to write or confess dependence upon their collaborators; and let any reader who believes that his favourite celebrity should be able to turn readily to writing try to compose just one thousand word article that would have the slightest chance of being printed and paid for.

The Cricketer, May 1956

A Critic's Concern

IN the Cricketer Winter Annual Mr EDR Eagar expressed a hope that first-class cricket might be entering a second Golden Age and suggested that the cricket Press carries a major responsibility in the promotion of so happy an era. The public attitude towards cricket, Mr. Eagar insists, is based primarily upon the attitude of cricket correspondents to the leading newspapers and he charges them to look with kindly eye upon the present and immediate future. In this instance Mr. Eagar argues rather dangerously from the particular to the general, but no cricket correspondent is likely to deny or deprecate the influence of the writer. It is obviously in the writer's own interests to maintain and stimulate the importance of his subject. Without that basic belief he cannot hope to keep his zest and consequent attraction. He lives by public favour and without public favour for his subject he will not live very long or very well. It is possible – just possible – to imagine the continuation of first-class cricket without written, spoken or visual reporting, but it is not possible to imagine the continuation of cricket reporting in the absence of cricketing interest.

Public interest can be, and undoubtedly is, stimulated by the reporting of cricket and in one sense there is no bad cricket reporting. The most severe condemnation, the gloomiest foreboding, does at least draw attention to the existence of the game. 'Say what you like about me,' concedes the publicity seeker, 'So long as you spell the name right'. Exaggerated praise can prove as stultifying as harsh criticism. Both, unrelieved, defeat their own object because in course of time they become disregarded. No critic, or criticism, can create or kill an interest. An interest is born of a desire, an impulse, and is either present or absent. It can be developed, it can be diminished, but it begins of its own accord and it ends of its own accord. Investigation of the interest follows. There was no cricket writing in the civilisation of ancient Greece and it was not cricket writing that brought about the first defence of a tree stump with a billet of wood against a round stone rolled, bowled or pitched. There is no current reporting of the chariot races in existence and it was not the commentaries upon them that caused their fall from public favour.

In its essence cricket interest is independent of cricket writing. The writer's influence lies in the expansion of interest and the development of cricket. He can spread the tidings of what is, what was and what might be. His interest is to widen cricket interest. In that endeavour honesty has proved to be the best policy, given enough time for honesty to be seen and appreciated. Expediency can enjoy temporary success, misjudgment can be momentarily veiled, vested interests can be briefly pursued. Sooner or later truth will out. Neither the cricket writer nor any other writer can conceal for long what he believes. The meretricious and the uninformed bring little lasting harm to cricket, to drama, to music, to any of the arts subject to criticism, because they are inevitably exposed. Of course there will be differences of critical opinion. Criticism is opinion, based on experience and observation, and experience and observation are attributes of the individual. No two spectators ever saw exactly the same cricket match and it is the primary purpose of the critic to describe and assess the cricket he saw. If he is to make his views acceptable to the reader (over an extended period) he must offer some attraction as a writer and show some trustworthiness as an observer. Few volunteers will concern themselves persistently with dull writing; demonstrable inaccuracy soon palls.

Cricket is a fortunate game in possessing a large following of interested readers. It is a game particularly adapted to the reflective satisfactions; it encourages, by 'emotion recollected in tranquillity,' the creation of evocative prose if not immortal poetry. No other game has inspired so much writing of enduring quality. Every age of cricket is established in character through contemporary comment and we know, or can know, the Hambledon men as well as we know the current Hampshire XI. Any danger to the future of cricket is less likely to arise from the pessimism of cricket writers than from the indifference of cricket writers. If cricket inspires there will be no indifference; if cricket does not inspire then the writer's indifference will be no more than a reflection of the general indifference. A critic cannot make his subject into what it never was and never could be. He can point excellences and shortcomings. He can set standards and mark distinctions. He can encourage and he can denigrate. What he cannot do, ultimately, is to deny the facts. Attractive cricket will, sooner or later, attract a following, whatever the critic may say against it. Dreary cricket will reduce the crowds, however much the critic may urge them to attend.

The greatest value of the critic to the subject of his writing lies in honest appraisement and the preservation of standards. It is his duty to see for his readers, in their absence from the actual performance, and relate his observation to known standards. The critic of any standing nails his colours firmly to the mast. He makes known, because he cannot avoid revealing himself in his writings, the principles upon which his judgments are founded. Without principles he has no judgment and is therefore no critic of any consequence.

It is his privilege to recommend what he believes to be admirable and to discourage acceptance of what he considers inadequate. In his own interests, to discard any higher motive, he will always tend to say, by implication, 'Come to the match and rejoice with me' or 'Come to the match and insist with me upon an improved performance'. He is at his most persuasive when his sincerity is beyond doubt and the measure of his sincerity is to be found in knowledge, integrity and feeling for his subject and his writing.

The Cricketer Spring Annual 1958

The Meaning of Sportsmanship

WHEN Sir Robert Menzies, speaking of Britain to Britain, said, 'This country ought to be the moral and intellectual leader of the world for generations to come, but it must not lose faith in itself,' he was not charging responsibility specifically in terms of cricket. In that context, however, his inspiration would have been both appropriate and welcome, for it is high time some forthright speaking was undertaken on moral attitudes towards cricket and all sport in England.

This is an age of protest before principle, of the pragmatist before the preacher, and in sport some plain re-statement of the meaning of honesty and sportsmanship is overdue. To say 'It isn't cricket' is now to invoke a sneer from the self-styled realist who never knew what cricket was and is and must be, if its life is valued. Honesty and sportsmanship are not inherent virtues. They have to be taught and acquired; they are attributes of community living. Organised society could not exist without a basis of trust in honesty; sportsmanship, which is the code of conduct for games, represents the social benefit from organised recreation. As children we are supposed to learn honesty at home and at school. As children in sport we are supposed to learn sportsmanship from the example of our seniors and from the experience derived from participation in games.

Honesty is conformity with the rules, a voluntary undertaking to abide by certain limitations imposed for mutual convenience. A burglar is dishonest because he does not accept society's rules of property; a cricketer would be dishonest if he used a bat bigger than the regulation size. Sportsmanship is a wider conception, more difficult to define and never, at any given moment, precisely formulated. A cricketer knows, or can know, when he is breaking the laws of cricket, but sportsmanship is measured in opinion. The unacceptable of yesterday may win today's approval; today's behaviour may become intolerable in the light of tomorrow.

Sportsmanship is so essentially an attitude of mind that it tends to be discussed with some embarrassment. Examination diminishes the strength and influence of the conception. To cry that 'it isn't fair' becomes in itself a breach of the flexible code of 'fair play'. To question what is or is not 'done' invites the counter-question of 'Who says so?' Leaders need faith to answer clearly and loudly, 'We do'. Even when sportsmanship is reduced to a simple issue of personal inclination and integrity, complications are introduced. A batsman caught at the wicket may walk or wait under conflict of responsibilities to the fielding side, to the umpire, to conscience and to his own team. A bowler deliberately wasting time in trying to save a match may be balancing his own interpretation of right and wrong against the team interests of the moment.

Further complications arise in matters of degree. Time wasting to avoid another over just before an interval might scarcely raise an eyebrow where the same practice at the end of a match – with the outcome in doubt – would raise a storm of controversy. There is no easy option for the leader. Sport grows increasingly vulnerable to ethical wounds as it grows increasingly professional. Winning a Test rubber, a County Championship, a World Cup, a boxing bout, carries a significance beyond the intrinsic rewards of participation and achievement. There is a cash conclusion, perfectly proper in itself and in no way incompatible with a code of sportsmanship but inevitably influential on playing attitude.

Few first-class cricketers spend any time on the field considering their match money or the financial implications of success, but professionals do play cricket with a professional interest. They must. A professional captain cannot view his players without regard for their professional interests because those interests are his own. The professional in any sphere seeks success because he lives by success. How he seeks success is his ethical problem.

The problem is of small consequence until it involves a community influence. The lone golfer whistling operatic airs on the green distracts no one but himself. League footballers could kick each other into hospital without creating a social disturbance if their performances went unseen and unrecorded. First-class cricketers could devise any principles and practices to meet their own requirements were there no other cricketers dependent on them. First-class cricketers do not play in isolation. By their special skills, by their conformity with the laws, by their example of attitude, they lead all cricket.

That responsibility for standard is at once the highest privilege and most exacting burden of the public cricketer. He above all others must display the warm heart and the cool head, the unflinching integrity, the capacity for moral distinctions that constitute sportsmanship. His outlook must be an outlook applicable to all cricket at all levels, making the game as much of a pleasure for all as it is a business for some. To this end he needs all the help he can be given in clearing his mind and establishing his code. He needs help from administrators who can simplify the objects of play by removing the shaded margins between profit and loss. He needs help from management to define his functions as player, as ambassador, as public figure. He needs help from cricket writers who have resolved a conflict of their own between cricket's welfare and a quest for personal aggrandisement through controversy. He needs help from a public recognising that they cannot receive more than they are prepared to give.

The faith to be honest, the faith to reject the mean and meretricious, the escape from pragmatism without principles, form steps on English cricket's way to 'moral and intellectual leadership of the world for generations to come'. The firmer the step the faster the following.

The Cricketer Spring Annual 1968

Moving Fingers

THROUGH nearly 40 years I have seen vast changes in the principles and mechanics of cricket-writing. Some I have accepted without enthusiasm, others have undoubtedly been beneficial to both the writers and the reading public. The most fundamental change has been in approach to the purpose of cricket journalism. In my early period – say, up to the war and for a few years afterwards – the writers were essentially supporters of cricket. Their basic object was to advance its cause or at least to preserve its existence and traditions. They were, of course, advancing their own cause at the same time. They sought to be professionally successful; to sell their cricket-writing. Their market, though, was inside cricket, among readers whose interests were also the wellbeing of cricket. Cricket-writing, consciously or unconsciously, was directed towards the preservation and embellishment of cricket because the writers cared, in varying degree, for cricket and for the cricket-writer's life. For most of them their professional undertaking was an end in itself.

Somewhere in the 1950s developed an iconoclastic mood. It expressed itself in politics; Winston Churchill was seen as a party member as distinct from a national leader. It expressed itself in industrial relations where all features of paternalism were scorned. It expressed itself in sport with separation of game from public entertainment and a consequent demand for payment not for playing but for exhibiting revenue-producing talent. It expressed itself in sports journalism by concentration on sport as a means to journalistic enterprise demanding the controversial. In the mildest form a description of the day's play justified less attention than a disputed umpire's decision. Increasingly the 'incident' more than the course of cricket became the writers' subject.

The older form of cricket-writing persisted and clearly retained a readership where it was allowed due scope, but a new form developed under editorial pressure for a supply of the sensational. Invective is more startling than admiration and, inevitably, failures, disagreements and their consequences were sought, exaggerated and emphasised until sports-writing became a close approach to search for scandal and dissension. The journalistic view of cricket veered away from calm consideration of a 'meadow game with a beautiful name' to a feverish anticipation and sometimes manufacture of misdemeanour. Cricket-writers came and went with remarkable rapidity, stepping through cricket on the way to wider and more profitable exploitation of the nose for news and the antagonistic pen.

The older cricket-writer was a specialist in cricket, seeking satisfaction and distinction in a limited activity. The later writer tended to be a specialist in provocative animation, working, sometimes temporarily, in a cricketing medium. The provocation, not the cricket, was his primary concern. Newspapers have always been 'angled'. They began as propaganda sheets and have remained so, the more responsible ones trying to distinguish between their presentation of news and views but not denying prejudice in politics or other areas of principle. Cricket-writing has always been angled, if in nothing more than emphasis on local interests. A Nottingham paper reporting Nottinghamshire cricket at Trent Bridge would inevitably tend to present the case of Nottinghamshire teams.

Cricket-writing has been angled to meet editorial wishes, to further specific causes and to illustrate talents in writing or observation. Cardus angled cricket to create character, to establish atmosphere, to express philosophy. The *Manchester Guardian* accepted the Cardus angle as its own. William Pollock of the pre-war *Daily Express* angled cricket to provide a daily witticism. The *Yorkshire Post*, and most provincial newspapers, angled cricket by regional emphasis. With the angling undisguised it was acceptable and appreciated. The

Daily Express reader looked for a Pollock sally rather than a balanced account of a day's play. Cardus was read with delight on his own terms or rejected in misunderstanding. He could be misunderstood. In my undergraduate days I once commended a Cardus column to a fellow-student who played cricket and was taking a degree in English language and literature. He read solemnly and conscientiously and then returned the *Guardian*. 'Well?' I said. 'Disgraceful,' he replied. 'I have never read a more biased report in my life. It's all about a Lancashire bowler.'

When I joined the cricket-writing fraternity I found an 'angle' already established for me. As a Yorkshireman representing a Yorkshire paper I was presumed to be a myopic observer and an unquestioning defender of county faith. This was never an editorial imposition. No *Yorkshire Post* editor has ever pressed on me a cricketing line of thought or approach or indicated that cricketing praise and blame were to be apportioned by regional label, but through correspondence and conversation I was made aware of an assumption that my brief was naturally to be always 'for' Yorkshire.

This illusion was, in great part, an inheritance from the distinguished work of AW Pullin, who, as 'Old Ebor', spent a lifetime in sports-writing for the *Yorkshire Post* and the *Yorkshire Evening Post*.

Nobody fulfilled an assignment more thoroughly than 'Old Ebor'. Through his voluminous reports and comments he contributed enormously to the spread and maintenance of public interest in Yorkshire cricket and he could fairly claim to have been responsible in large measure for the early growth in circulation of the *Evening Post*. He was the friend and attendant of Yorkshire cricket for more than thirty years and in his regional context he became a national figure in cricket-writing. His 'angle' was patent and unchanging. Yorkshire were inherently blameless. Their successes were natural justice and their failures were usually explicable in terms of misfortune or misunderstanding. Cricket may not have been a Yorkshire invention or entirely a Yorkshire preserve, but without a Yorkshire element the game lost significance for 'Old Ebor' and his newspapers. This attitude became a characteristic and Pullin became a character of the Press box. He was impressive in appearance, not tall but well built and bearded. He wrote, in his later years at least, with an assumption of authority that resented contradiction or even debate and he was inclined to be irascible under provocation. He wrote in the manner of his time, with a commendable attention to grammar but without much claim to wit or sparkle, which indeed he would have reproved as out of place in cricket-writing. Limitations of outlook, subject and circulation circumscribed his influence, but he was widely read in Yorkshire and respected for his research and industry. He was more of a mouthpiece for Lord Hawke and the Yorkshire cricket establishment than a contributor of original thought on cricket matters, but he used his position on his papers to draw attention helpfully to the old-age plight of some former Yorkshire players. Two major books, *Talks With Old English Cricketers* and *Talks With Old Yorkshire Cricketers,* were collections of journalistic interviews, stilted in style and resolutely directed towards a local market, but they have now become invaluable as historical background. In his *History of Yorkshire County Cricket 1903-1923* Pullin was in his element, officially commissioned and playing on his home ground.

As representative of Yorkshire cricket-writing and a senior of the Press box he gathered legendary attributes. His output was exceptional, even for his times. A day's work in summer would include a column report for the evening paper, prepared in three or four messages during morning and early afternoon; another column report for the morning paper, completed shortly after close of play: late evening might require composition of a weekly article. Everything was written by hand, the calligraphy adapted to speed before legibility.

On one such day at Worcester – so the story runs – Pullin had sent away his last bulky message for the evening paper. His Mercury for the match was aged casual labour whose function was to carry copy from the Press box at the riverside ground to the telegraph office in the town, perhaps half a mile away. With the last evening paper message completed and dispatched Pullin felt entitled to a period of recreational ease. He sat back from the desk, lit his pipe and surveyed the little world with satisfaction. Unexpectedly he found the messenger recently departed back at his elbow: 'Mester,' said the old man, with the calm of innocence, 'write some more papers. Them others blew out of my hand on the bridge and went into the river.'

Pullin was a conscientious journalist, proud of professional competence and happy in possession of exclusive information. At Trent Bridge the Post Office telegraphists allocated to cricket matches used to transmit from a room underneath the Press box, the reporters passing down messages through holes in the floor. During pre-play investigations Pullin had learned by chance one morning of the death of a world-famous cricketer. His first dispatch of the day was concentrated on this news item and appropriate obituary and when he handed his copy through the floor he surveyed his Press box colleagues with all the benevolent superiority of a journalist with a 'scoop'. Into the Press box silence floated a voice from the startled telegraphist below: 'Good God, Tom Emmett's dead'.

These stories and the many others associated with 'Old Ebor' came to me only as folklore. He and I were never contemporaries on the *Yorkshire Post* and I was not his immediate successor. After his retirement from staff appointment he continued in cricket-writing for a Sunday paper and the only occasion on which we met was during a match at Headingley in my first season. He confined himself to one sentence. 'Your work seems to pass muster,' he pronounced. In one aspect, at least, it could never have done more than pass muster in Pullin's eyes because of a difference in attitudes. 'Old Ebor' saw and reported cricket essentially in Yorkshire terms and association. His concern was proudly the Yorkshire viewpoint; his loyalty, professional and no doubt personal, embraced his county right or wrong. There are many like him and they form strong pillars of sport.

In contrast, I have not been able to convince myself, as a Yorkshireman, that the sun necessarily shines out of Yorkshire. My devotion is to cricket, not specifically Yorkshire cricket or England cricket or any locality or individual feature of cricket. I have always tried to see cricket and to assess cricket in terms of the highest quality within my experience and understanding. I have been called, accusingly, a perfectionist and I must accept the impeachment if perfection be a standard that can be assumed within reach because it has been touched. Standards, of course, change with widening education. Without knowledge of greatness we might be content with mediocrity; without illustration we cannot become aware of practical possibility.

I have been fortunate in my time of cricket. It has included the highest development, in context of the playing conditions, of every facet of cricketing art. To judge the acceptability of any performance I have only to measure it against what I know to have been achieved in similar circumstances. Often enough I have misjudged the given conditions, my recollections or my observations and have done less than justice or have over-praised, but, with hand on heart, I can swear that I have never borne false witness to my conception of cricket.

This principle of measurement against highest known achievement is not universally acceptable. Present-day tendencies certainly do not support it because the purpose of both play and comment on play has changed and is still changing. Values in sport, at the higher public levels, are no longer intrinsic. First-class cricket is not now based on essentially cricketing satisfactions for participants and supporters. It is following other forms of sport, with Association football an outstanding example, into the field of business entertainment. Test matches are much closer to theatrical presentations than to recreational undertakings. The ultimate object of players and promoters is financial success rather than contest in cricket. To this end outcome exceeds manner in importance. Winning the prize provides the major satisfaction and the prize is a credit balance in the bank. Ambitions are commercial and prosaic more than altruistic and imaginative. A Yorkshire captain of the 1960s asked for judgment by results without consideration of intrinsic merit. 'Don't compare us with great teams,' he said. 'Judge us by what we can do.'

Thanks to Cricket

Chapter Eight:
CLOSE OF PLAY

THE day at Old Trafford had been discouraging. Cricket of modest quality had ended shortly after lunch in a torrential downpour. Geoffrey Boycott, as Yorkshire's captain, had followed with public apology a conversational indiscretion in which he disparaged both his opponents and his companions of the match. Boycott had spoken wrongly and rashly and provocative journalism had mercilessly given quotation precedence over the social conventions*. I left Old Trafford with fear for the future of first-class cricket in reflection on Boycott's attitude towards it and with dismay for the course cricket-writing seemed to be taking. By the time I had reached the quiet hotel in which I was resident for the match the rainclouds had cleared to leave a lovely evening of early summer. The sky was new-washed blue, the sun, still high, gave sparkle to the innumerable greens of burgeoning foliage. I took my pessimism for a walk.

*Reports said Geoffrey Boycott had 'lashed out' in his criticisms of wide bowling from Lancashire. Boycott believed he was 'talking off the record'.

Unexpectedly I came upon a cricket field. It was clearly the home of a club of substance, the playing area extensive and well tended. Pavilion and scoreboard shone with fresh paint. The boundary line was neatly marked and accentuated with foot-high flags. The batting on soft turf was to slow bowling of a right-hander and a left-hander and though I could not read the scores from my distance, the concentration of the players suggested a critical stage in the match. An on-drive sent a fieldsman in pounding pursuit towards the boundary, the stroke assuring a comfortable two runs but a hazardous three. The third was attempted and was adjudged incomplete and the scampering batsman raised a hand of acknowledgment to the umpire's signal of dismissal and turned to walk briskly to the pavilion. He was passed on the field by his successor and the fielding side were in position, the bowler ready to run up as soon as guard had been taken. For all who were playing and watching there was nothing in mind beyond the next ball, the challenge of the moment, the absorption in good-natured contest. Time stood still in a distillation of delight. People and place and circumstances gave visual representation of a meaning, a conception, an ideal. Cricket was itself again and all was well with my world.

TRIBUTES

I WILL never forget Jim Kilburn, a great man, the voice of Yorkshire cricket, who became a wonderful friend to me throughout my career. It makes me very proud when I say that I could count Mr Kilburn as one of my very best friends. That's what I used to call him - Mr Kilburn. Always.

I can still remember him saying to me over breakfast: 'How many times have I got to tell you, Dickie, to call me Jim?' Yet I never changed. And I didn't change because I respected the man so much, he was a man of such great integrity.

I first came across Mr Kilburn when I was invited to the Yorkshire nets. I would have been 15 years old at the time.
He always used to come to the nets to watch Yorkshire practise. I can still see him now, as if it was yesterday, standing behind the nets, smoking on his pipe, just observing the players and what was going on.

I would later realise that he was simply doing his homework for the forthcoming season, building up a word picture in his mind of each of the players and some of their idiosyncrasies. Yet, for some reason, we just clicked. When I was in the second team and then made the Yorkshire 1st XI, one of the proudest days of my life, we would stay in the same hotel and share breakfast.

There were none of the diet fads that there are today. It was bacon and eggs. I was never a big breakfast person, but JM Kilburn used to enjoy everything. And he'd be smoking his pipe - I'm not quite sure what he would have made of the smoking ban!

It was a wonderful friendship, and because I was not one for pubs or nightclubs, we used to sit in the hotel in the evening and just discuss the day's play and any aspect of cricket. He had a great intellect; I learned so much from him. He knew the game inside out. This was an era when players and journalists travelled together and confidences were never broken. And, when you saw the byline 'JM Kilburn', you knew the words would have been written with the utmost authority; he was the very best of cricket writers. There could never be any complaints. If JM Kilburn said it, then it was right.

He was also a great source of encouragement when I chose to become an umpire. Typical journalist though, he knew I had applied before I had told him! Yet, that said, I will never, ever forget the words that he told me when it came to walking out to the middle in my white coat, and peaked cap, for the first time. 'Dickie,' he told me. 'Always be yourself. You always have a smile on your face. Have that smile when you are umpiring. And, if you treat the players as professional men, which they are, then they will treat you with respect in return.'

It is, of course, for others to judge, but I'd like to think that I stayed true to these words throughout my career. It's advice that is as relevant today as it was all those years ago in 1970. He also went on to say: 'You have to earn respect. You can not buy it'. He, of course, meant these words for me. But they equally apply to Jim – sorry Mr Kilburn. He was a great man, very sadly missed. He was such a loyal friend. I will never forget him.

Dickie Bird

I FELT a reverence towards JM Kilburn even before I first set eyes on him, for I had read his delightful book *In Search of Cricket*. In addition to being a writer of high quality he had been a close auxiliary to the mighty pre-war Yorkshire team, enjoying friendships with the players, and in particular Hedley Verity and the young Len Hutton (who happened to be a primary hero of my own). Jim Kilburn not only wrote with authority and elegance but in my enquiring mind he began to edge out Cardus as essayists go for the simple reason that he did not indulge himself in fantasy.

And now, in 1968, there sat Mr Kilburn in the front row of the press box at The Oval, with Bill Bowes at his side. What a pair. Soon I was to value a friendship with Big Bill, who greeted me like a favourite nephew in later years whenever I showed up at Headingley. But – initially at any rate – Mr Kilburn was not quite so easy to know.

During that classic Oval Test match of 1968 it was my duty to deliver his story to the office of the *Yorkshire Post* in Fleet Street as soon as he had completed it. Today's cricket writers would laugh at the ponderous process. JMK was probably the last journalist to write his copy with a fountain-pen, creating the same sort of broad sweeps of script as his Victorian predecessors. The sheets of paper were then carefully folded and placed in an envelope, which young Frith received with barely a glance from the writer. It was now time for the challenge of bus or tube journey followed by a sprint down

Fleet Street, culminating in a breathless hurtling up the stairs into the newspaper office. There was no duplicate copy should I have slipped off Waterloo Bridge and into the Thames, and there was little scope for late delivery either: the linotype operators were waiting each evening to drop the story into the blank column space.

Jim Kilburn, founding secretary of the Cricket Writers' Club in 1946, would have been as bemused by the transformation that has befallen that organisation as by the vulgarisation of cricket itself, transitions that would probably have persuaded him to add thirty minutes to his afternoon nap. Journalists used to nudge each other when the arms folded and that noble head slowly dipped forward onto his chest. Of course, at a time when there was no recourse to a fully informative television replay, he had his great pal Bill to cover for him.

From those Dickensian beginnings I'm proud to say that a friendship began to blossom, and, as is my wont, at every opportunity I plied Jim with questions about the great Yorkshire cricketers he had befriended. His comments were free of extravagance, reminiscences precisely expressed and unembellished. An unforgettable Test match lunch break was spent with him and EM Wellings, both veterans adamant that between the wars they had watched the best that cricket had ever had to offer. They pitied the likes of myself who had access only to the dull fare of the 1960s game.

The only serious blip in our friendship came when JMK tried to evict my 14-year-old son from the Lord's press box. I'd been fetching drinks in the bar, so Jim hadn't realised that Johnny was mine. I prefer to believe that, had he known, he would have let the situation be.

It was exciting to learn that Jim had taken film on England's 1954-55 tour of Australia under Hutton's captaincy. In the early 1980s I was compiling a video programme on great batsmen, and without hesitation he lent me the 16mm reel, an important discovery which opened with the scene at Caserta as the Yorkshire players visited the grave of war casualty Verity.

By now, though, Jim, was losing his sight. It was distressing for family and friends, but he bore this calamitous setback bravely and with characteristic dignity, as one would expect of a member of the Craven Gentlemen.

As I look around me now in the so-called 'media centres', with the predominantly history-allergic writers and their mass of electronic gadgetry, I do sometimes picture the reassuring figure of JMK with his solemn, shrewd gaze, his imposing nose. . . and, of course, that thick-nibbed pen which he used to put to such charming use.

David Frith

JIM Kilburn's writing, which was always authoritative and incisive yet restrained, earned him the respect of everyone who played and followed the game. During his time Yorkshire achieved 15 County Championship titles and in the absence of constant television and an electronic media it was through him that the great Yorkshire public lived out a triumphant age.

Unlike the modern journalist, Jim was part of the establishment and privileges were extended to him that would be unthinkable today. As a matter of course, every morning before play started, Jim and former Yorkshire and England bowler Bill Bowes, his main press companion who was cricket correspondent of the *Yorkshire Evening News*, would come into the players' dressing room for tea. The Yorkshire press travelled extensively with the team and for the most part relationships between players and press were mutually supportive of each other. Only for a very short time did my playing career overlap with Jim Kilburn, but he knew and understood my father as well as anyone. While Jim marvelled at his batting, he realised that his thought processes were not so orthodox. To some my father might have seemed enigmatic but Jim saw that he approached things tangentially, was oblique and astute, and held views that had not occurred to others.

My father drew strength from Jim Kilburn's previous career as a schoolmaster. Having been denied much of an education himself, he had a thirst for knowledge and information, and a respect for and interest in anyone that could impart them.

Richard Hutton

ONE of the most precious volumes in my quite ample cricket library is Jim Kilburn's *In Search of Cricket*, which I've always regarded as the finest book on the game from the pre-war years. As a Lancastrian, I might be expected to root for Kilburn's contemporary Cardus, but I believe that the Yorkshireman beats him by an innings and then some, if only because our Neville was intent on projecting himself as much as anything he watched at Old Trafford or the SCG and many places in-between, whereas Kilburn kept his eye on the ball at all times, diverting only now and then to consider some ambience close to the game. Read him on Worcestershire cricket and the baths at Droitwich Spa where 'the water is so saturated with brine that it is impossible for the bather to sink', and you'll see what I mean. No-one ever wrote more perceptively about the summer game itself and its peccadiloes – Herbert Sutcliffe batting in a trilby at Leicester (he wouldn't have dared to do that just over the hill!) and the heavy roller at Portsmouth that 'only Naval engineers could have built'.

Geoffrey Moorhouse

I'M DELIGHTED the cricket world will be reminded of Jim Kilburn's writing skills and his knowledge and love of the game. His first tour to Australia as correspondent for the *Yorkshire Post* coincided with my first appearance, aged 16, at a Test match – as a spectator. Bradman and Barnes both made 234 for Australia but the performance which most caught my attention was legspinner Colin McCool's eight wickets. Jim and I met when I was on tour in 1953, 1956 and 1961, and in 1960 in England I worked as a journalist and radio commentator, moving to the BBC Television commentary box in 1963. There were eventful matches at Headingley on those first three Australian tours, though there was no fixture at the ground when the South Africans toured in 1960. I look forward to being reminded of the articles from the *Yorkshire Post* as well as the contributions from *Wisden* and the books Jim wrote during a career covering more than 40 years.

Richie Benaud

I HAVE, sadly, only brief and distant memories of Jim Kilburn the man. I was introduced to him in the old press box at Headingley when he was a familiar and highly respected name, I a tyro. I remember an air of elderly distinction, a rawboned face of ruddy complexion and a friendly, courteous conversation from which the 'junior pro' emerged, rather pleased to have met a great member of the profession.

I 'subbed' him a little when he wrote for *The Cricketer* but in truth he needed no subbing and certainly not from me. The prose was clear, simple and elegant; a little, perhaps, like the batting of the Len Hutton he admired so much and wrote so much about.

Glancing at his *Thanks to Cricket* again the other day I was amused and enlightened by one paragraph about Hutton and the fact that he might not have captained England in Australia in 1954/55. Of his own approach to the question of whether Hutton or David Sheppard should have been chosen for the job, he wrote: 'Mine has not been an intimate professional association with England teams on tour or at home. I have not been required to investigate or speculate upon dressing-room concerns or personal idiosyncrasies and relationships. To the best of my recollection I have never sought a confidence or cultivated an acquaintanceship as a cricket writer amongst cricketers. What I have learned in private I have kept to myself'.

How journalism has changed, in the last 50 years, could hardly be better demonstrated than by that statement, one that would hardly be acceptable even to a 'blue top' sports editor these days. Revelations, at least of a genuine, cricketing nature, are positively encouraged and expected but I personally regret the feeling one gets when talking to some international cricketers that 'he' is a player and 'I' a writer. Perhaps sharing the Kilburn idealism to some extent, I would far rather that we were simply two people talking about a game we love and that 'he' would know instinctively that I would never want to do him or the game down.

Christopher Martin-Jenkins

JIM KILBURN wrote as he lived – with disciplined, somewhat austere urbanity. He was no more likely to construct an untidy sentence than to raise his voice. Indeed, of all one's colleagues in the cricket press box over many years he was the most imperturbable, and no-one's writing was more clearly a reflection of his character.

It was the good fortune of the readers of the *Yorkshire Post*, and for that matter of the Yorkshire cricket team themselves, to have Jim as their high-priest. Whether he would have welcomed the much wider recognition his work obviously merited, I rather doubt. He always seemed perfectly content as he was, keeping his own counsel and with Bill Bowes, once he had started with the *Yorkshire Evening News*, and John Bapty of the *Yorkshire Evening Post* for evening company. To the players, other than a few captains, he was very definitely 'Mr Kilburn'.

He would habitually take an afternoon nap before putting pen to paper in a small, neat hand. He never used a typewriter or attended a press conference or telephoned his own copy, a messenger having been told to be at his beck and call. Were he to find himself in the same job now, he would most likely go back to schoolmastering. Neither professionally nor emotionally would he or Neville Cardus come to that, be remotely suited by the demands of today or the modern game – a sad and sobering thought.

John Woodcock

JIM KILBURN was a member of the Empire Cricket Writers' Club, founded in Perth, Australia, after Wally Hammond's team landed to begin England's 1946-7 tour. Post-war shipping shortages meant that the team and media had to travel when space was available, which meant arriving a month before fixtures were due to start.

To fill in the time the writers formed a cricket club – after all, Englishmen had been doing this abroad since the mid-17th century – and the following spring, at Nottingham, the Club was re-named the Cricket Writers' and formally constituted. The first tie, a skull and crossbones motif, only adopted because it was available in bulk, was replaced by colours of printers'-ink blue and playing-field green.

Jim became treasurer, secretary and chairman (in 1950), following EW Swanton as the second member to be elected. He was proud of his links with the Club and when I last spoke to him in the late 1980s, as the Club's then Secretary, he was most helpful, explaining how, in the early days, he made it a practice of making himself known to every county secretary when visiting with Yorkshire or England.

Not until 1982 did the Club establish the office of President or Jim would certainly have been elected. He was also proud, in his last years, of being invited by Yorkshire to open the new press box in the Rugby stand at Headingley. His status in the Club is recognised on the honours boards at Lord's and Trent Bridge. His writings, especially his essays on Yorkshire personalities and grounds, will live. He would have been appalled by some of cricket's diversions.

When I first met him, in the late 1950s, he was one of those remote, fairly aloof figures who occupied the front seats at any Yorkshire match – Kilburn, Bill Bowes, Dick Williamson,

John Bapty, Eric Stanger . . . they could be as solemn as a bench of bishops. Jim, I felt, had no time for anyone he thought lacked respect for the game, a charge that could have then been levelled at many of the popular newspaper representatives, most of them football reporters obliged to find summer employment.

I was enormously impressed by his post-lunch nap, about 10-15 minutes, from which he would awake and resume writing without ever, in my experience, enquiring as to what had happened during his siesta. Jim asleep, or puffing his pipe, Jim Swanton's voice, John Arlott's bottle of claret, John Woodcock's bright smile and warm welcome to a newcomer – all dusty but precious memories.

Derek Hodgson, President Cricket Writers' Club

AS A YOUNG LAD, passionate about cricket I always thought JM Kilburn had the perfect job. Forty years covering Yorkshire cricket for the *Yorkshire Post* and at a time when the team was indisputably great, speaks for itself.

These days of course we have instant access to Yorkshire cricket. The internet, radio, TV commentators come and go. Few stay in our memory.

JMK most certainly did. He was an institution. He didn't so much cover a Yorkshire cricket match but give the reader an insight into the soul of Yorkshireman. Cricket then was more important than just about anything else.

I always remember one of his long summer essays about the East Coast. 'Is there a more beautiful phrase in the English language than cricket in Scarborough? The slow walk to the match, preferably taking in a sea view; the lumpen bag choked with food.'

This was how my love affair with the Scarborough Festival started and to this day I always followed his rules (even as President of the Festival).

'The first drink could be taken at noon . . . by tea one final go at the *Yorkshire Post* crossword!'

His eloquence made him a Lord in sport journalism. What I wonder would he have made of Twenty20 cricket? Coloured kits and the reverse sweep? Not a lot but I would have loved to have read his interpretation.

He once described Tom Graveney thus: 'His batting founded on the classical forward stroke contained an elegance that distinguished him in higher company'. But in the same article he could so easily have been writing about himself now in 2007.

'In an age preoccupied with accountancy he has given the game a warmth, colour and inspiration beyond the tally of the scorebook'. How true. Proper English. Proper Tyke. Proper journalist.

Harry Gration, President Scarborough Cricket Festival

WHEN I interview former cricketers about matches played years ago, I like to counterpoint their speech and the press reports of the time, to set the vernacular of the participant's voice against the formal prose of the reporter. It only works when I can find good copy in the old newspapers. I open them up, in bound volumes or on microfilm, with a sense of anticipation. Will the writer have an observant eye and a lovely turn of phrase, or will the report be a bare and lifeless summary of events?

The sight of certain reporters' names makes my heart leap, and chief among those are Alan Gibson of *The Times* and Jim Kilburn of the *Yorkshire Post*. People talk of EW Swanton as the doyen of cricket writers in the 1950s and '60s, but for me he does not create atmospheres or bring to life human character and passion, nor does he write prose to relish, as these two do.

I love the formality of Jim Kilburn's prose. The vocabulary and the sentence structures, the elaborateness of it all, tell me that cricket is important, Yorkshire cricket especially, and it must be written about properly. I love his insights into technique and character, his sense of occasion, his eye for the little detail – and, most of all, his feeling for the game and its traditions. The *Yorkshire Post* has been blessed with a long line of great cricket correspondents, a newspaper always keen to honour the passion with which the county plays its cricket, and Jim Kilburn was as good as any of them.

Here he is on a batting cameo by Gloucestershire's ever-cheerful Bomber Wells:

Wells is a skilful and enthusiastic bowler of off-breaks, and it is the enthusiasm rather than the skill that he carries into the sideline of batting, but 25 minutes of survival meant 32 invaluable runs for Gloucestershire and lively entertainment for the spectators who could appreciate a willing spirit and the humour of the game. Tail-enders do not customarily drive Trueman through the covers in the midst of a running conversation.

Here on Len Hutton's approach to his 100th hundred:

His batting in the morning had the calm and concentration characteristic of his approach to any important occasion. His habitual touch of the cap before he takes up his stance, his constant examination of the pitch between overs, his refusal to play any but the strokes of his choice or run any but the most carefully judged singles, always betokens a Hutton on business bent.

Here on a tense, low-scoring day's play between Yorkshire and Surrey:

This was one of two or three days to be found every season that build the memories of a lifetime and transmute a game from an entertainment to an experience. It was a day of recreation exhausting as a week of work, an occasion of restless anticipation, tautness of nerve and passionate opinion. It was filled with joy and shock and dream and doubting. An evening interruption was probably essential as a sedative.

The memories of a lifetime will die with the passing of the last participants and spectators, but Jim Kilburn's prose will survive, a reminder of an age when cricket was 'more than anything else a way of playing a game, of thinking a game, of caring for a game.'

It is not a livelihood, but a living; not an exercise or an entertainment but an experience . . . Cricket should see its line of development not as a commercial enterprise, not as a political weapon, not as a synthetic concern of ulterior motivation, but as a form of stability linking a way of life through yesterday, today and tomorrow in practical idealism.

They are still words worth reading.

Stephen Chalke

I REMEMBER making my first public speaking engagement to a rather packed hall. Jim could see I was nervous, and he came up to me and said very quietly: 'You see that man at the back of the hall? Just speak to him'.

That small story illustrates his kindly nature. He was always understanding of young players and took inexperience into account when judging them in the pieces he wrote.

Mind you, he set high standards when you became a hardened pro and were settled in the side. If you were a seam bowler, he measured you against Bill Bowes. If you were batsman, he measured you against Len Hutton. If, like me, you were spin bowler he measured you against Hedley Verity. He'd watched each one of them for years, and was able to compare and contrast for more than four decades.

He set his own standards high too. He was a lover of the game and he didn't want to let it, or himself, down.

I know one thing for certain about Jim. If he could see the antics of some of the players in today's game, he would be appalled. The spirit of the game was paramount to him.

Ray Illingworth

FOR those of us striving unsuccessfully to follow in his footsteps, JM Kilburn remains a source of inspiration and an unattainable model.

When I joined the *Yorkshire Post* in 2004, it was to take up a position which Kilburn had almost single-handedly glamorised and defined. A perfect blend of flair and good judgement, he wrote in a manner perhaps not dissimilar to the archetypal Yorkshire innings.

Solid in defence and scornful of ostentation, Kilburn knew instinctively the right ball to hit to the boundary and when to turn on his consummate style.

He was very much a product of a lost generation; indeed, Kilburn could never have flourished in the contemporary climate.

His enviable attitude towards journalism was perfectly encapsulated when he nonchalantly informed his *Yorkshire Post* superiors that he did not consider it to be his job, but rather that of a news reporter, to write about Yorkshire's sacking of Johnny Wardle in 1958. Instead, Kilburn felt that his duties commenced and concluded with events on the field, a concept that nowadays would not be tolerated.

Newspapers have changed greatly since Kilburn laid down his pen, and just as the harvesting of player quotes is among the expected duties of a modern cricket correspondent, so it would have been anathema to him.

Indeed, today's newspaper industry seems to place more value on player quotes than it does the type of finely crafted prose that was Kilburn's trademark, preferring hard-hitting impact to creative innovation.

Although Kilburn had eyes only for events on the pitch, one doubts whether that would have extended to the Twenty20 revolution.

What would the great man have made of being asked to compose 700 words on a Twenty20 match? My guess is that he would have nonchalantly informed his superiors that it was no job for a self-respecting journalist of any description.

Chris Waters

I CAN see Jim Kilburn now. He is tall and lean. He walks in a very upright way. He never seems to bend his neck or his head.

Jim always gave you the impression that he was still a

schoolmaster, which is exactly what he'd been before coming into journalism, and he commanded that type of classrsoom respect and appeal among the Yorkshire players. Even when I played golf with him – and he was a very good golfer – he didn't talk very much and, when he did, he spoke quietly.

I suppose he gave off a slightly lofty air, and yet it wasn't cold or off-putting. He was just a man who had a real command of his job and carried the responsibility of being the voice of Yorkshire cricket with real distinction.

These were the days when the press – including Jim and his great mate Bill Bowes – would come into the dressing room before the start of a day's play and share a pot of tea with the team. In fact, the two of them were part of the 'team' insofar as where we went, so did the two of them.

I think it helped Jim that the Yorkshire side was so successful during the period in which he covered us. It's always easier to follow a winning county. But what set Jim apart was his writing. He was a good writer and a good judge, who was always fair. You can't ask more than that.

Brian Close

I REMEMBER Jim Kilburn on the 1954-55 tour to Australia. You get to know a man when you spend nearly four weeks together on a boat and then cross a vast country alongside him too. The whole tour lasted six and a half months, and the boat wasn't like the enormous liners you see today. It was far smaller, and so we ran into one another every day.

What I liked about Jim – and what I grew to appreciate even more during the sea voyage – was his complete commitment to cricket. He wouldn't do anything sleazy to demean it. That's why I – and so many others – held writers like him and Neville Cardus in such high esteem.

I believe he is as much a part of the history of Yorkshire County Cricket Club as anyone who ever played for it.

Bob Appleyard

IN 1961 I was playing for Yorkshire at Worcester when I got injured and my arm had to be put into a cast. On the last day, it looked as if we might lose the match. I volunteered to bat one-handed. We needed about 40 odd runs to win with Bob Platt and I as the last wicket pair.

Worcester took the new ball and gave it to Jack Flavell, who had real pace. Given my injury, I was suddenly a bit scared, but I decided to have a go. I think I hit three one-handed sixes, made 29 not out and we won the game.

The following morning Jim Kilburn began his match report: 'Once upon a time . . .' He turned our unlikely victory – and my extremely unlikely part in it – into a fairy tale. I'd never known him to write in such a way before and I never saw him do the same thing afterwards. But I've still got the cutting and what he said means a lot to me.

When I came into the Yorkshire side in 1959, Jim was like a God. Everyone – the team and the members – always read what he wrote. He was a shy man, who didn't say much – even when we were traveling together in the same car to a match. But he still commanded our respect because he was so knowledgeable.

Don Wilson

FOR A WHILE, back in the days when Margaret Thatcher reigned, it became rather fashionable to read cricket reports and essays of the 1930s, or at least to read the reports of one man: Sir Neville Cardus. The Cardus nostalgia industry, which just stopped short of selling souvenir knick-knacks and T-shirts, reached almost alarming proportions; and his brilliant but idiosyncratic view of the '30s became received wisdom.

Jim Kilburn represents an equal but opposite tradition. Cardus was a cricket writer full of glorious improvised strokes but sometimes a little suspect in defence. Kilburn was much more of a grafter. He was not without deft touches of his own, but he represented – and became the epitome of – a different, harder school of cricket writing, which remains excellent.

I started reading Kilburn's *In Search of Cricket* after breakfast on a train between King's Cross and Leeds, which was the perfect setting. It is a book written by a Yorkshire cricket writer, largely but not entirely about Yorkshire cricket, and first published in 1937. It is very much a book of its time and place – perhaps THE book. Kilburn himself thinks he wrote much better later on. But there is a freshness about it that could only come from a young writer. It is like a very Yorkshire innings, full of textbook defensive shots leavened with the occasional perfectly-executed cover-drive. Thus, of the short boundaries at Tonbridge: 'a well-hit six can drop with a thrilling crash upon hard slates'; and 'Grimmett, of course, had to come back to look into this situation but Ames played the ball and not the bowler's name'; and 'Leyland's bowling is mostly a joke, but it is an extremely practical joke'. This represents masterful control of the language.

The cricket world has moved on and so have newspapers. It is hard to imagine Jim Kilburn, who for years resisted the innovation of a television in the press box, doing the job now, though for years it was impossible to imagine Yorkshire without him. I once asked him if he would do it all again. He thought not, but added: 'While I have had the best of cricket in my lifetime, there will be lifetimes to come when it will be good enough.'

Matthew Engel

Acknowledgements

IN 1973, not long into my teens and devouring every cricket book as soon as the small local library acquired it, I picked up a still gleaming copy of *Thanks to Cricket*. I'm fairly sure no one else in the village had read it before I did. I'd heard of neither JM Kilburn nor the *Yorkshire Post*. In fact, I was only dimly aware of some of the players Kilburn was writing about: for example, Hirst and Sutcliffe belonged to a dusty and sepia-washed era that initially seemed utterly remote and unreachable to me. But then I began to read . . .

What I'd previously understood about the history of cricket only stretched back to the tip of 1968. On our miniscule TV screen I'd watched Derek Underwood in blurry black and white as he jagged the ball around at the Oval pitch to defeat Australia.

Kilburn filled in the gaps. He guided me through the Golden and Silver Ages and introduced me properly to Bradman and Hutton, and the history of the Ashes. *Thanks to Cricket* did what any good book ought to do: it encouraged me to root out others just like it.

I'm indebted to Jim Kilburn, and I hope *Sweet Summers* partly repays him. It was written because I believe his work is worthy of re-discovery. I always intended to dedicate it to

Jim's wife Mary, who enjoyed cricket as much as he did. I didn't mention it to Mary because I wanted to surprise her on the day of publication. Her sudden death at the end of 2007 makes me regret that decision terribly. Her enthusiasm for the book – along with that of her son Robin – made it possible.

An author cum-editor owes many debts. I'm grateful to everyone who contributed to the tributes section, and did so not only without hesitation but also with a genuine respect and affection for JMK. I'd particularly like to thank Matthew Engel and Christopher Lane for allowing me to reproduce work from *Wisden* and *The Cricketer*. Peter Wynne-Thomas' vast accumulated knowledge, and his dedication to the history of cricket, is the 'hidden hand' behind so many books. His cataloguing of *The Cricketer* – as well as his company in Nottinghamshire's library – was indispensable.

At Great Northern Books, I leant on the expertise of Barry Cox, David Joy, Patricia Lennon, and David Burrill. At the *Yorkshire Post*, I received the unstinting support of my editor Peter Charlton, picture editor Ian Day, David Clay, the newspaper's library staff and my colleague and friend Tom Richmond.

And, of course, I could neither survive nor function without my wife Mandy. I was once asked:

'How did you find a woman who likes cricket?'

'How did I find Mandy, full stop?' I replied. It was pure luck . . .

Duncan Hamilton

Statham and Trueman: The Flood Tide and the Tempest originally appeared in the 1962 edition of *Wisden Cricketers' Almanack* and is reproduced by kind permission of John Wisden & Co Ltd.

Brian Close: The Art of Physical Courage originally appeared in the August 1970 edition of *The Cricketer* and is reproduced by kind permission of John Wisden & Co Ltd.

Percy Holmes and his Circus originally appeared in the October 1971 edition of *The Cricketer* and is reproduced by kind permission of John Wisden & Co Ltd.

Preserving Cricket's Future originally appeared in the November 1971 edition of *The Cricketer* and is reproduced by kind permission of John Wisden & Co Ltd.

Pleasures of the South originally appeared in the May 1937 edition of *The Cricketer* and is reproduced by kind permission of John Wisden & Co Ltd.

A Letter from the North originally appeared in the July 1938 edition of *The Cricketer* and is reproduced by kind permission of John Wisden & Co Ltd.

The Secret of Yorkshire's Success originally appeared in *The Cricketer Winter Annual 1935* and is reproduced by kind permission of John Wisden & Co Ltd.

An account of Yorkshire's game against the Australians originally appeared in the August 1938 edition of *The Cricketer* and is reproduced by kind permission of John Wisden & Co Ltd.

The End of an Age originally appeared in the August 1940 edition of *The Cricketer* and is reproduced by kind permission of John Wisden & Co Ltd.

Sir Neville Cardus: Lord of Lancashire originally appeared in the April 1971 edition of *The Cricketer* and is reproduced by kind permission of John Wisden & Co Ltd.

The Ghost in Cricket's Machine originally appeared in the May 1956 edition of *The Cricketer* and is reproduced by kind permission of John Wisden & Co Ltd.

A Critic's Concern originally appeared in *The Cricketer Spring Annual 1958* and is reproduced by kind permission of John Wisden & Co Ltd.

Editor's Note: Articles not identified are from the *Yorkshire Post.*

Other cricket books by JM Kilburn

In Search of Cricket

The Scarborough Cricket Festival

Yorkshire: County Cricket Series

Len Hutton: A Portrait

History of Yorkshire CCC 1924-1949

Yorkshire's 22 Championships (with EL Roberts)

Homes of Sport: Cricket (with NWD Yardley)

Cricket Decade

100 Years of Yorkshire Cricket

A History of Yorkshire Cricket

Thanks to Cricket

Overthrows

Barclays World of Cricket (contributor)

Cricket Heroes (contributor)

TRUEMAN'S TALES

'Fiery Fred' – Yorkshire's Cricketing Giant

by John Morgan and David Joy

With contributions from: Dickie Bird, Ian Botham, Geoffrey Boycott, Brian Close, Raymond Illingworth, Bill Pertwee and Harvey Smith.

This book began as a series of lengthy and memorable interviews that David Joy had with Fred Trueman in the first half of 2006. They were intended to form the basis of a collection of his humorous tales of life on and off the pitch. Then came Fred's untimely death, and it soon became apparent that many of his sporting colleagues and close friends wished to contribute to a work now clearly destined to form a tribute to a remarkable man.

John Morgan, the sports journalist who knew Fred over many years, has accordingly written a greatly enlarged text about one of England's true cricketing heroes.
Fully illustrated. Hardback.

TRUEMAN TALKS Audio CD

The last recording of 'Fiery Fred' – A Cricketing Giant

Presented by Harry Gration

Recorded in Fred's own sitting room, this unique CD allows you to listen in as Fred chats about his life as a top class cricketer, his fondness for the Yorkshire Dales; and some of his favourite stories and jokes.

THE VIEW FROM THE BOUNDARY

Signed Limited Edition Prints

by John Blakey

A strictly limited number of prints of this fabulous group portrait, A View from the Boundary, are available signed by the artist, John Blakey, and Ray Illingworth, Brian Close, Fred Trueman and Geoff Boycott.

Also available: signed limited edition prints of John Blakey's portraits of Ray Illingworth, Brian Close, Fred Trueman, Geoff Boycott and Dickie Bird.

THE YORKSHIRE COUNTY CRICKET CLUB YEARBOOK

Beautifully produced annually and bursting with facts and figures,the official yearbook of Yorkshire County Cricket Club is a detailed record of every match played throughout the season.   Featuring articles on players past and present, records from the history of Yorkshire Cricket and Internationals played at Headingley Carnegie, this book is essential reading for fans of Yorkshire cricket.

To find out more, visit **www.greatnorthernbooks.co.uk**